YOUR TEACHER TRAINING COMPANION

The second edition of *Your Teacher Training Companion* is your one-stop shop for the essential knowledge and skills you need to pass your course with confidence. Guiding you through your time in school and your studies, it will ensure you develop both the practical teaching skills and academic skills required to become a successful teacher.

Written in an accessible, no-nonsense style, it succinctly covers the most important aspects of becoming a teacher, showing you how to balance the competing demands of teaching in school, your course and social life. It is illustrated throughout with the case study of a fellow trainee teacher, focusing on developing best practice and ways in which you can pass on key skills to your learners.

Essential topics covered include:

- Classroom management
- Effective lesson planning
- Teaching methods
- Learning theory
- Assessment and feedback
- Delivering a highly successful lesson
- Making time and space for your studies
- Improving your writing skills
- Writing assignments and building your teaching portfolio
- Planning and delivering an effective presentation.

Designed for the very busy trainee on all routes to qualified teacher status, *Your Teacher Training Companion, Second edition* offers you the essential knowledge and skills you need to get the most out of your time with pupils, improve your study skills, successfully achieve qualified teacher status and manage your early career as a newly qualified teacher.

Jim McGrath was Course Director for the MA in Education and Professional Development at Birmingham City University, UK.

Anthony Coles is Reader in Post-Compulsory Education and Director of Continuous Professional Development for the Faculty of Education, Law and Social Sciences at Birmingham City University, UK.

YOUR TEACHER TRAINING COMPANION

Essential skills and knowledge for very busy trainees

Second edition

Jim McGrath and Anthony Coles

Routledge
Taylor & Francis Group

LONDON AND NEW YORK

Second edition published 2016
by Routledge
2 Park Square, Milton Park, Abingdon, Oxon OX14 4RN

and by Routledge
711 Third Avenue, New York, NY 10017

Routledge is an imprint of the Taylor & Francis Group, an informa business

© 2016 J. McGrath and A. Coles

First edition published by Routledge 2011

British Library Cataloguing in Publication Data
A catalogue record for this book is available from the British Library

Library of Congress Cataloging in Publication Data
A catalog record for this book has been requested

ISBN: 978-1-138-84196-3 (hbk)
ISBN: 978-1-138-84197-0 (pbk)
ISBN: 978-1-315-73192-6 (ebk)

Typeset in Interstate
by Swales & Willis Ltd, Exeter, Devon, UK
Printed in Great Britain by Ashford Colour Press Ltd,
Gosport, Hants

MIX
Paper from
responsible sources
FSC® C011748

For my mother-in-law, Saara Karjalainen, 95 years young and still going strong. Also in memory of my mother, Bridget McGrath, who always believed in the intrinsic value of education.

For William and Bea.

BRIEF CONTENTS

FULL CONTENTS

Tutorial 7   How to deliver a highly successful lesson   105

Part II   Managing your studies   123

Tutorial 8   How to make time and space for your studies   125

Tutorial 9   How to find and read the literature you need   138

Tutorial 13   How to plan and deliver an effective presentation   199

Tutorial 14   How to find your first job   212

FIGURES

HANDOUTS

ABOUT THE AUTHORS

Dr Jim McGrath qualified as an accountant in 1976 and for 20 years worked as an accountant, senior financial manager and management consultant in industry, local government and education. He was course director at Birmingham City University for the MA in Education and Professional Development and taught research skills and management and leadership on a wide range of undergraduate and postgraduate courses.

In 2012 he took early retirement to write full-time and spend more time complaining about his beloved West Bromwich Albion and their limitless ability to always let the faithful down.

Dr Anthony Coles spent his early career as a research chemist before he switched to teaching. Until his retirement in 2015 he was a Reader in Post-Compulsory Education and Director of Continuous Professional Development for the Faculty of Education, Law and Social Sciences at Birmingham City University. Much of his work involved research skills and supporting teachers in their professional development.

He was also responsible for developing links with a number of Chinese Universities and establishing the Faculty's MA in International Education and Ed.D. programmes.

Also by the same authors

Your Education Masters Companion
Your Education Research Project Companion
Your Education Leadership Handbook
Your Teacher Training Handbook

WHOM IS THIS BOOK FOR?

The simple answer is:

ANYONE ON A TEACHER TRAINING PROGRAMME!

This means that the book will be suitable for primary and secondary school teachers and lecturers in further education. Equally, it doesn't matter what type of training programme you are following. The book will meet the needs of those on any pathway, including:

- Assessment only route
- Initial teacher training programmes with qualified teacher status (QTS)
- Postgraduate certificate in education (PGCE)
- Researchers in Schools
- School Direct
- School-centred initial teacher training (SCITT)
- Teach First
- Troops to Teachers
- QTS for overseas teachers from Australia, Canada, New Zealand and the United States

How have we managed to meet what appears to be such diverse needs in one book? Simple. This book deals with the principles of teaching, not fine details. Providing precise instructions about how to do something is fine when the setting in which you operate is predictable and the environment consistent. This is not the case in teaching. You are operating in the messy reality of life in the classroom where no two teaching sessions are ever the same. That's why we want you to absorb and master the practice- and theory-based principles that underpin teaching. Once these have been mastered you will find that they can be applied in primary, secondary and tertiary settings, and in the teaching of any subject.

However, we need you to work in partnership with us. As you read the book it's essential that you constantly ask yourself, **'How is this relevant to my own teaching and learning?' 'How can I adapt it to meet my needs and those of my students?'** This ability to apply principles and ideas from other areas to your own situation is one that has grown in importance in recent years, with many working practices and ideas being imported into education from management, nursing and health care. This is a high-level skill and one that all teachers need to develop and master.

An example of this principle is provided by how we've dealt with teaching and learning standards. There are different sets of standards for the teaching in schools and the further education/lifelong learning sector, and they change regularly. We know this because we've had to implement such changes more than once in our careers. For that reason we do not spend endless pages discussing individual education standards. Instead we provide advice and guidance on how to identify opportunities in your daily work where a range of standards can be easily evidenced. We then leave it to you to identify those opportunities in your unique setting.

HOW TO GET THE MOST OUT OF THIS BOOK

The single most valuable piece of advice we can give you is:

READ TUTORIAL 7 FIRST!

As teachers we've found that it's useful to show students what they are aiming at. Not only can this motivate students but it provides them with a very clear of idea of what they need to do to achieve their objective. For that reason we suggest you read Tutorial 7 first. It explains what is required to deliver either a very successful lesson or, better still, a highly successful lesson. As a trainee teacher, that should be your objective. If you are just starting your training, no one will expect you to achieve such high standards. But as you progress you should be able to track your progress towards achieving these standards. Knowing from day one what your objective is will keep you on track.

Similarly, we suggest that you read the 'Record of mentor meeting' located at the end of each tutorial before you read the tutorial itself. Why? Because it provides you with a summary of what's covered in the tutorial. This overview will help you navigate the tutorial more effectively, and if you read it again after you have read the tutorial it will help embed in your memory the key issues we've covered.

Flipping through the book you will see that it contains a lot of free space. This wasn't done to pad out the book but was part of the design brief that we agreed with Routledge. Please use these spaces as an opportunity to reflect on what you have just read and try to identify how and when you might be able to apply the advice given in your teaching and/or studies. Feel free to also disagree with what's been said and raise these points with your placement mentor (PM) or personal development tutor (PDT).

Aim to turn this book into a personal set of notes. You don't have to spend a lot of time doing this but if you can make a quick note about an issue of interest as you are reading, it will help you to understand and remember what you have read.

This book is not a replacement for taught/training sessions. Good attendance at your teacher training sessions is essential. As Woody Allen said, '95 per cent of success is turning up'. But there are various ways that this book can enhance and support such training programmes, such as:

- Read the relevant chapter or chapters before attending a taught session on the same issues. This will familiarise you with the key concepts and enable you to clarify anything that you are unsure of with your lecturer.
- Read the appropriate chapter after a session. This will reinforce the learning that has already taken place and provide a different perspective on the issues discussed.

- Use the summary of each tutorial's main points and/or the figures in each tutorial to identify and understand the key issues. Visual learners may wish to study the diagram before reading the relevant tutorial to obtain an overview of the key issues discussed.
- Use Alex's action points as a starting point for your own development plan.
- Use the book as your primary learning resource when you have missed a session entirely, or found a lesson particularly difficult.
- Follow up the further reading recommendations provided at the end of each tutorial.
- When on placement, read the relevant chapter on how to deal with specific issues/problems as they arise.

We are conscious that long reading lists can demotivate rather than inspire students, and for that reason we have restricted the number of recommendations at the end of each tutorial. When following up a reference, you must decide how much of the recommended chapter/ article you need to read – some, most or all. You should apply the advice given in Tutorial 2 and develop the habit of using the book's index to trace key terms and ideas across the book. Occasionally in the text you will find a reference dated 20xx. This is a fictitious reference used solely by Dr Sue Storm who is Alex's university-based PDT, and Jane Gray, Alex's PM – for illustrative purposes.

THIS BOOK IS DIFFERENT FROM ANY TEXTBOOK YOU'VE EVER READ BEFORE

What you can expect to find in this book

As education tutors we have observed that many, if not most, trainees find the transition from student to teacher a stressful and challenging experience. Many trainees find the prospect of their first teaching placement little short of terrifying and some are overwhelmed by the sheer volume of work involved in their course. Others find it difficult to meet the academic demands of a teacher training course. The primary aim of this book is to address any concerns you may have and provide you with the essential information and skills that you need to pass your course and teaching practice.

Building on the approach that we first developed in *Your Education Research Project Companion*, each tutorial/chapter consists of a verbatim record of the tutorial between Alex and either his/her school-based PM or university-based PDT, interspersed with a series of reflections. It is hoped that this approach will help you to identify with Alex and realise that many of the problems you face are common amongst trainee teachers. We also hope that our approach has resulted in a more user-friendly and engaging book than is typical of the many texts aimed at the needs of trainee teachers.

Where appropriate, we have also discussed how Alex might pass on some of the study skills learnt to other learners. In some tutorials this is done using Alex's reflections, and in others as part of the discussions between Alex and either Jane Gray (PM) or Dr Sue Storm (PDT). This approach is our attempt to include an element of 'meta-teaching' as it is practised in our own teaching.

The book is written from the viewpoint of the student and not that of an academic dispensing words of wisdom. We believe that this approach helps us to simplify and make transparent the issues faced by trainee teachers. For that reason, the gender of Alex is never specified, nor do we disclose the subject/s that Alex teaches or the age of his/her students. Instead we invite you to create your own backstory for the character. Nor do we specify the pathway that Alex is taking into teaching. You may think that you recognise it, but the reality is that whichever route you are on it is highly likely that you will have a mentor in school and someone at a university or other recognised training organisation that is allocated to guide you.

Within each tutorial you will find:

- a short summary, not dissimilar to an abstract, outlining the contents of the tutorial;
- a verbatim record of the tutorial meeting between Alex and either Jane Gray or Dr Sue Storm;
- extracts from Alex's reflective journal. Please don't skip over these, as they often provide clarification of what has just been discussed in the tutorial and/or new information on the topic;

- space for your own notes/reflection;
- a summary of key learning points arising from Alex's tutorial with Dr Storm or Jane Gray;
- a list of agreed action points for Alex. You may wish to complete some of these yourself;
- a diagrammatical representation of key aspects of the learning in each tutorial;
- handouts provided by either the PM or PDT during the tutorial;
- advice on additional reading.

You can also use the book as a source of comfort and impartial advice. Every trainee teacher goes through a period of soul-searching as they come to terms with the demands of their chosen profession. One day a session goes well and you feel wonderful. The next week it all blows up in your face and you feel dispirited and ready to quit. It is at moments like these, when you are convinced that you will never make a half-decent teacher, that it is comforting to know that every teacher has gone through this stage and comes out the other side to find success and fulfilment in what we think is the best job in the world – teaching.

The book is divided into two parts:

Part I Managing your placement contains seven tutorials between Alex and the PM. It examines the practical challenges that you will encounter at your school/college as you try to apply what you have learnt about teaching and learning in the classroom. For many students the placement is both exciting and frightening. A once-familiar environment becomes alien because you are no longer sitting behind a desk listening to a teacher but are at the front managing a class of learners.

Part II Managing your studies contains seven tutorials between Alex and the PDT. It deals with the academic skills and knowledge that you need to complete successfully for the assignments that are required by most courses. The various tutorials will improve your reading, writing and presentational skills and show you how to find and critically evaluate the literature you need to complete your assignments. The last tutorial offers advice on how to get that all-important first teaching job.

A glossary of key terms that you may wish to refer to for clarification is provided at the end of the book. Each key term is shown in **_bold italics_** the first time it is used.

Health warning

It is essential that you refer to the assignment brief and assessment criteria used in your institution when tackling assignments and use the institution's recommended referencing system.

We wish you the very best of luck in your chosen career, and if you have any suggestions for how we could make this book more useful to the trainee teacher, please contact us at **writer7@hotmail.co.uk** with YTTC in the subject line.

Jim McGrath
Anthony Coles
Birmingham 2015

ACKNOWLEDGEMENTS

We would like to thank Simon Spencer at Birmingham City University for providing key information about the ever-changing pathways into teaching and for permission to adapt a range of documentation that is used by the university for inclusion in this book. We would also like to thank our colleagues in the School of Education; we have always enjoyed your company and have learnt a great deal from working with such gifted and committed teachers.

We would also like to thank Helen McGrath for reading and commenting on early drafts of several 'tutorials' and Laura Aston PGCE (PCET) and Andrew Walsh, MA Education, for permission to publish extracts of their work on the website www.routledge.com/cw/mcgrath that accompanies this book.

And finally, many thanks to our editor, Helen Pritt, for her encouragement, support and understanding throughout the writing of this book, and Sarah Tuckwell at Routledge, who continues to respond to our many enquiries with good grace.

Part I

Managing your placement

There are two crucial and complementary components of any teacher training course. One is the academic skills and knowledge that is delivered by universities and the other is practical experience of teaching.

This practical experience is obtained by placing each trainee in a suitable school or college where they will be given the opportunity to teach and join in the wider work of the organisation. This is essential if the trainee is going to be able to provide evidence that they have archived all the standards required for the award of QTS or qualified teacher learning and skills (QTLS).

When taking on a trainee teacher the vast majority of schools and colleges recognise the need to provide every trainee with the support and guidance they need to achieve qualification. This task usually falls to staff who have undergone mentor training. These mentors understand that to become a successful teacher the trainee must be supported, encouraged and challenged in equal measure.

How much you learn from your placement is largely down to you. You have to take responsibility and manage your placement. It's up to you to immerse yourself in school/ college life and wring from that experience every bit of learning and understanding that you can. Don't be a 'strategic learner' content just to do enough work to claim the QTS/QTLS standards. Go beyond that and immerse yourself in the life of the school/college. You will learn more, develop faster as a teacher and, who knows, may be offered a job at the end of your placement.

This section provides an insight into what you can expect on your placement and offers advice on how to manage your placement and get the most out of it and your mentor.

Tutorial 1   What you need to know to survive your placement

Aim of tutorial: To help you understand the priorities of your school/college and settle in quickly.

Tutorial overview: This tutorial identifies the importance of asking questions when on placement, the need to familiarise yourself with the aims and objectives of the school/college and where you can find essential documentation when you need it. In addition it offers advice on how not to alienate colleagues.

Contents

1.1 Alex's reflection

Well, here I am all grown up and facing my first day at school - again. I have to say I feel more nervous now than when I was five years old and attending St Augustine's Junior and Infant School for the very first time. Still, what can they do to me? Sack me? Actually, they could. Or, to be more precise, they could terminate my placement. Which amounts to the same thing. I really hope that I don't make a pig's ear of it!

(continued)

(continued)

I was able to visit my placement last week and have a chat with my mentor, Jane Gray. She seemed friendly enough. She's been teaching for six years and is already head of department. She's doing an M.Ed. at the university.

The school is on the border of Gotham and Metropolis, so the kids come from a wide range of backgrounds. Some are from the leafy suburbs and their parents are earning £100 grand plus, while other parents have never had a job in their life. It's going to be a challenge.

Jane said that during the first week I would just be shadowing her and that if all went to plan I could do a bit of team teaching with her in week 2. Depending on how that goes I can start to take some small classes of my own from week 3 or 4. So I'm not being thrown in at the deep end.

She also insisted that I must ask if I don't understand something. She doesn't expect me to know all the answers or to be the world's best teacher, but she does expect me to ask questions if I have any doubts about what I am doing or have been asked to do.

1.2 Don't be afraid to ask questions or say 'I don't know'

As agreed, I found Jane in her cubby-hole of an office after assembly. She pointed me in the direction of the kettle and I made us both a cup of coffee before we started.

'*So, on a scale of one to ten, with ten being the highest, how nervous are you about starting your placement?*' she asked.

'Eleven,' I replied.

'*Well, at least you're honest,*' she said laughing. '*I remember my first day – I was petrified. It took a full week for me to relax.*'

'Only a week?' I said, surprised.

'*Less, actually. I started to relax once I realised that no one expected me to know all the answers. That was very liberating.*'

'I know you said I should ask questions if I didn't understand something, but what about in the classroom. Won't the learners expect me to know all the answers?'

'*Surprisingly, no. They are perfectly happy if you say "I don't know. But I'll find out". What they don't like is if you try to fob them off with an incorrect or partial answer. They can smell farmyard manure at a thousand metres. So always be open with them. They'll respect you for it.*'

I nodded in agreement and waited for her to continue.

'*The same openness needs to be used with your colleagues. They know you are a trainee struggling to find your feet. They will be only too happy to answer your questions, so use them. Like all trainee teachers you are currently unconsciously incompetent, soon you'll* become consciously incompetent, later you will become consciously competent, and by the end of your training you will be unconsciously competent.' (See Figure 1.1.)

'I hope so,' I said uncertainly.

1.3 School targets and budgets

'Have you had any work experience?'

'Yes, but nothing really relevant to teaching. I worked on the market on a Saturday when I was at school, and at college I had a part-time job at a call centre. I hated it. After that I worked in an office for a few years before applying for teacher training.'

'I imagine a call centre can be tough. But it could prove very useful to you. You have been exposed to line management and the need to meet targets. If you are to understand what is going on in a school you have to have some idea of how the school operates. So, before you sit in on your first lesson I want to talk a little bit about the importance of meeting the school's targets.'

'OK,' I said, not at all sure where Jane was going with this.

*'Schools and colleges are increasingly judged on how well they perform against a range of targets and objectives that have been set by the government. For example, secondary schools are largely judged on how many learners gain five GCSEs, including maths and English, and primary schools on their **SAT** results. This means that schools and teachers are under enormous pressure to achieve their particular target. Similarly, all schools and colleges are concerned with how well they do in Ofsted inspections.'*

'Because Ofsted reports are public documents and can be used by parents and students when deciding the best place to send their children or study.'

*'Exactly. A poor report can cause many problems for a school or college. In theory, schools and colleges don't have to follow Ofsted's recommendations/advice, but it is a high-risk strategy. Many a head has lost their job after their school was placed in **special measures** following inspection. Heads can go it alone, but to survive they have to be successful in terms of exam results and student/parent satisfaction. Otherwise they are very exposed.'*

'So what are this school's key targets and objectives?'

'Like most schools, we are obsessed with our place in the league tables, so test results dominate our thinking. Any teacher who can improve the school's test results is likely to go far.'

'Does that mean that we are only interested in teaching learners how to do well in SATs and exams?'

'I wouldn't say that. It's possible to give learners an education and show them how to pass exams and tests. It's a balance. As you just said if our test results are poor, parents may send their children to another school and we will end up with fewer strong learners and worse results. This spiral of decline can make it difficult to attract good teachers and, before you know it, the school is in special measures or closed – which definitely doesn't help the local kids.'

'And what other targets and objectives do I need to look out for?'

'Take a look at the school's annual action plan and budget. The action plan lists all the things that the senior management team wants to achieve in the coming year and usually names the person responsible for making each action happen. Many of the items listed will have come from or been inspired by the school's latest **self-evaluation form (SEF)** *or Ofsted report. Some schools and all colleges will also have a strategic plan, which is concerned with targets and objectives for the next three years.'*

'Do all staff get a copy of the annual action plan?'

'Some schools and colleges do provide individual copies. But more often than not copies will be held by departmental heads. Most staff will just get to see the targets and objectives for their department or section. And it will be the responsibility of the department manager to ensure that all staff know what they have to achieve and to monitor that it's done.'

'So what about budgets?' I asked.

'A budget is just a business plan with a price ticket on it. It lists in financial terms what the school wants to do in the next year. It is usually broken down into departments, and the head of the department will be responsible for ensuring that the budget is neither under- nor overspent.'

'I can understand not wanting to overspend your budget, but I would have thought that management would like you to save money and underspend.'

'You would have thought so, wouldn't you? But think about it. The manager has been given a sum of money to spend on resources and activities that will help the school to achieve its objectives. If the money isn't spent, the objectives may not be achieved.'

'But what if they find a way to save money and still meet the objectives – surely they'd get a "well done" for that?'

'In the public sector, annual budgets are based on cash accounting. That means that if you don't spend your budget in the financial year, you are restricted in what, if any, balances you can carry over to the next year. So you lose that money and your budget for next year may be reduced.'

'So there is no incentive to stay under budget?'

'Not really. But what you have to try and avoid is "budget madness". This happens when, a month before the year end, the budget holders discover that they still have an unspent budget allocation and go mad trying to spend it.'

'And because they are in a rush I bet they don't always spend the money wisely.'

'Exactly. It's much more effective if you can identify a possible underspend a few months in advance and with your line manager decide if it can be transferred to another budget which is either under pressure or which would benefit from greater investment. But if you do that, make sure that you get the credit for your good deed as this may protect your budget being

reduced the following year. But it's also a good time for teachers to ask for funds to finance their pet projects!'

'If these targets and budgets are so important, I suppose the managers are constantly check-ing up on teachers and other staff?'

'The head of department should hold regular monitoring meetings with his or her staff to monitor how things are going and report back to the head or senior management team. In the main, you'll find the managers very supportive. They will tell you what needs to be done and then give you a fair amount of freedom to get on with it. But if you don't do what you are supposed to or you fail to meet your targets, they will take action – because their job depends on you completing the task and/or attaining the target.'

1.4 School management and how to avoid alienating people

'So they are more interested in the task and spending the budget than the people doing it?'

'That's not entirely fair. A good manager will have a high concern for both the task and the staff doing it. If you do end up working for a task-obsessed manager, at least you will always know where you stand. Do your job well and there is no problem. Mess up and you can find yourself in difficulties no matter how popular you are in the class or staffroom.'

'You make it sound like SPECTRE – fail and you end up in a chair connected to the electric grid.'

'If only. I can think of one or two people I'd cheerfully drop into a tank full of sharks. Which reminds me, don't alienate people. It's very easy to rub people up the wrong way. A few years ago we had a mature trainee who was constantly telling experienced staff that their **lesson plans** *were wrong and that they should be more student-centred in their choice of teaching methods. Now these staff had 20 years of experience dealing with kids while everything the trainee knew came straight out of a book. Needless to say, she did not make herself popular and not too many people volunteered to help her when she got into difficulties.'*

'But there are some poor and lazy teachers out there. What am I supposed to do – ignore them?'

'As a trainee or a newly qualified teacher it is not your job to sort out underperforming or ineffective teachers. That's management's responsibility. Besides, are you really sure that the teacher is incompetent? Instead of judging a teacher based on your limited experience and incomplete information, try asking them about their approach. Nearly always there will be a reason for why they work as they do and it will be based on years of experience of what works for them. Teaching is an art, not a science. There isn't a single perfect way to do it. Some people can get great results using a particular approach, but in other hands it might be a disaster. Everyone likes to be asked their opinion. So talk to the other teachers and find out what they do and why they do it. They will be only too happy to share their ideas and offer help and advice.'

1.5 Alex's reflection

I don't mind having targets and objectives as long as I know what they are. So I had better find out what it is that is expected of me. Once I know them I can set about developing a strategy to meet them. As I'm only on placement, my targets are likely to be the same as the teachers I'm working with. So that's another reason not to mess up. Not only could I let myself down, I could damage the reputation of a fellow teacher.

I also need to be careful that I don't incur any additional costs in my teaching – no marathon photocopying sessions without permission or promises of day trips to London. I'm not going to be popular with Jane or the head if I'm a drain on their finances.

I'm happy to follow the Ofsted model of teaching and learning – after all, that's the one they cover at uni. But I imagine in time I will develop my own style (at least that's what Sue my PDT says. What then? I suppose that I will need to justify why I have adopted the approach I have and be able to demonstrate that the results I get from it are at least as good as, or better than, the approach advocated by colleagues, the school or Ofsted.

I might be mistaken, but I think Jane was warning me, in the nicest possible way, of the need to be diplomatic with staff and not rub them up the wrong way by questioning their professional skills. It must be really annoying to get some wet-behind-the-ears trainee telling you the best way to teach when you have been doing it for 20 years.

SPACE FOR YOUR NOTES

Prompt

- Schools are organisations like any business. They need to be managed. What does this mean for you as a trainee teacher?

1.6 School structure

'Would it help me find my way around if I got hold of a school **organisation chart**?' I asked.

'Yes and no. My leadership tutor on the M.Ed. says that there are at least four versions of any organisation chart. There is the formal chart as it was written down when Adam was a lad and which no one has bothered to update. There is the formal organisation as it currently exists, which supersedes the written chart. There is the extant organisation chart. This is the unwritten chart which takes into account the power of individual staff. This chart, if ever written down, might show the head's secretary as the second most important person in the school because the head listens to her advice rather than that of the senior management team. And then there is the structure that staff think exists.'

'Which one am I supposed to work to?'

'All of them, none of them. You have to navigate that particular maze yourself. The only advice I can give you is to spend a month or so watching and observing. You will very quickly see who the players are. Whose voice is listened to, who is ignored, who has influence with the head and who wields the power. Once you've done that, start to make some alliances and, whatever you do, don't annoy the great and the good.'

1.7 School policies and procedures

'OK, let's move away from meeting targets and arguing with colleagues. I suppose you know that, like any school or college, we have policies and procedures for nearly every eventuality.'

'And you want me to read every one and commit them to memory,' I said.

*'Good Lord, no. That would be a nigh on impossible task. No, I want you to get a copy of each and give them a quick **skim read**. Have you done anything on speed reading?'*

'Yes. My PDT covered it with me.' (See Tutorial 9.)

'Good. That will save you a lot of time. What you need is just a rough idea of what each policy or procedure contains. Then, if you find yourself dealing with an issue in a particular area you can go back and read the material more carefully. Chances are that during your placement you will only need to know a small percentage of the stuff covered in any detail. But you must know where to find it when you need it. However, your first port of call should always be me. We can talk about the issue as well as find a copy of the relevant policy or procedure.'

'A case of strategic learning!'

'Yes. So what sort of policies and procedures do you think we have?'

I tried to remember what Hal Jordan had said in class on documentation. It had seemed pointless at the time and it took me a few seconds before I could reply. 'Well, there would be a staff handbook dealing with conditions of employment and things like the grievance procedure, discipline and performance reviews, etc. There would also be a health and safety policy and a school behaviour policy.'

'Anything else?'

I was scraping around for an answer when I remembered the importance of equal opportunities and said, 'There will probably be something on diversity and maybe a special educational needs policy.'

*'Good. The three documents that I think are essential reading for you are the school's behaviour policy, our teaching and learning strategy and the policy on **safeguarding**. Later, you can have a look at the departmental handbook, which will probably be more useful to you than the school's staff handbook as it deals with the day-to-day issues that you may get involved in.'*

Looking at her watch, Jane's eyes opened wide with surprise. *'Is that the time? You should have stopped me rattling on. I'm teaching in 5 minutes. I wanted to talk to you about what you can expect from me as your mentor and what I expect from you, but for the moment just read this handout. (See Handout 1.1.) It's important, so don't ignore it. We can talk about it later. Now get moving! You can sit in on my lesson. Afterwards I'll show you round the school.'*

1.8 Alex's reflection

It does appear that organisation charts aren't worth the paper they're written on as they are often out of date and don't actually show where the power and influence in the organisation lies. Still, it would be a good idea to get hold of the official chart just to see who's who in the organisation. Hang on, I've just had an idea. I could start with the organisation chart which shows the formal relationships in the school - for example, between the head and the deputies and the deputies and the assistant heads, etc. Then, as I learn how the real power and influence flows around the school I could show those relationships as separate lines on the same chart by using a different colour. Mind you, it would probably be wise not to show anyone at the school that particular chart! But it would give me a real insight into how the school works. Of course, on placement I may not be there long enough to do it. But I could certainly do it when I find a permanent post following qualification.

Thank goodness I don't have to read every policy and procedure in the school. As Jane suggested, I've got hold of the school's policies on behaviour, teaching and learning, and safeguarding. They don't look too intimidating. I'll read them over the weekend. I've already got a copy of the school's annual action plan. Jane was right, it's clear from the plan that test results and league table position are important to the school. They are looking for a 5 per cent improvement on the school's test scores across the board. But the plan also provides a good overview of where the school wants to go during the next year. It's got a lot of information in it. Reading it means that I'll understand what they are talking about in meetings and the staffroom and I'll be able to take part in the discussion. That's got to be worth some Brownie points!

*As for the list of mentee's and mentor's responsibilities, it's basically a **compact** setting out the responsibilities of both parties. I wonder if Jane has always used such an agreement or if she drew it up following problems with a trainee? I've just had another idea (I must be on a roll). If I go to another placement and there isn't a similar agreement, I could suggest that we draw one up using Jane's as a model.*

I'm tired. This week has been hectic. I think I need to head to bed to dream of eccentric teachers and how I need to understand them before I pass judgement. Or better still, leave it to more experienced teachers than me to judge them.

SPACE FOR YOUR NOTES

Prompts

- Reflect on the exercise of management in an organisation with which you are familiar, perhaps a part-time or holiday job. How might this experience help you in your teaching career?
- If you have never worked, ask friends or family about their experiences of starting a new job. What can you learn from them?

1.9 Record of mentor meeting

Trainee: Alex Croft

Summary of key learning points

- In response to a question in the classroom, it's OK to say 'I don't know. But I will find out and get back to you'. Don't try to fake it.
- It is OK to say to your mentor or any teacher on placement 'I don't understand. Can you explain it, please?' They would rather you asked for clarification than try and muddle through and possibly cause additional problems.
- Failure to meet targets can result in poorly performing organisations being criticised, placed in special measures, merged or closed down.
- Every school and college has numerous policies and procedures. Check with your mentor which you should read in detail. These will usually include the organisation's learning and teaching strategy, behaviour policy and safeguarding policy and procedure. Others you will only need to skim read or know where to find them if the need arises.

(continued)

(continued)

- Read the school's/college's annual action plan and/or strategic plan.
- The style of management will vary from school to school. Broadly speaking, management will either emphasise concern for achievement of the task or concern for the staff. The best environment is one in which there is a high concern for both the staff and the task.
- The organisation chart displayed on the wall will be out of date and is likely to be misleading. In time, you will work out which teachers and managers have credibility and influence with the head teacher and the senior management team. It is these people who can help you achieve your aims and objectives.
- Don't alienate people or make ill-informed judgements of staff. Just because they don't approach teaching the way you do does not make them bad teachers.
- Negotiate a written mentoring agreement with your mentor. (See Handout 1.1 for what should be covered in the agreement.)

Agreed action points

Alex will:

- Identify who holds copies of the policies and procedures identified above.
- Using a strategic reading approach, review the key policies and procedures identified above.
- Obtain and read the school's annual action plan and last Ofsted report.

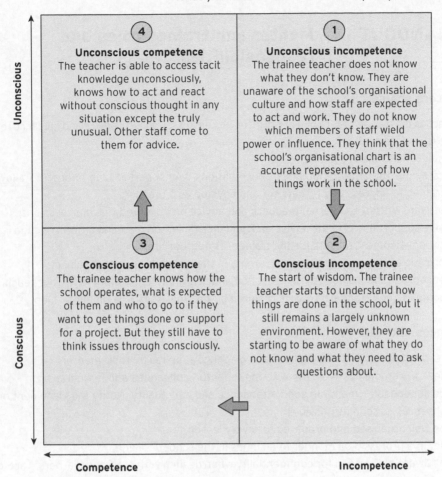

The figure shows four quadrants with two axes: the vertical axis ranges from **Conscious** (bottom) to **Unconscious** (top); the horizontal axis ranges from **Competence** (left) to **Incompetence** (right).

4. Unconscious competence
The teacher is able to access tacit knowledge unconsciously, knows how to act and react without conscious thought in any situation except the truly unusual. Other staff come to them for advice.

1. Unconscious incompetence
The trainee teacher does not know what they don't know. They are unaware of the school's organisational culture and how staff are expected to act and work. They do not know which members of staff wield power or influence. They think that the school's organisational chart is an accurate representation of how things work in the school.

3. Conscious competence
The trainee teacher knows how the school operates, what is expected of them and who to go to if they want to get things done or support for a project. But they still have to think issues through consciously.

2. Conscious incompetence
The start of wisdom. The trainee teacher starts to understand how things are done in the school, but it still remains a largely unknown environment. However, they are starting to be aware of what they do not know and what they need to ask questions about.

Note: You undergo the same 4 stage journey in the classroom as your teaching skills and knowledge develop.

Figure 1.1 Understanding your journey from unconscious incompetence to unconscious competence

Adapted from www.businessballs.com/consciouscompetencelearningmodel.htm.

HANDOUT 1.1 Mentor and trainee roles and responsibilities

Mentors should:

- act as the trainee's first point of call in the placement for general advice and guidance related to the placement;
- meet the trainee regularly;
- carry out the agreed number of observations over a period long enough to allow the trainee to address any targets set and develop as a teacher;
- provide written and verbal feedback and advice on observed teaching sessions;
- give support and provide advice and guidance on lesson planning and curriculum issues;
- set development targets for the trainee, as appropriate;
- provide advice on teaching and learning in the trainee's specialist subject;
- encourage the trainee to use reflection and self-analysis to improve his/her teaching;
- complete any standard reports required by the university in a timely fashion.

Trainees should:

- respond positively to any advice and guidance supplied by their mentor;
- seek to communicate clearly with their mentor, colleagues and learners;
- be dependable – maintain good attendance and punctuality. Notify the placement of any absences as soon as possible;
- be well organised and prepared for every lesson;
- act in a professional manner at all times in the school/college;
- be aware of the need for confidentiality when dealing with staff and learners. Tact, good humour and diplomacy go a long way;
- seek and act upon advice whenever they are unsure how to proceed;
- be flexible;
- be supportive of colleagues;
- follow the organisation's dress code;
- become familiar with the organisation's ethos/culture, routines, procedures and policies;
- keep up-to-date in their subject and any developments in teaching and learning;
- be accountable, responsible and trustworthy with both learners and colleagues;
- work collaboratively with others in teams and meetings.

Adapted from material issued by Birmingham City University to trainee teachers.

Further reading

Fletcher, S. (2012), *Mentoring in Schools: A Handbook of Good Practice*. London: Routledge.

Handy, C. (1993), *Understanding Organizations* (4th edn). London: Penguin Books.

Wallace, S. and Gravells, J. (2007), *Mentoring in the Lifelong Learning Sector* (2nd edn). Exeter: Learning Matters.

Tutorial 2 What you need to know about classroom management

> **Aim of tutorial:** To provide you with the information you require to feel confident in managing your learners and teaching environment.
>
> **Tutorial overview:** This tutorial on classroom management provides you with a range of strategies for establishing a good rapport with your learners and managing poor behaviour in the classroom. It also discusses the value of **reflection in action**, and on action, and suggests how to work effectively with classroom assistants.

Contents

2.1 Alex's reflection

> *I've always thought that classroom management would be a problem for me. I'm just not the asser-tive type. I can stand up for myself but I don't like conflict. It's probably going to be one of the trickiest aspects of teaching for me to get to grips with. It's a good job that Jane wants to talk to me about the different approaches to classroom management before she lets me free on a class.*

> *Maybe it would help the discussion if I listed some of the issues from my point of view. Firstly, I know I look young for my age - will that be a problem? To compensate should I go in hard at first and be authoritarian or should I try to be nice to them? If I do the latter I'm pretty sure that they will think I'm an easy touch. Secondly, as I'm not comfortable with conflict, how am I going to deal with the troublemakers and the ringleaders? Thirdly, most teaching assistants (TAs) are older than me and have a lot more experience of teaching - how can I tell them what to do? Enough already - I'm starting to worry!*

2.2 Behaviour management

Jane was finishing her lunch when I entered the staffroom. She quickly collected together the debris and dropped them in the waste bin. *'Right,'* she said. *'Before I let you loose on my lot I want to check out how you feel about behaviour management. This is the one area that most trainees worry about. So now is your chance to share your concerns.'*

I quickly outlined my worries about looking too young and being unsure about the type of relationship I wanted to establish with my learners.

'These are common concerns among trainees. But, based upon what I've seen of you in the classroom, your worries are unfounded. Let me explain. Most learners expect the teacher to give them directions. They have been conditioned to expect it by many years of school- ing. Indeed, they can become very confused if you don't exercise some authority. Now, that doesn't mean that you have to be authoritarian and unpleasant. You just need to act in an assertive manner.'

'What do you mean by "an assertive manner"?'

'Using a confident tone of voice, while looking relaxed and in control. If you can achieve that, very few learners will challenge your instructions or requests.'

'But what if you don't feel confident . . . Do I just fake confidence until I feel it?'

'Absolutely. Learners by and large despise teachers who try to be their friend and it can cause you all sorts of problems when it comes to marking their work or writing a reference for them. Not to mention the possibility that any unusual relationship could be seen as inap- propriate. No, it's safer all round if you maintain a professional distance from your learners. Yes, you want to help and support them but you are not their parent, friend or confidant - you are their teacher.'

'Those pointers are really helpful. Take your class, for example, they immediately do what you say but seem reluctant to follow my instructions when we're team teaching. Often they look to see if you agree with my requests.'

'As a trainee teacher you don't necessarily get off on the right foot. This is because you often meet the class after they have formed their own relationships with their teacher and you're an interloper, not part of their world. I tried to use a few strategies to help you with this when you started. Can you think what they were?'

'You gave me a great introduction, I remember! They must have thought that I was a celebrity. You also started a new topic, so I suppose they felt that we were turning a page in the course – new subject, new teacher. You also gave me specific things to do with groups of learners and didn't try to interfere; but I've got to say, I still think they saw me as your shadow – your sidekick. And these first impressions are important.'

'They certainly are. Many psychologists say that it can take as little as 15 to 30 seconds to form an impression of someone and that it's then very difficult to change your mind. So you need to make sure that you plan your first solo session meticulously so that you don't appear flustered. You must be there before them so that they're entering your territory. Your appearance should say that you mean business and you must start on time. Be assertive in asking latecomers for an explanation, but tell them to see you later. Don't dwell on them. Project your voice and use your whole body to convey your message. Of course, eye contact is important, and use directed questions.

You must address learners by name as soon as possible. You could try memorising names from photos, but that isn't easy. At the very minimum, get them to write their name on badges or cards and insist that they sit in the same place each session.'

'Sounds like a military exercise!'

'That's not a bad analogy. Have a strategy. Start by observing how good teachers and successful people in the media present themselves to their audience and use gesticulation to emphasise key points. Establish a set of ground rules that you and the learners will follow and always pick people up if they break one of these rules. Do this consistently and the rules will automatically kick in minutes after the session starts because of the learners' prior conditioning/expectations. It's worth mentioning that these tactics – to a greater or lesser extent – apply to teaching all age groups, even adults.'

'I get the picture. Adults can be difficult too. I remember trying to contribute to a staff development session at the call centre and the others wouldn't stop talking. We set ground rules at uni, so that seems like a good approach.'

'Certainly – ground rules or a classroom charter. But it needs to be done at the start or the classroom community will quickly make up their own. Try an activity in which you discuss absolutes, like not doing harm to anyone, then maybe negotiate rules like completing homework on time and a policy on putting your hand up to ask a question. Write up what rules have been agreed and give everyone a copy. It's also useful to get one laminated and put it on the wall. It is now a requirement for every school to have a home–school agreement, so it's important that the classroom charter reflects this too. Here's a handout as an example.' (See Handout 2.1.)

'Great, that's a start, but then it's downhill from there on. What do I do?'

'That sounded a bit defeatist, but there's an element of truth in it. I always think that classroom relationships go through three phases – mutual distrust, mutual trust, then mutual apathy. It's the transition to this last phase that you need to avoid. Most disruption is innocuous, low-level stuff. It doesn't threaten life or limb, but it impedes learning. Remember that

you're in charge: let your yes be yes and your no be no. Enforce school and classroom rules all the time, even when your mind's on going home for dinner. React decisively to any hint of low-level disruption, but don't shout; keep rebukes short, directed privately at the miscreant and if possible use their name. Again, use your body, gestures, eye contact and facial expression to enforce the rule. If this is done in the early stages, you've a good chance of maintaining order.'

'That sounds exhausting. But there's always that one who won't respond. What do I do then?'

'I know, the leader of the pack syndrome. Sometimes there's a case for ignoring low-level disruption. For example, if it's done for effect or to attract attention, then try to ignore it initially. Consider group management strategies to isolate ringleaders. Ensure that activities are focused and your instructions are clear. You could try making use of those leadership skills in group situations by letting different learners lead on different issues. Praise their success and try using peer evaluation and reflection to identify problems and isolate trouble-makers. Put problem learners in a situation where their peers can make their feelings known.'

'That sounds very fluffy. Sometimes I just want to tell them how I feel about them.'

'That's too personal. Public rebukes can often be detrimental to the task in hand. The individual trouble-maker may feel that they have won by getting you to react in public. Be prepared to ask the person to see you later and attempt a **restorative dialogue**. Allow them to put their point of view, but always end the conversation with a summary, conditions for re-establishing your relationship and indicators of how and when they will be achieved.'

'So what happens if this goes pear-shaped and someone loses control in class?'

'I'll come to that, but prevention is better than cure. Don't let unacceptable behaviour creep in by ignoring incidents and do ensure that you model the way that you expect learners to behave.'

'So if I shout, they see that as acceptable behaviour, or if I don't give work back on time, they will think that they don't have to hand it in on time.'

'Exactly. Also, be clear about punishments, issue them every time the rules are broken and ensure that they're stringent enough to discourage poor behaviour. You must be consistent in how you deal with each type of problem.'

'So I can't tar and feather one person for shouting in class and give a detention to another.'

'True. But less of the tar and feathering please. Try to avoid situations occurring by planning an engaging lesson – keep them busy. When you manage group work, plan to keep trouble-makers apart and make it easy to isolate them if needed. The psychologist Burrhus Skinner was the father of behaviourism. (See Tutorial 5.) He found that punishment did not change learned behaviour in animals. His conclusion was that undesirable behaviour should not be reinforced by undue attention; he considered that the only thing that is learned from punishment is how to avoid it. He considered **positive reinforcement** or reward preferable to punishment.'

'You still haven't answered my main question! Supposing someone kicks off. I could threaten all sorts of things, but the sanctions are limited.'

'OK. Let me try again. Your first strategy is to avoid confrontation, to diffuse the situation. If that fails, avoid making threats that won't be carried out. Once learners know that your threats are hollow, the behaviour will recur. Be prepared to downplay or ignore threats and insults. Often a reaction is expected and the situation can be diffused if one isn't provided. You can then address what was said at a time of your choosing. In extreme cases, be prepared to isolate the perpetrator or remove the audience. The trouble-maker will not want to lose face in front of the audience, so isolate them to avoid this. Look for a way out in which neither of you lose face; for example "I can see that you found that situation stressful and I empathise, but we need to make progress with this task, so we'll move on and talk about this at 12.30" – but make sure that the others see that you have pursued it. You can always call for help. For example, have a "time out" card with "please send help immediately to . . ." and ask a reliable learner to take it to a manager.'

'I know that the standard advice for new teachers is to discuss issues with other staff,' I said, 'but I can't help feeling that they will think I'm having a problem because I'm young/new to teaching/a useless teacher. It makes me feel inadequate.'

'That's quite common. But I can assure you that the problem is mainly in your head. All teachers remember what it was like to be a trainee and they will help if they can. If you have a problem with a particular class, discuss it with colleagues; they may have found strategies that work, offer support or raise it as an issue in a team meeting. You could even hold a class meeting in which the learners can feedback on what they think is working, what is not working and why. This could be an opportunity to bring peer pressure to bear. There is a policy on behaviour management, so make sure that you're aware of it and that you apply it.'

2.3 Alex's reflection

I'll definitely try out some of the behaviour management approaches suggested by Jane. Just as soon as I'm let free on a class of my own. At the moment I have Jane in the room to keep things under control. She seems to have eyes in the back of her head and is able to spot trouble minutes before it explodes into a full-scale problem. I wonder if this is another example of **tacit knowledge** *in action (see Tutorial 7) along with Jane's ability to reflect in action while delivering a lesson.*

I still think that I have very little, if any, tacit knowledge to draw on, but I have noticed that I am starting to find that I can work with a group while still monitoring what is going on in the wider classroom and be thinking about what I need to do to clarify issues for the learners before they arise. What was it that Wayne Kent said at uni . . . 'As a teacher you have to be able to deliver a lesson with one part of your brain while using another part to monitor everything that is going on in the classroom.' What could be easier than that?

What I could do is write up the next **critical incident** *that occurs in the classroom and then analyse it to see what lessons I can learn from it.*

SPACE FOR YOUR NOTES

Prompts

- What aspects of behaviour management worry you most?
- What can you do to remedy your concerns?
- How assertive are you? Do you need to undergo assertiveness training?

2.4 Classroom environment

'One of the standards talks about the classroom environment. I don't quite know what is meant by that. Is it just talking about the temperature and light and so on? If so, I don't have much control over that.'

'In some ways it does mean that and you do have some control. Remember that people need to have their physical needs met to learn effectively, so you need to ensure that the temperature and light levels are conducive to learning. However, the physical environment also extends to things like displays, so personalise your classroom and show that you value your learners' work by displaying it.'

'But that's about the limit, isn't it really? I mean I can't change much else in the classroom, can I?'

'You can quite easily designate areas for particular purposes. For example, a retreat area can be used to isolate trouble-makers. You can also encourage discipline and concern for others by insisting that the room is kept tidy and free from hazards at all times. You can try to make the environment warm and relaxing. You can do this by displaying learners' work, or photographs recording significant events – but make sure that you have the appropriate permissions before using photographs.'

'We're back to the school's policies and procedures on use of images and safeguarding of learners.' (See Tutorial 1.)

'Good point. The use of plants can also soften the environment, and music before the class starts can have a relaxing effect on even the most boisterous learners. But beware, some schools and colleges don't like music being played. What else do you think can contribute to a relaxed teaching environment that limits the opportunities for misbehaviour?'

'You can move the tables around, but the caretaker goes mad.'

'This is an important aspect of the classroom management because it affects communication between individuals. I suggest moving tables to suit the types of interaction required, but it's important to return desks to the standard layout in case others need to use the room. What sort of layouts have you come across?'

'Well, rows are common, but I think that table squares are better for group. I've been to seminars where tables have been arranged as a horseshoe too. Maybe I should try some of these arrangements to see how well they work.'

*'Certainly try them, but make sure that there's justification in your lesson plan for a particular arrangement. And, as you said, never upset the caretaker. If you annoy them they can make your life hell, so be nice to them. Anyway, here's a figure illustrating different layouts and how they relate to learner- and **teacher-centred** approaches.'* (See Figure 2.1.)

2.5 Alex's reflection

OK, let's see, classroom layout. What are the advantages and disadvantages of different layouts? Tables in rows - teacher-centred, so student-centred learning activities will be problematic. However, most of the learners will be able to see the board clearly. I can make eye contact with them and monitor their behaviour and there will be less opportunity for chatting. But it's inflexible in terms of allowing interaction between learners, but hang on, they could just turn round and work in fours! Now that's worth a fig roll and a cup of tea!

Now where was I?

*Table squares are student-centred. They allow for group work and collaboration and **differentiation** between groups - which would make completion of tasks much easier, with the focus much more on the learner. However, eye contact is a problem. I can't see them all from the front and they will chat more. But I could monitor the level of chat and off-task activities when I go round to see their work. Some of them will have to turn around to see the board - not a huge problem.*

Horseshoe arrangement - a sort of halfway house between the above two layouts which could be used for student-centred and teacher-centred activities. I can make eye contact with all of the learners. Learners have almost equal status - no front or back row - some communication between all learners is possible. Group work difficult, but pairs and threesomes would be OK. The major advantage is that I can get close to all of them and nip any disciplinary problems in the bud.

SPACE FOR YOUR NOTES

Prompts

- Which classroom layouts have you tried?
- What does your choice of layout say about your style of teaching?
- Which layouts do your learners seem to prefer?

2.6 Working in partnership with teaching assistants

'OK, I think that's about it for today. Any questions?'

'We've discussed most of my concerns, but what about TAs? Most of them are older and more experienced than me. I find them a bit intimidating. What's their role in the class and how do I deal with them?'

'If you are lucky enough to have a TA you should be grateful. They can play a very important role in any classroom. It's important that you show them respect, value what they have to say and include them in any decision-making and action planning. A good relationship with your TA is vital. Without it, you are working with one hand tied behind your back. They are there to support teachers, learners, specific aspects of the curriculum and the school in the widest sense.'

'I'd assumed that they were just there to support learners with special needs.'

'They do that, but they also try to develop the transferable skills of all learners, such as the ability to work independently, and improve social and problem-solving skills. Inclusion is really important, and many learners only remain in mainstream education because they can receive individual support from TAs. This includes learners with English as an additional language, those with additional physical needs, and the gifted and talented.'

'How does that differ from supporting the teacher, then?'

'The teacher often needs support with core subjects such as literacy and numeracy. In the case of group work, TAs can either free the teacher to work with particular groups, or they may work with those groups themselves and free the teacher to support the rest of the class. TAs can also fulfil an important role in behaviour management by working with those with challenging behaviour. In addition, they can watch for signs of bullying. This extra pair of eyes means that the teacher can be informed at the first sign of problems; communication with the teacher is a very important aspect of a TA's role. They may also help to prepare teaching materials.'

'I see, so when you say they can support aspects of the curriculum, that could include numeracy, literacy, IT and other language needs.'

'Absolutely, but let's not forget the wider school community. TAs can liaise with outside agencies, school psychologists and speech therapists, for example. Within the school they can work with special educational needs coordinators and also provide an important bridge between parents and teachers, particularly when language is an issue. It's also vital that they communicate with each other too, so they can share information on pupils. So treat them well. They can save you a load of work.'

2.7 Alex's reflection

It's clear that I need to form a good relationship with my TAs. I suppose this will involve regular meetings to discuss plans for forthcoming lessons – they could be involved in the planning of lessons – and sharing information on individual learners.

The group I'll be teaching for/with Jane has some learners who speak languages other than English at home. It would be a good idea if the TA could work with them to develop their language skills. Then there are the learners with dyslexia. There are five in that category. The TA could focus on helping them on some occasions.

It strikes me that a teacher is much more of a manager than I thought. They manage learners, their classroom and the role of support workers. Maybe I need to think more about improving my own management skills! Is the way I approach people for help or react to suggestions from colleagues appropriate and productive?

SPACE FOR YOUR NOTES

Prompts

- What has been your experience of working with TAs?
- Talk to several teachers in your school or college about how they use their TAs.
- How could you improve your relationships with TAs in your organisation?

2.8 Record of mentor meeting

Trainee: Alex Croft

Summary of key learning points

- From day one it is essential that you establish the correct relationship with your learners. They expect you to be their teacher, not their 'mate'. Be friendly and approachable but always maintain a professional distance from your learners.
- First impressions count. Be professional and assertive at all times – even if you don't feel confident.
- Address learners by their names as soon as possible.
- Watch out for signs of poor behaviour, and deter and defuse potential problems before they can ignite.

(continued)

(continued)

- Negotiate a classroom charter, give everyone a copy, display it and enforce it consistently.
- React decisively to low-level disruption, but don't shout; keep rebukes short, directed privately at the miscreant if possible and use their name. Don't reinforce bad behaviour with undue attention. Try to find the positive in people and praise it.
- Don't make idle threats. Be consistent in how you deal with behavioural problems. In extreme cases, isolate the perpetrator from the audience, speak to them individually at a time and place of your choosing and leave that meeting with a clear plan, having re-established a good relationship.
- Remember that you're not alone. Know the organisation's behaviour management policy, enforce it and be prepared to seek help from other staff if necessary.
- The physical environment of the classroom is an important aspect of learning. Maintain appropriate light and temperature levels. Personalise the classroom with displays and your learners' achievements. Try designating different areas for specific purposes.
- Classroom layout can be used to change the interactions between learners and between learners and the teacher, and to reduce the potential for behavioural problems. Troublesome learners can be kept separate and/or under observation rather than 'plotting' at the rear of the class. Rows, groups of tables and the horseshoe all have advantages and disadvantages. Justify their use by reference to your stated learning outcome.
- TAs can support the whole class, specific groups or individuals. They may also have a role in supporting curriculum subjects such as literacy, numeracy and IT. Their role in helping to foster independent learning is important.
- TAs often play an important role in inclusion; for example, working with those with special learning, language or physical needs, and gifted and talented learners.
- TAs can also work with learners who display challenging behaviour and monitor the class for signs of bullying.
- TAs may liaise with other stakeholders, such as psychologists and speech therapists. They may also work with parents, for example, when language is an issue. Good communication between the TA and the teacher is vital.

Agreed action points

Alex will:

- Try some of the behaviour management strategies discussed in the tutorial and reflect on the outcomes.
- Plan an activity using a classroom layout that has not been tried before.
- Talk to TAs about how they see their role and consider using this topic as the focus for a research assignment.

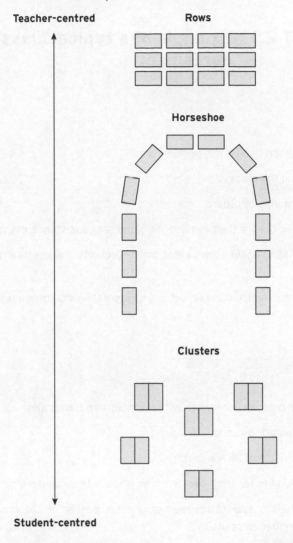

Figure 2.1 Consider using teacher- and learner-centred classroom layouts for classroom management purposes

HANDOUT 2.1 Example of a typical classroom agreement

Learners will:

- arrive on time;

- complete and hand in all homework on time;

- avoid disrupting the class in any way;

- respect the opinions of others;

- accept responsibility for their own learning and seek assistance whenever they need to;

- avoid discriminating against any person on the grounds of age, ethnic background, gender or sexuality;

- not bully any other learner and report any incident involving bullying to a member of staff immediately.

Teachers will:

- arrive on time;

- mark and hand back all homework within the agreed timescale;

- come well-prepared to class;

- respect the opinions of all learners;

- accept responsibility for their own learning and continue to develop as a teacher;

- avoid discriminating against any learner or other person on the grounds of age, ethnic background, gender or sexuality;

- respect the dignity of all learners and not bully any learner verbally or physically.

Further reading

www.routledge.com/cw/mcgrath

Rogers, B. (2011), *Classroom Behaviour: A Practical Guide to Effective Teaching, Behaviour Management and Colleague Support* (3rd edn). London: SAGE.

Department for Education, www.gov.uk/government/organisations/department-for-education.

Tutorial 3 What you need to know about effective lesson planning

Aim of tutorial: To provide you with the skills and knowledge required to draft a lesson plan.

Tutorial overview: This tutorial explores the preparation that is required prior to writing a lesson plan, the role that schemes of work play and the components of a successful lesson plan. The need for *lesson evaluation* is stressed as a means of improving future lesson plans. We return to these themes in Tutorial 7, which examines in detail the elements of a highly successful lesson.

Contents

3.1 Alex's reflection

It's been an interesting couple of weeks shadowing Jane. As the days have passed she has involved me more in the actual delivery of the lesson. At first I was largely passive, just watching what she did. Then I got promoted to classroom monitor in charge of distributing handouts and other resources. That developed into working with the learners in pairs and small groups. This week I have a terrible feeling that she is going to hand over a part of the session to me. I'm 90 per cent excited and 10 per cent scared out of my life. Or is that 10 per cent excited and 90 per cent scared?

3.2 Lesson preparation – the lesson rationale

It was lunch-time when I entered Jane's office. She was reading the latest copy of Empire, the cover of which was adorned with a picture of George Clooney. She caught my quizzical look and grinned sheepishly. *'I only have an interest in him,'* she said. *'I'm not obsessed. Honest.'*

'Isn't that what all stalkers say.'

'Enough cheek. Just remember I have an input to your final reference.'

'Absolutely, oh great one. You are definitely not obsessed.'

'Anyway, to business. You've probably guessed from our chat on Friday that you'll be teaching your first session this Thursday. Don't look so worried. It will only be 20 minutes and I'll be in the class with you.'

'Good,' I said, and meant it. 'Am I doing the start or the end of the lesson?'

'The start. What advice did the university give you about preparing for a lesson?'

'They said we should start with a rationale for the lesson (**lesson rationale**).'

'And what did they say should be covered in it?'

I was glad that I'd read the *Faculty's Practice of Teaching Workbook* over the weekend and was able to recite the list from memory. 'Well, you need to describe the context in which the teaching will take place, consider the needs of your learners and take into account any advantages or constraints that the classroom might have.'

'Such as,' asked Jane, breaking my concentration.

'Is the room too small or large for the group? Is it noisy? Has it got an interactive whiteboard and Internet access?'

'Ok, good. Carry on.'

'Where was I? Oh yeah – identify and justify my learning outcomes for the session; explain and justify why I have selected the teaching methods I have; consider how I will use information and communication technology (ICT) and other resources in the lesson; outline how I will assess the learning that has taken place and, finally, think about what methods I will use to evaluate the success of the lesson.' I sat back, feeling pleased with myself.

'That's very good. I'd add in identification and justification of any learning theories that you intend to use.'

'It seems a lot of work even before you get to the lesson plan,' I said.

'Indeed it is. Very few experienced teachers actually write rationales. Why do you think that is?'

After some thought, I said the obvious, 'Because they don't need one?'

'Correct. But why don't they need one?'

Finally the penny dropped. 'Because they already know the school, the learners and the environment.'

'Precisely. They have tacit knowledge which we talked about previously. We'll talk about this more in a future meeting. But basically you can think of it as background knowledge that the person uses subconsciously to inform their actions. So why do you think the uni wants you to draw up a rationale?'

'Because as a trainee I don't have any tacit knowledge. Therefore I need to think about the lesson consciously in advance. The rationale forces me to think about my learners, the environment I'm working in, and the theories and methods that I am going to use. When I have those straight in my head I'm in a good position to write my lesson plan.'

'Good answer. There is an old saying that "poor planning leads to poor performance". What you are doing is immersing yourself in the task ahead and thinking about it in broad terms before you get down to the detail of the lesson plan.'

3.3 Schemes of work

'What other document do you need before you tackle the lesson plan?'

That was easy. 'A **scheme of work**.'

'Exactly. So what is a scheme of work?'

'It's the link between the syllabus and the lesson plan,' I replied, remembering how Sue had described it. 'The syllabus is broken down into deliverable chunks and these chunks become lessons. Typically what you try to do is summarise in a few words the title and content of the lesson, aims and objectives of the session, teaching methods that you will use and activities that learners will undertake and resources and assessment methods that you will use – like this,' I said quickly, outlining the headings to be found in most schemes of work.

Date and lesson no.	Title of lesson	Aims and objectives	Teaching methods	Resources	Assessment strategy

'And the purpose of the scheme of work?'

'To ensure that the syllabus is fully covered and that nothing is missed.'

'And that it's delivered in some sort of logical order. There is nothing worse than delivering material to a group of learners in a haphazard order. Learning is incremental and each session should build on what has gone before. Most schools will have schemes of work, but when there isn't one you'll have to write it. Fortunately, we have a scheme of work in place that you will need to refer to when writing your rationale and lesson plan.'

3.4 Alex's reflection

> Thursday's deadline has certainly concentrated my mind. I've started to write my lesson rationale. There is a lot to think about. But working through one heading at a time and constantly referring to my university notes has made it doable.

Some sections are really easy to complete, such as describing the context in which the teaching will take place and the challenges and opportunities that the classroom poses. In fact, as most of my teaching is going to take place in the same or very similar classrooms, I should be able to cut and paste these sections into any future rationales and just make any minor amendments as required.

*Unfortunately, that can't be said for the remaining sections. Each session will have a different set of learning outcomes and the teaching and assessment strategies that I use are also likely to change. And what I teach will have an impact on what ICT and resources I use. But hang on a minute. What was it that Hal Jordan was on about in class? He said that 80 per cent of any piece of work could be done in 20 per cent of the time and that it then took 80 per cent of the time to complete the remaining 20 per cent. He called it the **Pareto Principle**. And, similarly, Sue said that I could meet about 80 per cent of all standards in a taught session. So maybe I can use these sections as the basis for any future rationales. They could be like my '80 per cent draft'. They will need significant amendment but it's better than starting with a blank page.*

I've got Jane's scheme of work. So I'll work to that. It seems pretty straightforward but then I didn't have to construct it from scratch. It's certainly logical and very clear. Maybe I can use it as a model for any future scheme of work that I have to write. After all, why reinvent the wheel?

I'm interested in this idea of tacit knowledge. Maybe I'll have a look on the Net and see what it's all about.

SPACE FOR YOUR NOTES

Prompt

- Review the example schemes of work and rationales produced by your university. Do you understand what has to be written under each heading?

3.5 Lesson plans

'OK, let's get on to lesson plans. Why do we need them?'

'They help you to identify what you are going to do, how you are going to do it and when you are going to do it.'

'What do you mean by when?'

'Well, on the back of the uni's lesson plan there is space to record what you are doing at each stage of the session. Here, I'll show you,' I said, grabbing a pen and sheet of paper. Quickly I sketched what I meant.

Stage and timing	Learning/teaching strategy	Learning outcomes	Aids and equipment	Assessment	Standards
0–10	Take, register, recap previous learning	Consolidation of previous learning	Register	Q&A	

Jane looked at my table, nodding her approval. *'Good. If you keep an eye on the first two columns, you can avoid spending too much time on one topic, ensure that you cover everything required and finish on time. But in my opinion the greatest advantage of a lesson plan for a trainee teacher is that it gives you confidence. A good lesson plan does not guarantee a good lesson but if you know what you are doing and have enough content to fill the time available, you are a long way towards having the basis of a decent lesson, which, if you are new to teaching, is a great comfort.'*

I nodded in agreement.

Jane handed my pad back to me and asked, *'So what does the rest of the lesson plan cover?'*

Jane was working me hard but I was well prepared and pleased to be able to show what I knew. 'Well, there is the obvious stuff, like date of session, details of the class being taught and the context of the lesson. Why am I teaching the session and how it fits into the scheme of work.'

*'Good. But what about your **lesson objectives**?'*

'They come next. It has been stressed to us time and time again at the university that we have to state our objectives in such a way that we can confirm, by some form of assessment, that they have been achieved.'

'And how do you do that?'

'By writing something like "By the end of the lesson learners will be able to: describe six features of x; explain how x works; list the causes of x or the advantages and disadvantages of x".'

'That's good. Basically, you have to provide the learners with the opportunity to demonstrate what they have learnt as a result of attending the session. You would be surprised how many teachers find it difficult to express their learning objectives in such terms. But if you think about it, the whole point of a lesson is to deliver learning. And the only way you can know if learning has taken place is to carry out some form of assessment.'

'So I need to think how I'm going to assess each objective as I write it?'

'Absolutely. But also think differentiation. How are you going to meet the different needs of your learners?'

'Well, if your objectives are assessable you can grade them. So, for example, all learners will be able to describe three features of x and some will be able to list six or more.'

'Good. There are other ways you can differentiate and we will look at them when we talk about delivering a highly successful lesson.'

'That's still some way off,' I said, with more feeling than I'd intended.

'No, you'll be there soon enough. Half of teaching is confidence and the remaining 50 per cent is being able to fake confidence.'

'Can I quote you on that?'

'No, I'd be out of a job.'

'So what else do you need to plan for?'

'Well, we've mentioned the assessment strategy,' I said.

'And what might that be?'

'The assessment methods that you use, such as Q&A, gapped handouts, completion of a task, a test or quiz, possibly an assignment . . .'

'That's good. You've got a range of strategies. The trick is to use complementary approaches . . .'

'What do you mean by complementary?' I asked.

'Well, you can ask questions to check if people understand something, but you could also give them a task to see if they can apply their knowledge. We can look at **formative assessment** and **summative assessment** if you like in the future (see Tutorial 6), but for the moment what else do you need to record in your lesson plan?'

'I need to outline the resources that I am going to use. Sue said that I should avoid over-reliance on PowerPoint and to think about using artefacts, video clips, models, photos and the like.'

'I agree with her. Teachers are becoming too dependent on PowerPoint and the kids are getting fed up. It's become the twenty-first century's equivalent to the nineteenth century's blackboard.'

Keen to list all I could remember before it went out of my mind, I pushed on. 'Vitally, I've got to consider what activities the learners are going to be involved in. I can't spend the majority of the lesson talking at them. I have to get them to do something.'

'Such as?'

'Individual work, pair working, small group working, discovery learning, any activity that is **learner-centred** and focuses on them being active learners rather than passive listeners.'

'What you are talking about is the different teaching methods that you can employ and the need to match them to the learning styles of your learners. Now, both of these subjects are huge. So I suggest that we look at them separately in future sessions, after I've had a chance to see you teach. (See Tutorials 5 and 6.) For the moment, can we just agree that your choice of teaching methods is crucial to the success of any lesson.'

'OK,' I said.

'So, what else do you need to take into account?'

'I need to identify if any of my learners need literacy, numeracy or ICT support.'

'How would you know if they did need help?'

'Well, learners with significant needs would be **statemented**. So I would have a copy of their report. Those with less-serious needs would be known to me if I had been teaching the class for a while, and if they were a new group I could look at their prior attainments and speak to their previous teachers.'

'There is a huge amount of information available in schools and colleges about each learner. Don't be afraid to ask questions of your colleagues or to check out what records exist on a specific learner if you have any concerns. The information is there to be used and it will help your teaching and the learner's performance. OK, we're almost at the end. What else can you include in the lesson plan?'

I was beginning to run out of ideas and, after a pause, Jane answered her own question. *'Consider how you are going to start the session and how you are going to end it. These plenary sessions are vital. As any actor or politician knows, entrances and exits are important. You need to make an impact when you start the session and leave a good impression when you finish. Try to have a starter activity that will grab the attention of the learners and involve everyone in the class.'*

'So I need to be very clear about what I expect the group to cover during the session and equally clear in summing up about what we have done,' I said.

'Absolutely. You should also give some thought to any potential problems that might arise in the session and how you might deal with them.'

'Such as?'

'Anything you can think of, from the mundane, such as the projector not working, to the unusual. I once had a student who had undiagnosed narcolepsy and kept falling asleep in the class. Rare or what?'

'All human life on show.'

'And then some. Once you have been observed you will also have a list of targets from the previous observation. Make sure that you address these issues specifically in your next lesson. Append a note to your lesson plan explaining how you will meet these targets. It will help you and whoever is observing you. But what is the one thing we have not mentioned so far that you must include on your plan?'

I sat for what seemed an age before the answer came. 'The standards!'

'Exactly – you must record on your lesson plan any standards that you wish to claim against that session. Now, because standards are boring, trainees find every excuse they can to avoid studying them properly. The result is that they under-claim on their early sessions and then start to panic as the year draws to a close. To avoid this, and to ensure that you don't become bored, I suggest that you study one section of standards a day. It won't take long and the more familiar you are with the standards the easier it will be to identify when you have met them in your work.'

I didn't say that I'd already looked at them. Something at the back of my mind had been nagging me. Finally, it popped into my consciousness and I asked, 'Is there a common lesson plan or template that most teachers work to?'

'Lesson plans vary a lot and when training it's best to stick to the one that your university uses. Once you start working you'll obviously use your organisation's standard lesson plan. But every plan will address most of the issues that we've covered today.'

'Does every teacher write a lesson plan for every session?'

'Hmm! It all depends. All teachers will have some sort of lesson plan. They will range from the highly detailed to the fairly informal depending on the how experienced the teacher is and how they view lesson plans.'

3.6 Lesson evaluations

'Now there is just one last issue to discuss before we finish – **evaluation** of your lessons. You should get into the habit of evaluating every lesson that you deliver. When you are not being observed you only need to spend a few minutes at the end of the session thinking about what went well, what could have gone better, how the session could be improved, etc. You can record these thoughts as a series of bullet points on your lesson plan if you like. However, when you are formally observed, your evaluation should be more extensive. What do you think you need to cover in these more extensive evaluations?'

I was getting better at taking a few seconds to consider my response before replying. Finally I said, 'How well did I meet the needs of my learners? How appropriate and relevant were my learning objectives and the teaching and learning strategies that I used? Did I use a range of effective differentiation strategies? And how useful were my learning aids and resources to the learners?' I paused, unable to think of anything else.

'That's impressive,' said Jane. 'I'd just add two more; to what extent did your strategies for assessment of learning assist learning and how successful were you in meeting the development targets that were set for you in the previous session?'

'Basically, what you are saying is that the formal evaluation covers exactly the same ground as the lesson rationale and lesson plan. But it looks at the issues from a different perspective.'

'That's very perceptive. You are indeed covering the same issues but you are looking at them from a different angle and stage of the process. The rationale is a strategic overview which looks forward. The lesson plan is a practical "how am I going to do it" document, and the evaluation **critically evaluates** what you did. Anyway, that's enough for today. Off you go and start preparing for your first taught session.'

As I packed up my things, Jane started to hum the funeral march. I looked at her quizzically and she burst out laughing. Some people!

3.7 Alex's reflection

I've been thinking all day about how I can minimise the work of writing up a new lesson plan for each session that I deliver while not missing anything. I think I've come up with a solution. I'm going to get an electronic copy of the uni's lesson plan. In each box I'm going to type myself a note reminding me what I have to cover under that heading. There could be different types of notes for different sections; for example, under objectives I could write, 'By the end of the lesson learners will be able to complete an action that I can assess and these actions can be differentiated.' But under teaching methods I might just list all the methods that I could use to teach my subject. Such a list would remind me of what is available and maybe stop me using just one or two methods that I'm comfortable with. Then, when writing a new lesson plan I can 'type over' the notes, give the document a new name and save it as a separate file. That way I'll still have my 'skeleton lesson plan' to use next time.

I'm also going to studiously evaluate each session that I do. I know that Jane said just write a few lines of evaluation on each session that is not observed but, thinking about this tacit knowledge thing, surely the quickest way to build up such knowledge is to reflect critically on what I've done in class. And learn from what went well, what went badly and, more importantly, try and work out why something went well or badly. If I'm going to do this I'll have to be self-disciplined and write up my evaluation as soon as possible after each session. Which won't always be easy, but at a minimum I could do it daily.

I'm dreading the thought of ploughing through the standards again, but it has to be done. As a first step I'm going to identify against each standard the type of activity I need to undertake to stand a chance of gathering evidence for that standard. Thinking about it, there are probably not that many activities. Let's see - teaching (which of course covers everything mentioned in this tutorial as well as giving and receiving **feedback**), working with colleagues, attending meetings with colleagues, learners and managers, setting assessment tasks, planning, completion of assignments, **continuing professional development (CPD)** activities, etc.

SPACE FOR YOUR NOTES

Prompts

- Which areas of lesson planning do you find most difficult? Why do you think this is? Who could help you with these problems?
- What process do you use to critically evaluate sessions that you deliver?

3.8 Record of mentor meeting

Trainee: Alex Croft

Summary of key learning points

- Lesson planning starts with the rationale which establishes the context in which the lesson will be delivered, the learners' backgrounds and needs, the teaching methods to be used, resources required, the intended learning outcomes and methods of assessment. **(Please note: some institutions do not require lesson rationales to be completed.)**
- Tacit knowledge is gained from experience, reflection and study. It is the knowledge that an expert accesses unconsciously and which they would find impossible to express verbally and therefore can't communicate to others.
- Schemes of work show how a single lesson fits into the overall programme of study or syllabus. They are summary documents that record the date, time and title of the session, the session's aims and objectives, the teaching methods to be used, resources required and assessment strategy.

(continued)

(continued)

- Lesson plans provide trainee teachers with a sense of confidence. The better the plan, the more likely the session will be successful.
- A good lesson plan will ensure that the trainee considers the key elements of a lesson, i.e. aims and objectives, timing, content, teaching methods, differentiation, inclusivity, resources and assessment strategy.
- Always state the aims of the lesson in such a way that you can assess whether they have been met. For example, 'By the end of the session all learners will be able to name all the planets in the solar system and stronger students 4 of the 62 moons of Saturn.'
- Think about how you will differentiate your aims, resources (including handouts) and assessment methods to meet the needs of all learners.
- Use formative assessment throughout the session to monitor the level of learning that is taking place. Consider to what extent a summative assessment at the end of the session would be appropriate. Try to develop a range of interesting assessment tools and don't rely on a few old favourites, such as **pop quizzes** and Q&A exchanges.
- Only use a resource if it will enhance the students' learning experience. Think carefully about the purpose of each resource and consider whether there is a better way to achieve the same result. Avoid 'death by PowerPoint'.
- It is vital that learners are actively engaged in their own learning. Therefore, use a range of learner-centred methods and activities to engage learners.
- Always take into account and provide for students with special needs. Where such needs have been identified, the school or college will have details of what provisions need to be made for the learner. However, many learners with special needs go unrecognised. As a teacher, you need to look out for learners who appear to be struggling and ask yourself why.
- Reference any standards that you are claiming on the lesson plan. Do this from the first session that you teach. Become familiar with the standards required. Seek out experiences that will enable you to claim standards that cannot be met in the course of teaching, e.g. attending staff and moderation meetings. Keep a written record of all such experiences.
- Always take the time to evaluate each session that you teach. For unobserved sessions the evaluation might be relatively brief with just a few comments added to the lesson plan. For observed sessions you should undertake a full evaluation using the feedback received from mentor and/or PDT.
- Always try to address any relevant targets given to you by your PDT or mentor in the next lesson that you deliver. As a source of evidence, record how you have done this on your lesson plan.

Agreed action points

Alex will:

- In the next two weeks, read the standards and identify how they can be met.
- Obtain a minimum of three different lesson plans used in other schools or colleges and examine the differences and similarities between them.

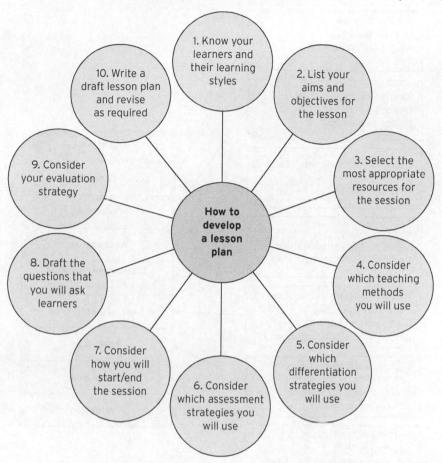

Figure 3.1 Evolution of a lesson plan

Note: Go through the cycle as many times as necessary until you are satisfied with the resultant plan.

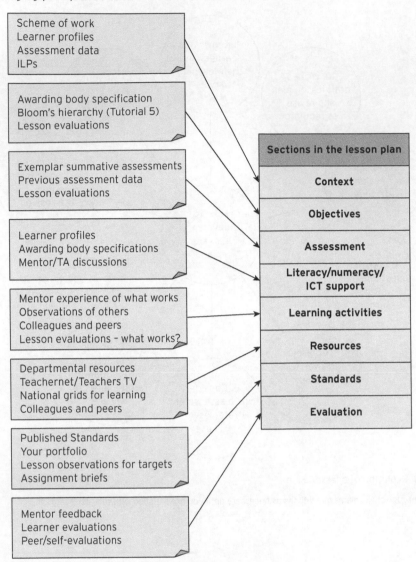

Figure 3.2 Sources of inspiration for a lesson plan

HANDOUT 3.1 Example of a completed lesson plan

PGCE PCET/DPS PCET Lesson plan		
Date 01/03/XX	Year/Group PGCE PCET level 6 Module EMOM10	SVUK and minimum core stds
Context of lesson (Why are you teaching this element? How does it fit into the scheme of work?) This is the penultimate session of the module. All the necessary theory has been covered, the majority of students will have had their teaching observed by a critical friend and the selection of resources they used evaluated. They will use this information in their next assignment. We wish to consolidate the action points arising from observed sessions and encourage students to reflect on these, the impact on their teaching and progress towards the Standards. An assignment surgery was held at the end of January at which a number of questions were raised. These questions have been answered via postings on Moodle or the intranet, but we considered that an opportunity was needed for trainees to share their experiences of completing the tasks for the assignment. Assignment tutorials will be held during the final session of the module, so this is the last whole group session. This is an opportunity to celebrate the end of the module with students and identify any further assignment-related issues as preparation for the tutorials.		CP 1.1 CP 3.2 DK 1.1 DK 1.3 DP 1.1 DP 1.3
Assessment strategy (How will you know if the learning has been successful? How will you measure this learning?) • ultimately in the quality of assignments submitted; • during feedback at assignment tutorials; • by observing the contributions on the 'tablecloths'; • by listening to the discussions during the evaluation café; • by reading feedback on Moodle following the session.		BP 1.3 EK 2.3 EK 3.2 DP 2.1 EP 1.1 EP 2.1
Note: This lesson plan is based on a session delivered to a group of PGCE students aiming to work in the post-compulsory education and training sector.		

(continued)

(continued)

Resources	BP 1.1
(How will you use ICT [create resources/PowerPoint/Smartboard]? What other resources will you use?) ICT: • PowerPoint • Smartboard • Digital audio • Digital camera • Moodle postings Other resources: • Number cards to mix groups • Flip chart • Paper tablecloths • Sweets • Markers (six colours) • Question cards • Instructions for each table, including roles • Extension activity cards • Post-it notes	BP 2.1 BP 2.2

Learning objectives	How will you differentiate?	
By the end of the lesson – All students should be able to: • assess the impact made by target setting on learning; • evaluate progress towards meeting the standards; • describe the use of an evaluation café as a teaching and learning tool; • identify areas of weakness in policy, curriculum, inclusion, resources, using ICT and learning theory aspects of the assignment in preparation for the assignment surgery; • evaluate their progress towards the assignment to determine areas for which additional support is required.	• the learning and teaching activities will be varied to suit different learning styles; • through the learning outcomes. Learners will be engaged in the same task but will not be expected to achieve the same outcomes; • more able students will be challenged further by giving them an extension exercise; • use group work so that peers can support each other; • level of individual support from tutor; • the variety of resources used; • the separation of Level 6 and 7 groups.	AP 1.1 BP 1.1 BP 2.1 DP 1.1 DP 1.2 DK 1.1

Most students will be able to: • use an evaluation cafe in their own teaching; • improve their assignment as a result of reflection. Some students will be able to: • adapt the evaluation café approach for their specialist subject area; • formulate new understanding of pedagogic approaches.	
Shared time activities (e.g. group work, learner-centred activities, individual/pair work, differentiated activities?) Class activity: starter; initial Q&A; feedback by groups at the end of the session; summary. Group work: during the sharing of targets, speed dating and evaluation café. Individual work: students identify their own action points in relation to their targets, take individual roles during the evaluation café. Completion of the assignment is an individual exercise. Pair work: speed dating	AP 4.1 BK 2.1 BP 2.2 BP 2.3 BP 2.4
Literacy, numeracy, ESOL and ICT support ICT will be addressed in the pre-session activity. Written communication will be addressed in the evaluation café. Safeguarding/ECM issues Criminal Records Bureau checks in place. Some students have addressed ECM for their assignment and their input will share their ideas and findings.	BP 3.1 MC 2.1 MC 2.2 MC 2.3 MC 2.8 MC 9.1 MC 9.3 MC 9.5 MC 9.7
Plenary (How will you open/begin/conclude/summarise your lesson?) The morning session opens with a whole group discussion on the significance of targets. The session ends with individual action planning in response to sharing targets with others.	BP 1.2 BP 2.2 EP 4.1

(continued)

(continued)

The morning session opens with a whole group discussion on the significance of targets. The session ends with individual action planning in response to sharing targets with others.	
I will open the afternoon session with an IWB session as students settle, followed by a Q&A relating to the Moodle task set at the end of the last session.	
Students feedback to the group at the end of the session and the plenary asks them to identify and share one key learning point. Tablecloths will be photographed and posted on Moodle.	
Anticipated problems/solutions • Trainees may be reluctant to share their feedback with others, so we will ask them to share targets rather than detailed feedback. • The warm-up speed dating can be difficult with large numbers. A variation involving pair work round a table will be trialled. • Some students will dominate discussions. Roles will be assigned and exchanged on each change of table. • Some may find the instructions complicated. The speed dating and evaluation café will be modelled. • Technology might not work properly. I will have copies of the instructions to hand out.	DP 1.1 BP 2.2

Further reading

www.routledge.com/cw/mcgrath
Cohen, L., Manion, L. and Morrison, K. (2010), *A Guide to Teaching Practice* (5th edn). London: Routledge.

Tutorial 4 What you need to know about teaching methods

Aim of tutorial: To give you the confidence to use a wide range of teaching methods.

Tutorial overview: This tutorial reviews a wide range of teaching methods, broadly divided into tutor-centred and student-centred methods. Many of the methods you will be familiar with, some you won't. The importance of teachers having the knowledge, skills and confidence to be able to use a range of teaching methods effectively, if they are to meet the diverse needs of learners, is stressed.

Contents

4.1 Alex's reflection

Well, my teaching session wasn't a complete disaster but it wasn't great either. I wasn't particularly nervous but I froze when one of the learners asked me about the previous week's session and I was unable to give a very convincing answer. I could feel my face flush as my mind scrabbled about for an answer that I knew wasn't there. Every second I remained silent seemed like an hour.

Jane said it didn't show and that I did OK for a first outing. But she would say that, wouldn't she? And I'd worked so hard to get everything just right. Maybe I'm not meant to be a teacher. No, come on, snap out of it. You are just feeling sorry for yourself. The session wasn't that bad. I always expect too much. I'm sure that others have had a much worse introduction to teaching and survived to become good teachers.

As for the actual incident itself, Jane said that all I had to do was say, 'I'm sorry, I don't know the answer to that question. But I'll find out and give you an answer by the end of the session.' Or just pass the question over to her. After all, she was sitting there at the back of the class. But, no, I had to try and bluff my way through. I must remember that it is not a weakness to say 'I don't know'.

4.2 Teaching methods

Jane looked up from her reading as I entered, *'So, you didn't take the honourable way out then?'* she said, smiling.

I gave a grimace in response. The wounds to my self-image were still seeping blood. 'No, I thought that it would be a bit of an over-reaction.'

'Good, because as I said in the debrief, you did OK for a first outing. Most trainee teachers expect too much from themselves. What they fail to realise is that even very experienced teachers have days when everything they do turns to dust. The important thing is to "get on the bike as soon as possible again". That's why I want you to do 30 minutes on Thursday with the same group. You did fine; now you need to build on it.'

I hadn't expected to be teaching again quite so soon, but instead of feeling anxious I felt strangely exhilarated. 'I'll be better next time,' I said with real feeling.

'I know you will. What I'd like you to think about for Thursday is using a greater range of teaching methods. At the moment you are tending to use teacher-centred teaching methods. This is understandable as they tend to give you the greatest control over what is going on in the class – even if some of that control is illusory. What you need to do is develop your use of learner-centred teaching methods. Here's a handout that will help.' (See Handout 4.1.)

4.3 Learner-centred teaching methods

'So give me some examples of learner-centred teaching methods.'

'What about discussion, discovery learning, role play and pair or small group work.'

'Good, that's a fair list to be going on with. So when might you be able to use discussions in your lesson?'

'Well, I was told that they were useful when you were working in **Bloom's affective domain** and you were trying to change people's ideas or feelings about an issue.'

'That's true, but they are also useful when you want to encourage an exchange of ideas between learners and learners or learners and teacher. They can also be used to check out

the learners' understanding of what they have been taught in a class, or seen at a cinema, theatre, on a DVD or at a presentation. But what do you think are their drawbacks?'

'Well, they can become competitive, with some kids wanting to "win" the discussion, so you need to control that. Also, one or two extroverts can end up dominating the discussion.'

'*So how do you deal with that?*'

'You need to establish ground rules before you start and actively chair the discussion, making sure that everyone has a chance to express their views and encouraging those who are shy.'

'*Any other dangers?*'

'You can get some really daft arguments that are based on personal attitudes and prejudices and have no actual knowledge or theory to underpin them.'

'*In other words, the typical pub bore. If you get that you have to explore and challenge the learner's attitudes and prejudices in such a way that they will go away and think more deeply about what they claim to believe. But what you mustn't do is embarrass them in front of the class. You might also need to consider why you feel uncomfortable with what the learner is saying. Is it your own prejudices that are being challenged?*'

'Another case of having to **reflect in action**,' I said.

'*Indeed. In addition, as the chair you have to ensure that the discussion stays on topic. For example, don't let it descend into a discussion on the "X Factor" if your focus is on the wider question of the rise of celebrity culture in the twenty-first century. But at the same time you need to avoid talking too much or jumping in to fill silences. Hold the group on a sort of loose/tight leash, giving them plenty of rope to explore the subject, but pulling them back when they go off on a tangent. OK, what about pairs and small group working?*'

'Well, that's where you split the learners into smaller subgroups to work on a particular issue or task.'

'*And what's the point of doing that?*'

'It gives the learners a chance to show what they know or can do. It also gives them some responsibility for their own learning and encourages them to show initiative. And, of course, if you set the groups up in competition with each other it can also motivate the students and keep them awake!'

'*Very true. If they have to listen, to you or me, for half an hour non-stop on a hot Friday afternoon, the chances of them falling asleep grows with each passing minute. Get them doing something. Get them active. Get them thinking. But what must you do if you are going to use small groups?*'

I tried to think, but there was nothing there and, after a pause, Jane continued: '*Every group activity must be well planned and any materials required prepared in advance. It's essential that you give clear instructions and that the learners know exactly what is required of them. Otherwise, it will be chaos.*'

'So I need to manage it and check out that the learners know what they have to do.'

'*And how are you going to do that?*'

'Give them their instructions and then ask if they understand what they have to do.'

'*You need to go further than that. Don't ask a general question such as "Do you under-stand?" Instead, ask specific questions about the instructions you have just given, such as "What is the first thing that I said you have to do?"*'

'OK.'

'*And remember – never, ever, use a task just to fill in time or to break up the session. It has to have a real purpose. It has to aid learning. If it doesn't, the learners will know and they won't take the task seriously, which can lead to all sorts of behavioural problems. Now, how can pair working or group working help you to assess learning?*'

I didn't have to think too much about the question and replied, 'You can monitor what is going on in the groups as you walk about and you can get each group or pair to feedback to the whole class at the end of the task. That way, you get a fair idea of the learners' understanding.'

'*Good. And remember, you can use questions to dig into their feedback as well and identify any issues that they may have missed. In fact, it's useful to have your own list of answers or issues and tick them off as the learners identify them and then . . .*'

'You can mention any they have missed at the end,' I said, 'but what's the best way to organise the groups?'

'*There isn't a single favoured approach. Consider your learning outcomes and the character-istics of your learners. You can group them according to ability – either mixed or groups of individuals with similar abilities – by learning preferences or native language, if relevant. In fact, any criterion, providing that it's justifiable. It's probably best if each group is then set a different task according to its characteristics.*'

'What about getting them to move from their normal seat?'

'*It sounds as if we are back to your lack of self-confidence.*'

I felt my face and neck blush but remained quiet. Was I that easy to read?

'*You could place resources on specific tables so that they have to move to access the resources. Or you could give them coloured cards or group names as they walk in. You can do this randomly or with group composition in mind. I like to put coloured Post-its under chairs with each colour representing a different group. There's an element of surprise in that!*'

'Cunning! What about group size? Is there an optimum?'

'*Quite a lot of research has been done on that. Apparently, the optimum is supposed to be four. More than that and roles can be unclear, although you can do something about that*' *by giving each learner a specific role. Some possibles are scribe, reporter – if they have to feedback to the group – coordinator, ideas person, evaluator, resource investigator and so on. If necessary, ensure that each learner produces something. This can ensure that everyone contributes. If you wanted to maximise participation, you could start with pairs and then merge two or more pairs into larger groups.'*

'We do quite a lot of **peer assessment** at the uni – I could use that. They could evaluate each other's contribution. That may serve to motivate next time.'

'Good idea provided that your learners are mature enough to take feedback from peers. Otherwise . . .'

'I could have a riot on my hands.'

*'Now I've told you millions of times not to exaggerate. If you are going to use small groups you need to reconsider your role. You move from being teacher to **facilitator**. This means that you must circulate between the groups, ensuring that everyone is on task. Listen to the conversations, provide prompts when needed and resolve any problems and note any issues that you need to change next time. An alternative approach is to use group work for guided learning. In this case you set different tasks for each group and then take the opportunity to work with each group for part of the lesson.'*

'That would give me the opportunity to support weaker learners, or challenge the more able. But if I did that, I would need to ensure that the tasks that the others do are well planned and keep them occupied.'

4.4 Alex's reflection

As luck would have it, John Steed covered aspects of group work today at uni. Some of them seem a bit complicated, so I'll really need to be organised if I'm to use them. Now where are my notes . . .

Evaluation café – Paper tablecloths are placed on tables together with a topic to consider. Each group has their own coloured pen and writes their comments on the tablecloth. They then move to the next table where they comment on the topic allocated to that table and at the same time comment on the previous groups' ideas. When each group gets back to base they reflect on their tablecloth and present a summary to the whole class at plenary. This could work with different aspects of a topic such as the Second World War, with groups working on subtopics such as politics, the home front, America and the war, etc.

Snowballing – You start with individuals thinking about a topic. They then share their thoughts in pairs, discuss in threes and then sixes, and then each group of six feeds back to the whole class.

Jigsaws – Each group works on a subtopic and then the groups are reconfigured so that each subtopic is represented in one of the new groups. Each member of the group takes the role of an expert and teaches the new group their subtopic. An example could be climate change, with subtopics of human sources of carbon, natural sources, effects of climate change, etc. Reconfigure groups by giving each learner a colour and ensure that learners on tables for subtopics have different colours. Then give each table a colour and ask learners to go to the table with their colour.

Mantle of the expert - each learner takes the role of a different expert to solve a problem. For example, the task could be to devise a package holiday, with someone being an expert on hotels, another on flights and another on the culture of the country, etc.

But what do they do then??? I've forgotten! I'd better have a look at the website John Jonzz recommended: www.mantleoftheexpert.com.

As for what Jane said, I already know that I expect too much of myself. My problem is how do I wind back from that position? It's like part of my DNA. No, that's not right, it's just my way of thinking. It's a habit and, as I've already proven by increasing my reading speed (see Tutorial 9), habits can be broken. It just takes time and patience. There are enough people out there willing to criticise me - I don't need to help them. So for the next six weeks, every time I find myself being unreasonably self-critical, I'll change the record in my brain. Maybe I could wear an elastic band on my wrist and snap it every time I find that I'm running myself down - or is that too pseudo-psychological?

Jane is right about my reliance on teacher-centred methods. It's definitely a hangover from my own school days. Most teachers I had emphasised the teaching element of teaching and learning, and personally I've always been perfectly happy to sit and listen to what they said as long as I was allowed to ask questions. But that doesn't suit everyone. I do need to use a more balanced mix of teacher- and student-centred methods.

But by just shadowing Jane I've already noticed that not every learner wants to 'take responsibility' for their own learning. What am I supposed to do with them? The learners who want to be passive and spoon-fed? What would Sue say? At a guess she would tell me that it was my job to wean them off dependency on the teacher because once out of school or college they have to take responsibility for their own learning. The problem is, how do I do it? Slowly and in stages, I would imagine.

SPACE FOR YOUR NOTES

Prompts

- What is your preferred teaching method?
- Why do you use that method?
- What teaching methods have you never tried? Why?
- Can you think of any other group work activities?

4.5 Learner-centred teaching methods continued

'What was the next method you mentioned?'

'Discovery learning. Mind you, I sometimes think that it's just an excuse for the teacher to do nothing.'

'It sounds like you've had a bad experience of discovery learning.'

'Well, I had this teacher in sixth form. He said he wanted us to be independent learners, but personally I think he just wanted to read the "Racing Post". So he used to send us off to the learning resources centre to research what he should have been teaching us.'

'Alas, it can be misused. But it can be incredibly powerful when properly applied. It allows learners to take responsibility for their own learning, make their own discoveries and develop a wide range of skills and qualities, including personal responsibility, initiative, problem-solving, planning, decision-making and communication. But to achieve these lofty aims it has to be properly organised and, as with group work, it's essential that learners know precisely what is required of them and that there is a clear system of monitoring and feedback in place. The teacher can't just abrogate responsibility for the learners' learning. They have to monitor the exercise, ensure that learners don't go off at a tangent and put in place mechanisms to assess the learning that has taken place.'

'All the things my old teacher didn't.'

'There are a few lazy rogues in every profession. But, properly done, discovery learning can motivate learners, involve students who are disenchanted with other teaching approaches and be used very effectively as a strategy for differentiation, with each student effectively differentiating the task according to the level at which they engage with it.'

'I'd never thought of it in terms of differentiation but I can see how it might work. In the same way, I suppose role play could be used to promote differentiation.'

'Possibly. For a role play to work, learners must be given enough information about the character they are playing and the situation that they face. They need to be briefed beforehand. Without that they won't be able to react appropriately to the situation they find themselves in.'

'So, again, it's a teaching method that has to be planned for and set up. If I use it I'll need to give lots of information to the learner in advance. But wait, I could give them a written briefing note. That would save time and I could reuse the notes.'

'Correct. If done properly, learners can experience what it's like to play a particular role in real life. Such as a sales assistant responding to an angry customer or going for a job interview. The difference is that they can practise and receive advice and criticism in the safety of the classroom. What do you think are the benefits of such an approach?'

'It can help you understand where people are coming from.'

'How so?' Jane asked.

'Well, we've all complained at some time or another. But we have not all had the experience of facing an angry customer. The role play gives us a chance to see things from the other side.'

'*It's also a good method for learners who are activists and learn by doing things. But what are the disadvantages of role play?*'

'Lots of learners hate them. I know I did at school.'

'*Why?*' Jane asked.

'Embarrassment, fear of making a fool of yourself in front of the class, a lack of confidence and classmates taking the mickey if you take it too seriously. Do I need to go on?'

'*So how can you combat this?*'

'You need to plan the role play carefully. You also have to agree to some ground rules that everyone in the class signs up to. And, finally, you have to fully brief both those taking part in the drama and those observing. Because both participants and observers have a part to play in making the exercise a good learning experience.'

'*I couldn't have said it better myself. You can see that there is a theme emerging here. The more you plan and prepare your teaching methods the more likely they are to be successful. Always think about the instructions that you have to give. Are they clear and unambiguous? Will the learners understand what is required? How am I going to assess that learning has taken place? Now, there are other learner-centred methods that you can use, but I'm going to apply a bit of discovery learning. I want you to take this handout (see Handout 4.1) and fill in the last column which asks you to consider how and to what extent you could use each teaching method in your own teaching.*'

'OK. Learner-centred methods seem to be the flavour of the decade, but they must have some downsides?'

'*In recent years learner-centred strategies have become the new orthodoxy in teaching, along with the idea that learning must be fun. But things are changing. It's become recognised that poorly motivated learners may regard the freedom provided by these strategies as an opportunity to do very little or to misbehave. They tend to be most successful with highly motivated, self-disciplined learners. I'm pleased to say that in the past few years there has been a rebalancing of the education scales. With a recognition that great learning requires great teaching.*'

4.6 Alex's reflection

Everything keeps coming back to the need to plan things in advance. It doesn't matter which learner-centred approach I adopt - I have to plan the activity carefully. I suppose that's the price I pay for having to do less active teaching in the classroom - I've already done most of it before I arrive - and more facilitation.

If I'm going to use more learner-centred methods in my teaching I'll have to work on my questioning technique. I've never thought about using specific directed questions to check out if the learners know what they have to do. But it's obvious really. I'll try and make an extra effort in my next session. I should note that as a personal target on my lesson plan.

SPACE FOR YOUR NOTES

Prompts

- What are the benefits of using learner-centred teaching methods?
- What are the drawbacks or difficulties of using learner-centred methods? How can these be minimised?

4.7 Teacher-centred teaching methods

'OK, let's look at teacher-centred methods. How many can you list?'

'How about lecture, formal teaching, team teaching and maybe a demonstration.'

'OK. How would you describe lecturing?'

'It's a bit like a presentation given to an audience with little (if any) interaction or feedback. It can be useful when you have a large group of learners.'

'Very good – and what do you think are its strengths?'

I had to think before answering. 'The lecture can be pre-planned, written and practised in advance of delivery. It's also a good way to convey a large amount of information to an audience in a short space of time.'

'Be careful about the idea that you can deliver a lot of information. It's still true that a learner could cover more ground in an hour by reading a textbook than by attending a lecture. Good lectures provide a framework for learning that students can build on outside the classroom. So you need to cover the main points, explain difficult issues and enthuse the learners with what you have to say.'

'You mean motivate them to do some personal study or discovery learning?'

Exactly. A good lecture is motivating and interesting. The best can inspire a love for the subject that lasts a lifetime. A bad lecture is an hour of sheer boredom. But what we have just described is the formal lecture. Far more useful to a teacher is its near relative, the short interactive lecture. This is where you deliver information, but seek to check out the learners' understanding by using a series of directed and open questions to members of the group. That way you can still cover a wide range of material but involve the learners in the process.'

'So they don't just sit there passively.'

'Precisely. Keep them alert, keep them attentive.'

'But where does an interactive lecture end and formal teaching take over?'

'That's a fair question. Formal teaching is concerned with presenting information to the learners using a variety of techniques, including mini-lectures and demonstrations. But it also encourages the learner's active participation in the lesson. This is done by allowing space for dialogue, discussions, and question and answer between the teacher and the learners and between learners.'

'So you are looking for the learners' active involvement but you set the parameters within which the learners can take part,' I said.

'That's about it. You build the box within which they study. You determine to a large extent what they need to know or should know.'

'Sounds very 1984ish.'

'Maybe, but learners need guidance on what to learn. On what is important and why. And sometimes the best way to deliver that is by formal teaching. But, as with lectures, you need to keep the learners interested, otherwise they will become bored, and that can lead to behaviour problems, as we've previously discussed.' (See Tutorial 2.)

'It still sounds as if most of the talking is done by the teacher.'

'That's why it's called teacher-centred,' said Jane, stressing each word as if she were talking to a dimwit.

I felt like striking my head with the palm of my hand and saying Doh! Instead, I changed the subject and asked, 'What about demonstrations? I always thought that they were student-centred.'

'It all depends on who does the demonstration. Very often the teacher will demonstrate the skill or technique that they want the learner to master and then give the learner the opportunity to do it themselves. But that performance will be done under the watchful eye of the teacher.'

'With health and safety so important in schools, that would be expected.'

'True. Most demonstrations will involve the teacher in breaking down the task into its constituent parts and showing how each part is performed. Then they will link the various parts together and perform the task slowly. Only when they are sure that the learners understand what is required will they perform it at normal speed.'

'I can see how demonstrations are relevant to the teaching and learning of physical skills, but . . .'

'Not just physical skills. Accountants will show how tax is calculated using a series of PowerPoint slides, drama teachers will show learners how to deliver their lines or react to other actors. Scientists will show trainees how to read instruments.'

'OK, OK, I get it,' I said. 'There are all types of demonstrations.'

'Demonstrations can be used in Bloom's cognitive, affective and psychomotor domains. Of course, for a skill to be mastered it has to be practised. So it's essential that the learners consolidate their learning by practise and repetition.'

'So, what are the weaknesses of demonstrations as a teaching method?'

'Well, oddly enough, if the task is done too well, learners may not appreciate the complexity of the task or the skill involved. It works best when it is possible to show all the components of the task and then get the learner to practise the skill through repetition. Conversely, if the teacher is poorly prepared and makes a mess of the demonstration or fails to explain what is required, they can very quickly lose credibility with the learners.'

'So you are only as good as your last performance?'

'It's not quite that cut-throat but you get the idea. Which leaves us with team teaching. We've done a bit of that so this should be easy. How would you describe team teaching?'

'Well, based on what we did I'd say it involves two or more teachers working together as a team in the same class. They have one set of aims and objectives and each has a distinct role to play, which they have discussed and agreed in advance.'

'And what might those roles be?'

'They may divide the session into separate sections, with each taking it in turns to deliver part of the course, or they may decide that one person leads the entire lesson and the other adds in comments and additional information as they judge appropriate while helping to maintain discipline and assist the learners, either individually or in groups, with any tasks they have to do.'

'So what are the strengths of such an arrangement?'

'Well, it can allow staff to play to their strengths and deal with those things that they are best at or most interested in. It also provides more opportunities for a teacher to support students in the classroom. And, of course, it means that the job of preparing lesson plans and resources can be shared.'

'Good. It can also be useful as a means of introducing new or trainee teachers into the culture of the school and its working practices. It also reduces the burden of marking and, as you said, it can help with classroom management. But I have always thought that the greatest advantage to the learner is that it provides them with the opportunity to work with a wider range of teachers . . .'

'And a change can be as good as a rest?' I said.

'It depends on what you are changing to, but I do think it keeps things fresh. I have a couple of lecturers at university who regularly team teach. One is quite serious and very knowledgeable. The other likes to provoke mock arguments with him to add spice to the session, entertain students and present an alternative view on the issues. Sometimes it's quite funny and it works really well.'

'I suppose it also has some advantages for the school in that larger groups can be accommodated and several groups can be taught at the same time.'

'True, but then accommodation and the size of the classroom can become a problem.'

'I suppose if the group becomes too large there is a temptation to use lectures or formal teaching as your preferred teaching method.'

'That can be a risk. Big groups can work against learner participation as many learners don't like talking in front of a large audience. So learners may become disengaged. If you are demonstrating a skill or procedure, not everyone may be able to see what you are doing, and discussions can become very hard to develop and manage. Anyway, the handout I gave you earlier (see Handout 4.1) also lists teacher-centred methods and, as before, I want you to fill in the missing information.'

4.8 Alex's reflection

I've been mulling over what Jane said for the last couple of days and even discussed it with a couple of friends on the course. I think we came to the conclusion that the right mix of teaching methods is dependent on choice, balance and timing. Now let's see if I can remember what we meant by that fancy phrase!

Firstly, we thought that some methods would be better suited to some subjects. So while it might be possible to role play aspects of a maths lesson, there are better ways to deliver the session. It's the teacher's job to select the best methods available, and to do that they have to be able to use every method. Otherwise, their choice is artificially restricted to those methods they feel comfortable with.

Secondly, we all agreed that it is very likely that we will have to use some teacher-directed methods in most sessions, perhaps to deliver information or contextualise the issues. But that we should also try to involve the learners actively. The precise balance of methods used will be a judgement call by us and will depend upon the requirements of the subject, the facilities and resources available, and time available to deliver the lesson and course.

Thirdly, and we found this the hardest to get to grips with, timing. We not only have to make a judgement about how much responsibility our learners are capable of taking on board, we have to decide when they are capable of taking on greater responsibility for their own learning. It is no use saying to a highly dependent group that as of tomorrow they are responsible for their own learning. No, we have to monitor the learners and pass over responsibility when they are ready for it. But sometimes we may have to pull it back if the learners run into difficulty or if we start to work in a new area which they know very little about.

So this choice between teacher-centred and learner-centred methods isn't an either/or choice. We need both types of methods, but the trick is knowing when to apply a particular approach and when not to. I think I may be back to tacit knowledge again!

Time for tea!

SPACE FOR YOUR NOTES

Prompts

- How would you classify your learners, dependent or independent?
- What strategies, if any, have you used to help them become independent learners?

4.9 Record of mentor meeting

Trainee: Alex Croft

Summary of key learning points

- Teaching methods can be broadly divided into teacher-centred and learner-centred methods, but, as Figure 4.1 shows, there is considerable overlap.
- Avoid assuming that everyone learns the way that you do. Don't only use teaching methods which you, as a learner, liked. Experiment and don't be afraid of failure.
- Discussions can be used to explore contentious issues and to change learners' attitudes and beliefs. It is essential that they are well chaired, stay on topic and that all participants sign up to a set of ground rules. Mutual respect and tolerance must be at the heart of any ground rules.
- Pairs and small group working provide learners with the opportunity for independent learning and thought. It is vital that you plan the activity in advance and give clear instructions to the groups as to what their tasks are.
- While the groups are working you should act as a facilitator, offering advice and guidance as required.
- The optimum size for a group is four and you should consider beforehand on what basis you want to split the class up, e.g. mixing weak with strong learners, having two females and two males in each group, splitting friends or trouble-makers.

- As an extension to group working, think how you might use evaluation cafés, snowballing, jigsaws and the mantle of the expert in your teaching.
- Discovery learning requires learners to take personal responsibility for their own learning and requires them to communicate effectively and exercise initiative, problem-solving and decision-making skills.
- However, teachers cannot abrogate their responsibility by using discovery learning. They must plan and monitor the activity in great detail and ensure that all learners remain on task.
- Role play enables a learner to experience an event from someone else's perspective. Such insights can be a very valuable learning experience. Again, it is important that the role play is well prepared and that the participants are fully briefed as to the role they are to play.
- Many learners feel embarrassed undertaking role plays, so ensure that ground rules are drawn up and that the whole class complies with them.
- A lecture is a teacher-centred teaching method that enables a significant amount of information to be disseminated to a large or small group of learners simultaneously. Unless it is an interactive lecture, interaction between the teacher and learners may be restricted to a question-and-answer session at the end of the lecture.
- A good lecture will provide a framework of knowledge around a particular topic and motivate the learners to go away and fill in the detail.
- Interactive lectures involve the teacher posing questions to the learners throughout the lecture and responding to points made by students.
- Formal teaching involves the teacher using a range of teacher-centred approaches, including mini-lectures and demonstrations. It also encourages the learners' active participation by allowing space for dialogue between learners and teacher.
- Team teaching involves two or more teachers working together with a single class while sharing common aims and objectives. Exactly what role each teacher will play in the session is agreed in advance and may be based on areas of expertise or professional interest. Very often, team teaching is used as part of the induction process for new teachers.
- Demonstrations involve the teacher demonstrating a skill at normal speed. The process is then broken down into its component parts and each part is demonstrated slowly. Learners then attempt to perform each part of the process before attempting the entire process.
- Demonstrations move from being very teacher-centred to learner-centred during the course of the session, with the teacher acting as a facilitator when learners attempt to copy the teacher's actions.

Agreed action points

Alex will:

- List the teaching methods employed to date.
- Consider why these methods were chosen. To what extent was it a case of "teaching as you like to be taught"?
- Consider whether different methods would have been more effective.

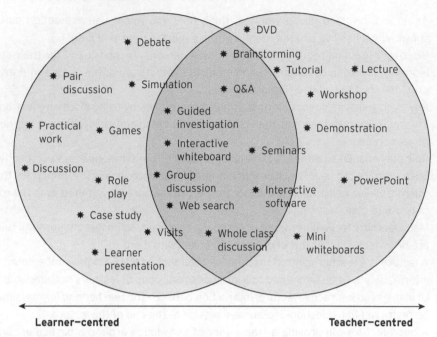

Figure 4.1 Learner- and teacher-centred teaching methods

Note: The placement of the ❋ indicates where on the teacher-/learner-centred continuum each descriptor resides.

HANDOUT 4.1 Teacher- and learner-centred teaching worksheet

The following tables list a range of teacher-centred and learner-centred teaching methods. You should:

- Consider each entry in turn and list at least one further benefit and limitation for each method.
- In the application column, consider to what extent you could apply the method in your teaching.

Teacher-centred methods	Strengths	Weaknesses	Application
Demonstration	Potential to be interesting and novel. Attractive to kinaesthetic and activist learners.	Can go wrong. Not suitable for large groups of learners.	
Formal teaching	Teacher retains control of the entire session. Enables a lot of information to be covered.	Learners have little input into or control over the session. Learners are generally passive throughout.	
Lecture	Teacher retains complete control of the session. Enables a large amount of information to be delivered quickly.	Learners are reduced to the passive role of note-takers. Allows very little room for clarification of points.	
Team teaching	Two or more teachers in the classroom can lead to greater support for learners. Teachers can play to their strengths while supporting colleagues.	Learners have little input into or control over the session. Learners are generally passive throughout.	

(continued)

(continued)

Learner-centred methods	Benefits	Limitations	Application
Brainstorming	Can be used to identify existing level of knowledge about an issue and get everyone involved. Generates new ideas.	Requires good group management.	
Case study	Provides opportunity to take a dispassionate look at an issue and exchange ideas. Provides training in decision-making.	Requires careful planning and the preparation of significant amounts of material.	
Discussion	Suitable where content involves opinion. Useful way to challenge attitudes.	Learners may stray from the subject. Session can become unfocused. Certain individuals may monopolise the discussion.	
Games and ice-breakers	Encourages initiative and creativity.	Badly handled, can go wrong or be embarrassing.	
Individual work, projects and assignments	Encourages independent learning, initiative and creativity. Provides feedback on learners' knowledge and attitudes.	Learners must be motivated to complete task. Work may be copied or plagiarised.	
Open learning	Learning can be individualised. Learner autonomy promoted.	High-quality materials must be prepared in advance. Learners may not wish to be autonomous learners.	
Pair and small group work	Can be highly motivating. Learners able to display learning and initiative.	Work must be well-planned and relevant. Learners need knowledge of task before starting.	

Role play	Learners can practise and receive feedback in safety. Provides guidelines for future behaviour.	Learners may be embarrassed, shy, lose confidence or not take the role play seriously.	
Search or discovery	Promotes active learning. Develops a wide range of skills.	Poorly motivated learners can regard this as an opportunity to do nothing.	
Seminars	Challenging and stimulating. Develops skills in stating and arguing a case.	Some prior training in how to argue and present a case is required. Labour-intensive.	
Simulations	Opportunities to make decisions in life-like situations. Learners can experience what real life is like.	Must be realistic. Can be expensive and time-consuming to set up.	
Tutorials	Individual guidance can be provided. Individual progress can be monitored.	Time-consuming. Learners need to prepare for tutorial to get the most from it.	

Adapted from Birmingham City University handout.

Further reading

www.routledge.com/cw/mcgrath

Cohen, L., Manion, L. and Morrison, K. (2010), *A Guide to Teaching Practice* (5th edn). London: Routledge.

Tutorial 5 What you need to know about learning theory

Aim of tutorial: To provide you with the knowledge and skills to be able to identify the learning styles of your learners and respond accordingly.

Tutorial overview: This tutorial examines the claims made for a number of learning theories, including *Honey and Mumford's learning styles*, *VAK*, the humanistic, behaviourist and cognitivist schools, and Blooms taxonomy of learning. It ends with a brief review of *constructivism*. The tutorial suggests that all education theories are but a simplification of the complex reality that they seek to explain/represent.

Contents

5.1 Alex's reflection

> Jane has been giving me more and more opportunities to teach, which is great, but she's concerned that I don't pay enough attention to the students' learning style preferences when designing my lesson plans. So she asked me to look at visual, auditory, and kinaesthetic (VAK) and complete Honey and Mumford's Learning Style Questionnaire.
>
> She's also asked me to select a range of resources that she uses in her teaching and asked me to select those that I liked the most. Not sure what that was about.
>
> I've got a feeling that today could be interesting.

5.2 Honey and Mumford, VAK and the Coffield Report

Jane's door was half open when I arrived and she was sitting back in her chair staring at the ceiling. If she was going to have a nap, at least she could shut the door.

I sidled up to her and said, 'Jane?' She beckoned to the chair, showing no surprise whatsoever. She swung round with such aplomb that I felt she would do a full circle, but she stopped with a jerk as the back of her chair hit the desk, sending her near-empty coffee cup flying. That seemed to wake her from her trance.

'*Is it that time already?*' she asked, mopping up the spill with last month's copy of *Empire* film magazine.

'I'm actually a bit late. I've had so much to do recently that I've only just managed to finish the Honey and Mumford questionnaire. I kept putting it down and thinking about my answers. I was thinking about the relevance of the questions to me and how they fitted into what I had learnt previously about VAK approaches to learning.'

'*So you didn't just think "I'd better get on with it and complete it as quickly as possible".*'

'No. I'm never that decisive!'

'*That's interesting. It's clearly an important aspect of your approach to learning. You prefer to reflect on what you have done and spend time making links between that new learning and previous learning. You don't like making rash assumptions and take things at face value. Let's have a look at your questionnaire results.*'

Jane took the sheets and spent a few minutes looking at my answers and the descriptors of my learning style. '*Well your tendency to think and reflect upon things is backed up by the results of your learning style questionnaire. When the questionnaire is graded, it indicates the extent to which you are a:*

- *pragmatist who prefers to learn what they need to know when they need to know it and do so in a focused way. Their learning is closely linked to outcomes;*
- *theorist who is interested in ideas and linking ideas together;*

- *reflector who prefers to consider and evaluate their learning before internalising it and linking it to theory;*
- *activist who prefers a practical, hands-on approach.*

Your results show that you have dominant reflector and theorist styles.'

'That does sound about right. As you're still concerned about the range of teaching methods I use, I assume you want me to use the questionnaire with my learners and, based on that, perhaps change how I teach.'

'Hang on, you are making some big assumptions there. You say that the results would tell you how your learners like to learn. How can you be sure about that?'

'Because you gave me the questionnaire and I assume that the people who produced it are respected in their field.'

'They're certainly respected, yes, but don't accept everything at face value. They have made a valuable contribution to the field, but to say that they're right is rash. The questions are grounded in psychological theory, but we can still argue about how much they actually measure degrees of pragmatism, reflection and so on. There's a danger of building houses on quicksand if you take these learning style questionnaires too literally, and equally, if you base your judgements on one set of preferences only. For example, do you really think that these are the only criteria that can be used to describe how people prefer to learn?'

'No of course not. There's also VAK approaches to learning.'

'So now you're saying that people only learn by either seeing, hearing or doing?'

I was surprised by Jane's cross-examination; this wasn't like her. 'I don't really mean that. I suppose that people have a balance between these, so someone might be dominantly kinaesthetic, but have visual and auditory characteristics too,' I said.

'At last. That's what I was trying to impress on you – people's learning preference is really a combination of preferences. And it's extremely difficult to identify those preferences. VAK and Honey and Mumford have useful things to say about how people learn. But don't take them as the truth carved in stone.'

'Hmm . . . so is that why you use the term learning preference, rather than learning style? A preference means that there's a tendency; a style is more definitive.'

'Very perceptive. That's exactly the case. There are lots of arguments about the value of different learning style theories. They're what's known as contested. Some people prefer one theory to another and some suggest that none of the theories reflect the complexity of real life.'

'My PDT says that all theories in education are at best just a simplified model of reality.'

'Which is what I've just said. But I wouldn't want you to think that I'm arguing against the value of trying to understand the characteristics of learners. The more we try to understand our learners, the more we can design teaching sessions that engage them and try to differentiate the learning experience.'

'OK, I'll go back and re-read what I've got on learning theory.'

'While you're at it, have a look at the Coffield Report. You can Google it. He and his panel tried to evaluate critically a range of learning theories and what they found is really interesting.'

'OK, so let's say I gather this information on my learners. How do I avoid building on quicksand? In other words, what can I usefully do with it?'

'We've an idea that you're a reflector and I know that you keep a reflective diary, so why don't you have a think about it and make some notes?'

'Gee, thanks a bundle,' I said, but Jane just grinned at me.

5.3 Alex's reflection

Trust me to ask a question! It either gets thrown back at me, or I get extra work to do. Now, let's see. What could I do if I gather all this info on my learners?

I suppose I could turn it on its head. I could actually share the results of the questionnaires with my learners. I'm sure the information is just as useful to them as it is for me – learning to learn and all that. They could reflect on their own preferences and discuss them with people who have different preferences. That way they might be able to strengthen their less-dominant areas and become better all-rounders. I could even get them to plot their two highest scores on a chart, and then group them together based upon these scores. That way they could see who had similar learning styles to them and who were different. It would also help me to visualise the class as a series of loose learning groups. A bit like this:

Group 1   Reflector/pragmatist – unusual

Group 2   Reflector/activist – very unusual

Group 3   Reflector/theorist – common

Group 4   Pragmatist/activist – common

Group 5   Pragmatist/theorist – unusual

Group 6   Activist/theorist – very unusual

Obviously I must do something to incorporate the findings into my planning. This will really help with differentiation. I can't devise an individual lesson for everyone based on their learning preferences, but I can make sure that I take the profile of the group into account in the activities that I plan. It will also ensure that I consider a range of different learning style approaches when I prepare my lesson. I could also vary the make-up of groups. It would be interesting to group those with similar learning preferences together, then switch it around and group those with dissimilar preferences.

I should also take account of VAK and include visual, auditory and kinaesthetic activities and resources in my teaching.

Wait, if these learning preferences are such contested descriptors why don't I get my group to think about how they learn themselves? After all, surely it's better that they come up with the vocabulary and idea themselves. They could do this in groups and discuss how different activities might help them. I'm sure that VAK, activist and reflector wouldn't mean much to them – but they're really the ones who need to understand their own way of learning!

SPACE FOR YOUR NOTES

Prompts

- What do you think your learning preferences are?
- Which learning style models do you use in your teaching? Why these models?

5.4 The humanistic school

'Now what about the resources I chose from web links, articles in the Times Educational Supplement (TES) *and a copy of the PowerPoint slides that I use in class. Which of them did you choose as your favourite?'*

'I'm not sure why, but I did like some better than others. But I chose as my number one pick the electronic resources with web links.'

'So what made you choose that particular resource? Think.'

'I suppose I selected it according to what I like. So I probably chose it according to my preferences and without regard to what my learners might like. I see what you're getting at. Cunning!'

'You could call it that. I call it teaching. I was trying to illustrate one particular school of learning by giving you the opportunity to choose the type of resources that you like. I'd given you the power to select resources according to your learning preferences, but also according to lots of other criteria, some of which you would not be consciously aware of.

*Essentially you were in control and acting independently. The philosophy behind this approach is called **humanistic** and arose out of the work of two psychologists, Carl Rogers and Abraham Maslow.*

Rogers felt that self-identity and the gap between who we think we are and who we would like to be is important. From this Rogers developed a form of person-control therapy based on unconditional positive regard, which is essentially non-judgemental. As teachers we assist our learners to learn as they feel is best for them.

*Maslow worked on theories of motivation. You may have heard of **Maslow's hierarchy of needs** too. He believed that people learn when they are motivated, but for this to happen their basic needs must be satisfied, such as food and shelter. So how did you feel about this humanistic approach?'*

'OK. I was aware that I was exercising my choices and that felt **empowering**. As if you trusted me to make good decisions. Does that make sense?'

'Perfect sense. That feeling of empowerment can motivate learners to achieve great things because you are not setting limits on what they can do or achieve.'

'I know that we have talked about this before (see Tutorial 4) and I've covered it at uni, but what exactly do you mean by, firstly, the term "school" and, secondly, "humanistic"?'

'A school is the name given to a group whose ideas are supported by a canon of literature. There were a number of followers of the humanistic approach and we could say that they are members of that school. The key features of the humanistic school are that teachers should encourage learners to exercise self-direction and encourage them to become independent, autonomous and self-reflective. So you have demonstrated this aspect of the humanistic approach by acting independently and thinking about how you chose your resources. You have evaluated your learning. This is also an important aspect of the humanistic school. Now, can you think of some disadvantages of this?'

'I suppose a disadvantage is that if someone doesn't feel like doing the work, it's easier to avoid as no one is watching over their shoulder. Also, it's possible that I would impose my beliefs on my learners through my selection of resources. But looking at your resources they must have taken an age to prepare.'

'Those certainly can be the disadvantages. In terms of your learners engaging with the tasks, it's really important to follow them up. Of course, formative and summative assessment is vital for this purpose. (See Tutorial 6.) As far as your selection of resources goes, it is the case that you need to try to suspend your own preferences, but that applies to the selection of all resources, not just those used for independent learning. Time-consuming? Yes, but once you have the resources you can use them continuously, just updating them as required.'

'I just thought. If you adopt this approach are you really teaching them or are you just acting as a facilitator?'

'Yes, the role of the teacher changes. You do become more of a facilitator. But you also become a learning resource yourself. This changes the teaching experience and some regard it as less stressful. Hopefully, you can see that the focus is on the individual; the personal, hence its role in personalised learning. We will talk about assessment later (see Tutorial 6), but individual needs assessment is related to this approach. In essence, valuing and motivating the individual is at the heart of the humanistic approach to teaching.'

'I remember Bloom's taxonomy – the cognitive, affective and psychomotor domains – this sounds like this is one way of addressing the affective domain.'

That's a very good point. The affective domain is about attitudes, feelings and beliefs, and the humanistic school certainly addresses these. Steiner and Montessori schools follow the philosophy, as does Summerhill School, a famous private school in Suffolk. We'll look at Bloom in a bit.'

5.5 Alex's reflection

The humanistic approach looks like a good way to introduce aspects of the affective domain into subjects that don't normally lend themselves to it. We could discuss their attitudes to the selection of resources I use. Which would help me to update my resources in the future.

There are lots of opportunities to introduce ICT here too. Certainly discussion forums, **blogs** and **wikis** are relevant to the humanistic approach, as they allow learners to express themselves, their attitudes, beliefs, etc. But it can also help a lot with putting the resources together. If I find relevant websites, all I need to do is put the addresses in a file on the virtual learning environment (VLE), or even embed them into the task sheet, and the learners can check the sites out and make up their own minds. I mustn't be too narrow in my choice of resources. Jane mentioned that people could be used as a source of information too - I'd have to ask them, of course. Maybe the learners themselves are a resource; some may have particular expertise. And I bet a lot of the kids are better at navigating the Internet than I am.

Engagement does worry me though. Maybe if I got them into groups and asked them to negotiate roles - scribe, evaluator, ideas person, etc. - they could monitor themselves. I bet they would soon tell me if someone wasn't pulling their weight.

SPACE FOR YOUR NOTES

Prompt

- Have you experienced any humanistic approaches? How did you feel about them?

5.6 The behaviourist school

'The work of the humanistic school was quite revolutionary, really. Prior to that the behaviourists had probably led the field. They did a lot of experimental work on the psychology of learning. Much of this was performed on animals, but some on humans. Much of it was done during the late nineteenth and early twentieth centuries and involved researchers such as Skinner, Thorndike, Watson and, perhaps most famously, Pavlov.'

'I've heard of Pavlov. He did all that work on dogs. They were fed when a bell was rung. I remember that after a time they continued to salivate whenever the bell was rung, even if they weren't fed.'

'Yes, pretty controversial stuff these days, but it did lead to biological theories of learning. In many ways the debate is still raging. How much learning is programmed into our genes and with us from birth and how much is as a result of our experiences. It's the old nature or nurture debate. So, which do you think is most important?'

'Sounds as if you expect me to know! From our conversation so far there seems to be evidence that what we do is important – the humanistic school, for example – and the work of Pavlov is still pretty well respected, so my guess is that it's a bit of both?'

*'That's perceptive. Too often people think that an either/or choice has to be made. During all this research we're building up evidence for the factors that contribute to our ability to learn. Pavlov explained his results in terms of the **conditioned reflex**, in which a stimulus – when repeated regularly – led to a response. This was in contrast to **unconditioned reflexes**, such as blinking, which are automatic and not under our control. Nurture and nature.*

*It was this work that gave rise to the **behaviourist school** of learning. But, what's the relevance of all of this to teaching? Can you give me some examples of how you would use behaviourist theory in your own teaching. For example, what sort of rewards could you give in order to provide reinforcement?'*

'OK, here goes. The reward would usually be praise, but I suppose just my attention and encouragement might be enough. With younger learners I could occasionally give stickers or a bar of chocolate.'

'Hmm, good points. Suppose I tell you that the reward should follow the desired behaviour as soon as possible?'

'That means that I have to do my marking on time! If I don't they'll become demotivated. I also need to praise regularly in the classroom.'

'Yes, but not just praise. You should engage with your learners regularly and provide continuous encouragement. It is also the case that repeated success strengthens learning. Learners remain motivated if they experience at least some success. And the younger they achieve a bit of success the better. Now, the idea that learners need to experience repeated success means that a series of discrete activities with short-term goals provides the best chance of repeated success.'

'This sounds like differentiation. I need to ensure that all my learners can experience some success. As we discussed when we looked at lesson planning, I do differentiate my objectives – all learners, most learners, some learners will be able to . . . , but I accept that this isn't always translated into my resources or my assessments. Hang on, I've just thought of something . . . Perhaps it's important that they don't compare themselves with others, but with their own previous achievements. That would fit into the use of **individual learning plans** and **negotiated learning**. Maybe this is another strength of the humanistic approach. With guidance from me they could make their own decisions according to their preferences and ability. Also, I know from my very first session with my PDT that setting short-term achievable goals is really important.' (See Tutorial 8.)

'Good, so this can be summed up as frequency and recency; learning is most effective if the stimulus is received regularly and without too much delay. I like the phrase "medal and a mission" coined by Geoff Petty in his book Teaching Today. *This means that you need to reward achievement, but also set further short-term achievable goals. Have a think about how you can embed behaviourist principles in your teaching.'*

5.7 Alex's reflection

Frequency, recency, and medal and mission. So much to remember, so little brain space! I need to draft out some principles that I'll apply consistently in class in terms of giving praise and setting future targets.

Clearly, recapping the previous session with a Q and A at the beginning of a session is important, as it's an opportunity for checking on previous learning but also for giving feedback and praise to individuals and the class. Wait. I could even use self and peer assessment as a way of revisiting earlier themes. To help them with this I could produce a PowerPoint with gaps for them to complete. That would both test and embed knowledge. It would also provide feedback to me and my learners on individuals' learning.

I'm starting to see how important this recap and summary thing is. It's actually vital because students' learning develops progressively as topics are revisited in different contexts. Previous learning becomes part of their life experience, so they can build on that, not just what they bring to school or college. I need to think about how often I should summarise learning in my sessions.

SPACE FOR YOUR NOTES

Prompt

- How would you plan a lesson just using behaviourist principles?

5.8 Cognitivism and Bloom's taxonomy

'You've mentioned some experiments that investigated behaviour and gave rise to the behaviourist school, but there seems to be a gap here. You haven't really said anything about how we process the information that we receive. Surely this has to be at the centre of the learning process? The humanistic approach doesn't seem to say much about that either,' I said.

'*Good point. It could almost be argued that a lot of teacher intervention is needed for the behaviourist approach, but less so for the humanistic approach. You're right that thinking processes haven't really figured in our discussion. That's where* **cognitivism** *comes in. It has been investigated by experiments too.*'

'We did some work on cognitivism at uni but, to be honest, it wasn't the most inspiring session. All I really remember about it was that it deals with how we think and process information. I also remember Bloom's cognitive domains with its hierarchy of knowledge, synthesis and evaluation. The two are linked, aren't they?'

'*In the sense that it's about thinking processes, yes. In fact, Bloom's taxonomy of the cognitive domain was modified by Lorin Anderson and David Krathwohl. Bloom's original hierarchy went from knowledge as the lowest cognitive activity to evaluation as the highest. Anderson and Krathwohl's modification went from recalling knowledge through evaluating to creating as the highest order skill. Here, their ideas are summarised on this handout which I got on my MA course. (See Handout 5.1.) These ideas can be used as an aid to planning lessons covering these different knowledge dimensions and cognitive domains.*'

'But there are other domains as well.'

'*Yes, the psychomotor and affective domains, as you mentioned. As well as the cognitive domain, Bloom also wrote about the affective and psychomotor domains. These arose from work done by Robert Gagné. The affective domain is concerned with changing or influencing people's attitudes, values and beliefs. For example, a lot of equal opportunity training uses this domain when designing courses that challenge racist and sexist attitudes. The psycho-motor domain is concerned with how physical skills are taught/ranked. Here, I've done a handout that shows Bloom's three domains.*' (See Handout 5.2.)

'All this stuff about information processing reminds me of my laptop; I suppose there are some similarities between the brain and a computer.'

'*That's a very good way of putting it. In fact, cognitivist ideas do represent the brain as a computer, receiving information, or data, from the senses, processing it and storing it in short- or long-term memory. Learning a skill – or knowing how to do something – represents the amalgam of many of these programmes. Of course, we may retrieve and process that information further. There are other parallels with computers too. We can only process ver-bal information serially – as we receive it – and we can only deal with a limited number of simultaneous tasks. Too much data and cognitive overload is the result. In practical terms, learning how to process data – how to learn – and controlling the environment to reduce cognitive overload are important.*'

5.9 Alex's reflection

*So cognitivism is all about thinking and learning how to think - **metacognition** - I like that word; I'll have to see if I can sneak it in to one of my taught sessions and see how Jane reacts! So, what can I do in the classroom to address the cognitive domain? I suppose I could pay closer attention to the learning environment. Try to control the flow of information by pacing the learning activities. They need to be broken down into manageable chunks so that learning can proceed in a step-by-step way. Now I see why pace and environment are on the lesson observation form; there is a reason after all! Of course, different learners will be able to process information at different speeds and probably in different ways. I can see a link with learning preferences here, so it's back to differentiation in terms of pace and managing the cognitive level - knowledge, understanding, etc. Tricky if a specification requires me to work at a specific level.*

I also need to think more about developing the learners' own thinking skills - learning how to learn. This must be really fundamental, but we just don't spend enough time on it. It's really about providing them with a range of learning tools. That means giving them more opportunity to reflect on how they approach problems and share their reflections with others.

SPACE FOR YOUR NOTES

Prompt

- Consider an activity that you could use to develop thinking skills with your learners.

5.10 Constructivism

'OK, any more schools I need to take into account in my lessons?'

'Well, you must have covered the constructivist and the work of people like Piaget, Vygotsky and Bruner at university.'

'I was only joking – I thought we'd finished! I can't believe there's more. How am I supposed to fit them all into my lesson planning?'

'You don't. What the uni and I want you to do is choose from the widest possible range of options when preparing a lesson. It doesn't mean that you have to use every theory in every lesson or even one theory in its entirety. Someone once said to me "If you only have a hammer in your tool bag, then every problem you come across will look like a nail." We want you to have a full range of tools to choose from. Anyway, so far our emphasis has been on the individual and their capacity to learn. We haven't really discussed a role for human experience.'

'But you did mention making links with prior learning in the lesson planning tutorial.' (See Tutorial 3.)

'Yes, prior learning; not necessarily prior experience.'

'Isn't all learning experience?'

'Good point, but learning tends to be defined as a change in behaviour. I suppose it's debatable whether all experiences change behaviour. Maybe some experiences do change behaviour but an awful lot don't. Nonetheless, I'd like to spend a few minutes considering the role of experience and social interaction in learning.'

'If we must.'

'Yes, we must because it's an aspect of learning that really excites me,' Jane said with just a touch of malicious glee.

I was speechless for a moment. The thought that any learning theory could be exciting was way beyond anything I could imagine. I nearly said "You need to get a life," but instead said, 'Well, of course, if that's what turns you on . . .'

'You try reading Bruner and Lave and Wenger and you'll see what I mean. I don't think enough trainees read original work. There's too much "cited in".'

'OK,' I said, not wanting to start a pointless argument.

'Basically, constructivism is the idea that we learn best from our own experiences. For example, Jean Piaget was a developmental psychologist. He believed that children were not just small adults, but that they go through specific developmental stages and that interaction with their environment is key to development. Here the situation was considered vital. Similarly, Lev Vygotsky considered that new learning is conceptualised first in a social context through dialogue, then in an individual's consciousness. So in this case, other individuals are the environment; the theory became known as social constructivism for this reason.'

'How does this differ from cognitivism if it's about the thinking process?'

'Cognitivist ideas really focus on the biological nature of thinking, rather than the effects of external influences. A particularly useful example is Lev Vygotsky's **zone of proximal development (ZPD)**. *Essentially this is the transition between a child being able to do something with adult help and being able to do it independently. He considered it vital that children were presented with problems of increasing complexity to develop cognitively.'*

'ZPD sounds like something out of Dr Who! I can see that the transition is an important part of learning. If someone can't do something independently, then presumably learning hasn't taken place. How can we avoid that happening?'

'You've heard of scaffolding – progressively building on prior learning – it's similar to that. Jerome Bruner was very influential in this area. He considered that meaning making was important to learning. In other words, learning is not about internalising isolated facts, but establishing a rationale for the knowledge in the context of prior experience through discovery. He suggested that learners are the agents of their own learning. He believed that approaches based on learner-centred discovery in which trial and error play a major role would be most effective.'

'Yes, we learn from our mistakes.'

'Finally, it's worth mentioning some more contemporary researchers in constructivism. Jean Lave and Étienne Wenger did a lot of work on apprenticeship and how interaction with more experienced others promotes learning. They proposed that learning is situated within **communities of practice**. The community could be at home, school or work, for example, but they considered that there had to be a domain of shared interest. The members of the community share practice, literally in the sense of resources, approaches to problem-solving and so on. Active participation and the consequent construction of identities are important. They also used the term "legitimate peripheral participation", in which members initially interact on the margins of the community, but it is this interaction which helps them move towards full participation and consequent mastery of the skills and knowledge. They made a number of fascinating studies of diverse apprenticeship situations, such as Yucatec midwives and Vai and Gola tailors.'

'I begin to see what you mean about constructivism; it is interesting and it does seem that there's still a lot to do in this area. I'll have a think about its application in my reflective account. There, that's saved you from saying it!'

5.11 Alex's reflection

Thinking about this in practice I must ensure that I scaffold learning. If experience is so important, then I need to plan some of it into my lessons. I need to develop learning by progressively introducing more complex ideas and requiring higher order thinking skills.

I also need to consider how I can use others in the learning process. If communities are important, then I need to involve as many stakeholders as possible, such as my learners' peers, their parents and maybe other members of the community, too, like those in business, politics and so on.

Learning to learn. Bruner's interesting point about meaning making and the role of the learner as an agent means that I also need to equip my learners with the appropriate skills to understand their own learning preferences. Work on problem-solving skills will be important here.

I'm exhausted. Time for tea, biscuits and bed . . .

SPACE FOR YOUR NOTES

Prompt

- Review your lesson plans for aspects of constructivist theory.

5.12 Record of mentor meeting

Trainee: Alex Croft

Summary of key learning points

- There are a range of ways in which learning preferences can be described. For example, Honey and Mumford's Learning Style Questionnaire divides learners into four categories:

  1 Pragmatists are concerned with outcomes and develop a learning strategy to maximise their learning outcomes.
  2 Theorists are interested in ideas and how they link together.
  3 Reflectors like to evaluate new learning and understand how it fits with their existing ideas and theories before they adopt it.
  4 Activists learn by doing.

In contrast, VAK suggests that learners have a preference for either visual, audio or kinaesthetic learning (learning though performance of an activity).

- Learning preferences shouldn't be taken at face value. They aren't set in stone. They change as people grow and develop and find themselves in different learning and life situations. Indeed, the *validity* of many is open to debate. Read the Coffield Report on learning styles available online (Google 'Coffield Report').
- The contested nature of specific learning preferences/styles shouldn't detract from the value of trying to understand the characteristics of our learners.
- Most importantly, teachers should think about how to use information on students' learning preferences to inform their lesson planning, resource design and differentiation strategy.
- The humanistic school of teaching was developed by Carl Rogers and influenced by Maslow's hierarchy of needs. Teachers offer students unconditional positive regard. They are non-judgmental and seek to facilitate and support the student in their learning. Typically they would employ many of the student-centred teaching methods discussed in Tutorial 4.
- Teachers who follow the humanistic approach want learners to become self-directed and reflective learners. Following humanistic principles means valuing learners as individuals and considering their motivation. Student-centred teaching and independent learning is central.
- Lessons involving humanistic approaches can be time-consuming to prepare as they're resource-intensive. Learner engagement can be an issue. Therefore, it's essential that teachers do not abrogate their responsibilities and continue to monitor student progress and achievement and take appropriate action when required.
- Teachers should avoid designing lessons and resources that suit their learning preferences and instead seek to understand the learning preferences of their learners and plan accordingly.
- Behaviourist approaches to learning were pioneered in the early part of the twentieth century by Skinner, Thorndike, Watson and, perhaps most famously, Pavlov. Behaviourists aim to establish a conditioned reflex by providing the learner with a stimulus when the desired behaviour is demonstrated. For example, supply rewards such as recognition, praise, a certificate or even a sticker or star for younger learners. Such rewards need to be delivered as soon after the desired behaviour is observed as possible and must be repeated each time the required behaviour is seen (frequency and recency).
- This approach is what underpins Petty's medal-and-mission approach, where completion of the mission is the required task and the medal is the reward.
- To assure that all students achieve some level of success, and therefore reward, use differentiation when setting your learning outcomes.
- Bloom's taxonomy outlines the three domains of learning (see Handout 5.2). Namely, the cognitive, the affective and the psychomotor. Each is represented by

(continued)

(continued)

five or six levels of learning, from the very basic to complete mastery. Each level in the taxonomy has to be achieved before learners can hope to master the next. For example, in the cognitive domain learners must remember information before they can understand it and they must understand it before they can apply it with confidence.

- Key workers in the field of constructivism were Piaget, Vygotsky, Bruner, Lave and Wenger. Constructivism is about individuals building on previous experience in collaboration with others to make meaning out of knowledge. Basically, it argues that people learn from their own experiences and their interaction with other people. This implies that the individual is the agent of their own change.
- Vygotsky's ZPD is actually the transition of the child/learner being able to do something with the assistance of others to being able to do it independently.
- Jerome Bruner has championed the concept of scaffolded learning. The theory suggests that teachers should build progressively on what students have learnt previously. To do otherwise would be like trying to build the second floor of a house before the first. The implications of this for teachers is that they must carefully plan for logical progression in their lesson plans.
- Jean Lave and Étienne Wenger have championed the joint concepts of apprenticeship and communities of practice. This is not a new idea but it highlights the value of working alongside experts as apprentices. This may be a particularly valuable way for learners who are described as pragmatic, kinaesthetic or psychomotor to learn.

Agreed action points

Alex will:

- Use one approach to determining the learners' learning preferences and involve them in the feedback.
- Take one topic area and plan to use humanistic, cognitivist and behaviourist approaches in selected sessions.
- Given the significance of constructivist theories, review the lesson planning approach to ensure that scaffolding is included, stakeholders are involved and thinking skills are included.

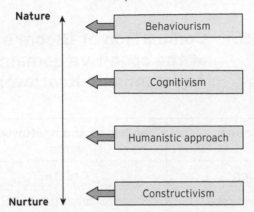

Nature: Built into our genetic make-up; inherited or innate.
Nurture: Develops as a result of exposure to the physical
and social environment.

Figure 5.1 Relationship between schools of learning and nature vs nurture

HANDOUT 5.1 Comparison of Bloom's taxonomy of the cognitive domain with Anderson and Krathwohl's

Bloom's nouns	Anderson and Krathwohl's verbs	
Evaluation Make judgements and recommendations.	**Create** Assembly of parts into a coherent whole.	Higher order cognitive skill ↑
Synthesis Assembly of parts into a coherent whole.	**Evaluate** Making judgements and recommendations.	
Analysis Breaking learned material into its component parts for understanding.	**Analyse** Breaking learned material into its component parts for understanding.	
Application Using learned material.	**Apply** Using learned material.	
Comprehension Constructing meaning.	**Understand** Constructing meaning.	
Knowledge Recalling learned material.	**Recall** Recalling learned material.	↓ Lower order cognitive skill

Adapted from Anderson and Krathwohl (2013).

HANDOUT 5.2   Bloom's domains of learning worksheet

See how far you can complete the missing information in columns two and three before you log onto www.businessballs.com and search for Bloom's taxonomy of learning domains in the alphabetical index. One example in each domain has been provided to show what is required.

Bloom's taxonomy	Behaviour required/ descriptor	Evidenced by
Cognitive (knowledge)		
Recall information	Remember and recognise data/ information.	Ability to recount facts, rules and definitions.
Understand		
Apply information		
Analyse		
Synthesise		
Evaluate		
Affective (attitudes)		
Receive information		
Respond to information		
Value	Express and explain personal values.	Evaluate the worth of different ideas and commit to a set of values.
Organise		
Internalise		
Psychomotor (skills)		
Imitate		
Manipulate		
Develop precision	Execute skill without assistance.	Displays high level of skill in performance of function and can train others.
Articulation		
Naturalisation		

Adapted from www.businessballs.com.

Further reading

Anderson, L.W. and Krathwohl, D.R. (eds) (2013), *A Taxonomy for Learning, Teaching, and Assessing: A Revision of Bloom's Taxonomy of Educational Objectives* (Abridged edition). Boston: Allyn & Bacon (Pearson Education Group).

Coffield, F., Moseley, D., Hall., E and Ecclestone, K. (2004), *Learning Styles and Pedagogy in Post-16 Learning: A Systematic and Critical Review*. London: Learning and Skills Research Centre.

Petty, G. (2014), *Teaching Today: A Practical Guide* (5th edn). Oxford: Open University Press.

www.businessballs.com.

Tutorial 6   What you need to know about assessment and feedback

Aim of tutorial: To provide you with the knowledge and skills to choose the most effective method of assessment for your learners and to give and receive feedback.

Tutorial overview: This tutorial explores initial, diagnostic and formative assessment before exploring the use of questioning in teaching. The discussion then returns to summative assessment and the difference between norm, criterion and mastery referenced approaches to assessment.

Contents

6.1 Alex's reflection

> *Jane asked me to think about assessment before our meeting and list the ways that I have been assessed since the start of the course and how I've assessed my learners, so here goes.*
>
> *I had to complete a piece of writing in preparation for the interview. They used that to check my writing skills to make sure that I could cope with the assignments.*
>
> *During induction I did some audits of my ICT skills and my numeracy. I've completed a few written assignments and my teaching has been observed, so that's assessment.*
>
> *I think she's trying to get me to think about different types of assessment, so I wonder if* **portfolio**-*building counts? I have to gather all sorts of evidence from my teaching to show that I have met certain standards. But then that's assessed as part of an assignment, so maybe it's not so different.*
>
> *As for how I've assessed my learners – well, I've used questions and answers,* **pub quizzes***, and pair and group work where they had to feed answers back to the class.*

6.2 Initial assessment

Jane waited for me to sit down and set up my recorder before asking, *'OK, so let's have a look at the list of assessments that I asked you to make.'*

'I wasn't sure what to include. When you said assessment, I thought of all the times that I had to write something which was marked. That mostly happens at uni. Then I thought of here, where my teaching is assessed. I assume that you were getting me to think about the differences between the two locations. Because assessment isn't just about writing things down and having them marked, it can be about people, such as you or my PDT watching me and commenting on what I do, rather than what I write.'

'Hang on a minute, you're trying to second guess me, which isn't a bad thing. I was encouraging you to think about your own experiences to get an idea of your thoughts on assessment. Now let's look at this list . . . You talk about your first experiences of assessment before you went to uni. You mention that you did a writing task, but do you think that was the only assessment taking place when you went to the interview?'

'I suppose the whole interview was an assessment. They were trying to see if I was suitable for the course.'

'In that case, when did the assessment begin?'

'You mean I was being assessed before I got there? I guess that the fact that I was selected for interview means that I had passed some hurdles. They wouldn't have bothered interviewing me otherwise.'

'Let's try to get away from the idea of hurdles. Schools and colleges don't try to put barriers in the way of people. Certainly it's important that people meet the basic entry requirements. So you needed to have the requisite maths, English and science qualifications to get on the course. But remember that you are studying for a professional qualification. Not everyone who meets the basic requirements is suitable. Teacher training colleges want to ensure that whoever joins their courses has the right aptitude, motivation and personal qualities

to become a teacher. Now, just because they think you have what it takes to be a teacher doesn't mean that you have to go it alone. Many people have the potential to become a good teacher, but have additional support needs, be that in terms of confidence-building or academic skills. In fact, people who find the going hard are often the best teachers because they have empathy with their own learners. So let's go back to your early experience on the course and consider other factors that you were assessed on.'

'OK. I was asked to write a personal statement about why I wanted to become a teacher and what my aspirations were. This was presumably about my aptitude for the profession and whether I had potential to become a good teacher. Personal experience was relevant too as I had to explain about any previous teaching work that I had done.'

'Fine, so what about the interview. What were they looking for there?'

'That was their opportunity to find out about my personal attributes. Did I have the sort of personality that would make a good teacher? They were a bit nosey too and wanted to discuss, for example, if I had any learning support needs. I also had to complete the Criminal Records Bureau check and answer all the usual questions about my ethnicity, religion and so on.'

'You have a good memory! So what about induction. What happened then?'

'I think that we're getting away from assessment now, aren't we? What's induction got to do with it?'

'Humour me for a while longer. Just tell me about some of the things that you got up to.'

'OK. We did some team-building activities, an exercise on learning styles, and we observed some lessons.'

'That's quite a comprehensive description of your experience at the beginning of the course. Essentially you have listed many aspects of **initial assessment**. This is where schools and colleges collect qualitative and quantitative data on someone with a view to determining their suitability and support needs for a programme of study. Now, as a teacher, I think it is really important that you try and collect similar information on your learners. I suggest that you go back to your list, identify examples of initial assessment, add some further examples from our chat and write a sentence or two about the purpose of each one.'

6.3 Alex's reflection

I thought that these were my reflections. Now she's telling me what to write! Anyway, I suppose there must be some method in her madness. Back to the list.

Preparatory writing, ICT and numeracy audits - these were to assess my basic skills. I had met the requirements, but I needed some additional numeracy support, so my support needs were important here, particularly with those mandatory skills tests. They didn't want to set me up to fail. They could also have shown up any additional learning difficulties that I may have had so that they could refer me to Student Support.

(continued)

(continued)

My personal statement and application form for the course had details about my previous learning. This showed that I met the requirements, but it could also help my tutor understand my needs.

All that information about ethnicity and so on would help them to ensure equality of opportunity and tell them if I was likely to have any particular needs, like prayer rooms or issues around fasting.

My interview for the course was about personal attributes and my suitability, both for the course and for teaching. They could have recommended further tasks if they didn't feel that I was prepared.

They said the learning styles test was to help them plan their teaching, but I think that it was more beneficial to me to come to some understanding about how I learnt best.

During the team-building exercises I got the feeling that we were being watched. Of course, I could just be paranoid, but I suspect that they were checking out my professional attributes and suitability. I bet I'd have heard about it in tutorials if there was a problem with, say, team-working. This is a qualification for the job, so both uni and I need to know that I'm suitable. Best to find this out early rather than late, which brings us back to the lesson observations.

SPACE FOR YOUR NOTES

Prompts

- Does the above match with your experience of initial assessment?
- List ways in which your prior learning and experience have been assessed.
- How might you undertake an initial assessment of your learners?

6.4 Diagnostic and formative assessment

'There's one thing that puzzles me about those examples of initial assessment and that's the point about the **skills audits**. Why were they necessary when I already had GCSEs? Surely it's duplication?'

'*That's a good point. Trainers have to prepare you for the skills tests, so they need to know how far you meet their specific requirements. It's part of your initial assessment, but the purpose is specifically to diagnose the extent to which further help is needed in this area, rather than to examine experience and attributes. It's called* **diagnostic assessment**.'

'We often have a quiz or question-and-answer sessions at the beginning of a new topic. I suppose that's the same. The tutor can diagnose our learning needs in a particular area to help plan the teaching to meet those needs. In fact, that's what I use quizzes for in my class. Mind you, it still seems a bit like initial assessment.'

'*Well, it's a moot point and we shouldn't get too hung up on definitions like this. I suppose if we must, the initial assessment that happens before the course starts, or very early on, is usually about determining* **entry behaviour**. *Diagnostic assessment tends to happen once the programme has started and it's very much an ongoing process. As you say, it would certainly be used at the beginning of a topic. After all, there wouldn't be much point in starting from first principles if everyone in the group had a good understanding in a particular area. Essentially, it's part of the learning process and it's important to vary the experience of diagnostic assessment. So let's think about other ways that you have been assessed at uni . . .*'

'I've a feeling this isn't what you're after, but I suppose assignments and my placement?'

'*Go on,*' Jane said.

'Well, we do presentations and . . .'

'*Think about what we have just been discussing,*' Jane said, sucking the air between her teeth.

'You mean approaches to assessment, rather than methods?'

'*That's what we have been discussing. We talked about initial and diagnostic assessment. These approaches could use a range of different methods. It's the purpose of the assessment that's at issue, not the method.*'

'So my examples are mostly about the uni assessing me to see if I have the relevant skills and knowledge?'

'*Possibly, but we'll come on to that in a minute. What other purposes of assessment can you think of?*'

'Tutors may want to understand gaps in my learning to help them plan their teaching.'

'*At last!*' Jane said, sitting back in her chair and fixing her gaze on the ceiling as if searching for the source of inspiration. '*When we use the word assessment, too often we think about exams and assignments. In fact, the majority of assessment carried out by teachers doesn't have anything to do with these.*'

But aren't you talking about evaluation too? Aren't assessment and evaluation the same thing?'

'*No. We've talked about this, evaluation covers more than assessment. Assessment is about gathering data to help you to make informed judgements about a learner's progress, whilst evaluation is about using those data to make judgements about the extent to which your learning objectives have been met. In the wider sense, evaluation can also apply to teachers and educational institutions and can be used to identify priorities for improvement. They're quite different. But we're getting sidetracked. You said that teachers use assessment to help them plan. Of course, the purpose of this is to develop learners' knowledge, skills and under-standing. This is formative assessment. Just think for a minute about this and jot down some of the ways that you think teachers assess formatively . . .'*

I scribbled away for a couple of minutes and then handed Jane my rough note, which read:

- watching as their learners work;
- using questioning and monitoring the questions they ask;
- homework tasks as a source of evidence;
- working with learners during activities;
- they may get evidence from others – staff and parents, for example.

'We'll talk about questioning in a minute, but you have some good points there. You can use other tricks too, like mini-whiteboards that learners can write on and hold up. This can be less threatening than answering questions. Traffic lights are popular in primary schools. Each learner holds up a green, yellow or red card to indicate their level of understanding on a point. You could also add reflective diaries. These can be very revealing in terms of indicating whether learners understand. I like your last point. It shows that you're thinking outside the box.'

6.5 Assessment for learning, peer assessment and self-assessment

'Talking of boxes, one of the teachers here recommended that I read Inside the Black Box, *which is about assessment. What's the Black Box bit?'*

*'Black box theory is understanding something entirely in terms of its function, not what makes it work. So "inside the black box" means that we open the box and find out how some-thing – in this case how **assessment for learning** – works. Of course, it's also a parody on one of the authors' names: Paul Black. The other one was Dylan Wiliam. It was they who brought formative assessment to the fore over the past 20 years.'*

'Hang on. I've just realised it's assessment for learning, not learning for assessment. The two are significantly different.'

'Absolutely. That's why you have to think of all assessment as a two-way process. Crucially, it involves feedback to learners on their learning and the setting of short-term goals so that both you and they can monitor them and judge whether they have been met. This enables you to modify your teaching plan to vary the level of challenge and the methods in the event that appropriate learning styles are not being satisfied. Now it's this area that I think you are weak at. You certainly plan assessment activities, but I don't feel that you're fully in tune with the group. You need to monitor constantly how your learners are learning. Petty calls this "withitness".'

'So what you're saying is that I need to hold discussions with my learners about their progress?'

'Yes and no. You're important, but you're not the only person able to give feedback. Often we learn best from people in the same circumstances as ourselves. Our peers. In this case peer assessment is important. Try to incorporate opportunities for your learners to comment on each other's work.'

'That's a recipe for chaos,' I said, with a sceptical look.

'So ground rules are vital. Negotiate them at the start and try to let your learners police them. After all, they will be providing feedback to each other, so if they're helpful and constructive then maybe their partner will be the same. You can try to do this in groups, too, so that personalities are less of an issue. I wouldn't do it with the whole class at once, though. Try to get some learners working on a task and some assessing each other. That way you can listen in and consider the impact of the learning.'

'Sounds like the **critical friend** idea.' (See Tutorial 10.)

'Very similar. There's one other dimension, though, and that's the notion of **self-assessment**. If we learn well from peers, then surely we learn best from ourselves? From our mistakes and times when we don't understand. Bafflement is one of the most powerful drives to learn.'

'This comes back to reflection then. I can see that providing opportunities for my learners to consider their own learning is important, though I can imagine that letting them sit and think for 10 minutes wouldn't go down too well.'

'It wouldn't. So try to devise activities in which reflection is implicit rather than explicit. Have a think about how you could do this.'

6.6 Alex's reflection

This all sounds great, but how can I possibly manage to assess all my learners constantly in this way? I would have to gather all sorts of evidence about their progress. And then I'd need to change my teaching to accommodate everyone's needs. This sounds like **personalisation** to me. I can see that assessment for learning is just one part of this. I guess that learner-centred teaching and learning strategies, ensuring learner choice and partnership are very important to this. Maybe that's part of the answer. Learner choice. I always think that I have to do the work, but I should remember the adage 'less teaching, more learning'.

But what activities can I devise in which reflection is implicit rather than explicit. Right, I could get them to compile a scrapbook of their best work. That would involve implicit reflection. I could then ask them to include notes on why they chose each item. That would make explicit what had previously been implicit. They could also discuss their learning using a blog on the VLE.

I'm not sure about using peer assessment. I suppose it will depend on how mature the group is that I'm teaching. Then if I think that they will benefit I need to lay down some ground rules about feedback and how it is to be given and received. If I do this, I'll have to monitor it very closely at first to ensure that it's working as it should.

SPACE FOR YOUR NOTES

Prompt

- From your own experience, what are the best ways to get learners to reflect critically on their own learning?

6.7 Use of questioning

'I want to come back to questioning. Why do you think that it's important to discuss questioning?' asked Jane.

'Because it can be used to enable learners to make links with prior experience,' I said confidently.

'Can you give me an example of how links could be made with prior experience?'

'I could ask a learner to describe a previous incident relating to the topic under discussion.'

'You certainly could, but can you suggest some assumptions made in your last question?'

'I would be assuming that the learner has had a relevant experience and that they understood the question.'

'You also assume that they would be prepared to talk about the incident. We're talking about questioning, but what evidence do you have that questioning is an effective teaching method?'

'I remember that it has helped me to learn in the past. But I was always afraid of getting the wrong answer, though, and I was self-conscious about speaking in class.'

'As teachers, we need to be aware of such feelings and attitudes and the implications they have on the effectiveness of questioning. Can you tell me how some of your learners might respond to the use of questioning?'

'Some may find it challenging, or become frustrated because I don't immediately provide answers. Just like this conversation! I feel like there's an agenda here.'

'Well, there is. In the past few minutes I've tried to give you an example of **Socratic questioning**.'

'The old Greek guy,' I said, waiting for Jane to explode.

'Socrates was not some old Greek guy. He was a philosopher and teacher and he developed the Socratic approach to teaching. Dialogue is really important here and it's sometimes called the **dialectical** approach to knowledge construction. Questions are formulated as if from an expert and are used to guide the learner towards accessing their own prior knowledge and experience.'

'But you were asking different types of question. Was that intentional?'

'Yes, it was. Here, on this handout (see Handout 6.1) I've indicated the different types of question. Of course, you don't have to follow the whole sequence all the time; you can select different approaches according to the circumstances. The idea is that you plan the questions into your lesson as far as possible. This helps you to express them clearly. When you ask a question, don't answer it yourself. Include wait time. Be prepared to wait for a minute if needed.'

'A minute is a long time in teaching!'

'It will seem like it, but learners will soon get the message that you won't give them an easy way out. Ask for elaboration if the answer is limited and pause occasionally to summarise the discussion. Of course, questions should be as open as possible. Remember the rhyme "Six little words I use them now and then, how and what and why, who and where and when." Closed yes/no questions don't encourage deep thinking, so avoid them. What if . . .? is a good way to start a question.'

'I'm worried that I'm not as inclusive in my questioning as I should be. I tend to ask people who sit at the front or those who I think know the answer because I don't like embarrassing people.'

'So tailor your questions to the recipient: differentiate them. Try addressing a question to a group sometimes. If someone dominates, try a no-hands-up policy where only you choose who answers, or try giving tokens, say three each. Each time someone answers a question they lose a token and can't answer another question when they're all gone. But coming back to Socrates – and I can see that your attention is waning on this one! – a key point is that questioning is a two-way process. Initiate – response – feedback, or IRF. The feedback bit is vital to motivate and positively reinforce.'

6.8 Alex's reflection

I've been using questions off the cuff. Now I realise that I need to use them as a resource. Just as I might plan a handout, or a game, I should plan my questioning too. I can't plan every question, but I'll start by including a range of planned questions – perhaps using some of the Socratic ideas – in one lesson a week. I'll soon build up a stock of appropriate questions. I could put them

(continued)

(continued)

in a file to draw on as I need. By reviewing the file regularly they'll become part of my long-term memory and I'll be able to access the material without conscious thought. In this way my questioning technique will appear spontaneous and not planned.

We discussed my asking the questions, but what about the learners? I could encourage them to ask questions by using those tokens, but instead of taking a token off them I could give them an additional token.

If I used mini-whiteboards I could get them to write questions and hold them up. Post-it notes are another idea. They could write the question on a Post-it and stick them on the board for me to answer at the end of the session.

SPACE FOR YOUR NOTES

Prompt

* Write a Socratic sequence of questions for your next lesson.

6.9 Feedback

'Now let's turn to feedback.'

'Feedback,' I said, trying to fight off a yawn.

'Yes, feedback,' Jane said, an edge of irritation in her voice. *'Or to give it its new trendy name, feedforward. A strange term, but it does exemplify the principle that this is about continuous improvement. Now tell me about some of your experiences of feedback.'*

'My first lesson observation. You thought that my teaching methods were too teacher-centred.'

'That's interesting – you have focused on my negative comments. Haven't you had any positive ones?'

'I have, but I tend to remember the bad experiences.'

'And so do most learners, so beware of how you feedback negative comments. As a teacher you're constantly giving feedback. It may be formal and planned, but in many ways the informal feedback that should go on all the time is more important, often because it involves nonverbal cues that convey all sorts of meanings to the learner, such as impatience or annoyance. It can be direct or indirect in the sense that it may specifically be targeted at an individual or to the group or class as a whole. The latter can be less threatening.'

'So it's a continuous process. Another thing to think about!'

'Exactly. Now, I've mentioned that the purpose is developmental, but for whom?'

'For the learner, of course,' I said, before adding, 'unless you mean that it's like formative assessment in that it guides the teacher, too?'

'The response to feedback must guide the teacher. It's a two-way process. The teacher and learner negotiate manageable short-term targets – you've probably heard of SMART targets that are specific, measurable, achievable, relevant and time bound – well, once they are set you have to review them regularly. The success or failure at meeting those targets provides invaluable feedback for both the teacher and the learner. So it's as much about the process of giving feedback as what is actually said. Clarity is important though. The targets must be recorded by both parties. Some say that they need to be focused on the learning outcomes, but often transferable skills are worthy of discussion, as they help the learner to become autonomous.'

'That's all very well, but sometimes I just want to know what I've done right and what I've done wrong. I can't bear this beating about the bush – for example, you asking me what I thought went well when I was just glad to get through the session, let alone think about how it went.'

*'I do have some sympathy with that. In some ways you're talking about **formative** versus **summative feedback**. But it can be really helpful to reflect on your learning. If you identify your own weaknesses, you're more likely to remember how to address them in the future.'*

'I see, experiential learning. OK, so summative feedback is more my kind of thing.'

'It's not a choice. There are times when summative feedback is required, following an assignment, for example. That is about your destination. Formative feedback is to help you along the journey. You do have a valid point, though. The method of feedback needs to be tailored to the individual and their characteristics; their learning styles, for example.'

'So what's the best place and time to give feedback?'

'Don't leave it too long. The sooner the better, but allow yourself some time to think about what you want to say. The environment can be important. It needs to be comfortable and private. I do think a short period of shared reflection is important, but it's certainly important to be clear about the targets for development, how they could be achieved and what sort of evidence for them will be needed. This is an opportunity to build confidence and motivate, so do find the strengths of the work and praise them. Always end on a positive note and ask your learner to recap the targets so that you both understand what has to be done. Finally we need to look at summative assessment.'

6.10 Summative assessment

'At last! When you said assessment, I was expecting to spend the session on assignments and exams and we've hardly mentioned them.'

'That was intentional. Summative assessment is about determining the extent to which the learning outcomes have been met. Of course it's important, but it's only a part of the vital role of assessment in learning. You're aware that there are different summative assessment methods. Jot down a few that come to mind.'

I scribbled away, then handed my list to Jane.

- Essay
- Portfolio
- Presentation
- Multiple choice test
- Written exam
- Practical assessment
- Reflection
- Structured assignment
- Poster

*'Good. Of course there are others, including oral tests and contributions to online discussions, for example. The key point is to ensure that your assessment is **valid**, i.e. that it does actually test the learning outcomes that have been shared with learners. Instructions must also be clear because a good assessment tool can be used repeatedly and produce consistent results – in other words it must be reliable. So depending on what you are assessing, your assessment tool may need to measure the student's recall, understanding and application of knowledge and their ability to analyse and evaluate information. It's not unusual for groups to complain that they haven't covered a topic appearing on an exam paper, when in fact*

the paper merely presented a familiar topic in an unfamiliar scenario which required some interpretation on the part of the learner.'

'But how can I develop that sort of understanding and expertise?'

'In the case of awarding bodies, they all have support sessions, which are usually free. They can really help you to understand what is required and are essential if you're assessing practical work. And, remember, attendance will help you to claim some standards.'

6.11 Norm, criterion and mastery approaches to assessment

'It's also worth mentioning a few approaches to summative assessment, rather than assessment methods. These are **norm-referenced** *and* **criterion-referenced assessments** *and mastery assessment.'*

'Shouldn't all assessment aim at mastery?'

'You could argue that, but mastery assessment – and mastery learning for that matter – is just what the term implies. For example, if you go to the dentist, would you want to be treated by someone scoring 40 per cent in the root filling exam?'

'Hell, no. I expect every dentist to be skilled in the process.'

'So mastery assessments have a high pass mark – say 80 per cent – generally the principle is that they can be retaken until passed, but this isn't always the case. Mastery assessment can be motivating as people feel that they have achieved to a high standard.'

'And norm-referenced?'

'For example, in professional exams it used to be the case that, say, the top 10 per cent of each cohort passed the exam regardless of the mark achieved. Effectively they were competing against each other and the supply of new entrants to the profession was controlled.'

'So in such a scenario the difficulty of the questions is less of an issue?'

'Yes. But it is also possible when using norm-referenced assessment to include a basic bench-mark that a candidate must pass in addition to being in the top 10 per cent. Just in case one group contains a larger-than-usual number of less able candidates. Now, criterion-referenced assessment relates to competencies, so potentially everyone can pass providing that they can demonstrate achievement of a competence. The critical thing here is the assessment or mark scheme, as it must be consistently applied.'

'So the driving test is criterion-referenced?'

'Yes.'

'Well, that explains all the lousy drivers on the road!'

6.12 Alex's reflection

Where do I start with feedback? There is so much of it! I'll need to read this section again to get all the terminology right.

Jane was right to pick me up on only hearing the bad feedback and not listening to the positive stuff. I've always done that and I'm sure that many of my learners do the same. I really need to take the sandwich approach to feedback. Start by saying something positive. Move onto the negative and then end with something positive. I also need to ensure that learners hear the good stuff and that they don't go away deflated. This is probably most important with the less able learners who doubt their ability and have been hearing for ages that they aren't very good.

Many of the points that Jane made on verbal feedback could apply to written feedback too. We didn't discuss this, but I can see that a written dialogue is needed and that it's important to concentrate on significant issues for development and not feel that I have to comment on everything. In a conversation I can emphasise the important points but if I list five points for improvement in writing, I really need to show the learner which are the really important issues that they need to address as a priority.

I also need to spend more time thinking about what I will say to my learners and, more importantly, how I say it. I need to give myself some time to think about how I will handle the feedback and not just jump in feet first. This is especially important when I'm annoyed, 'cos then I'm not thinking straight.

The trouble with summative assessment is that for most courses I'm constrained by the awarding body. They decide how the assessment will be carried out. Even so, I still need to do my own summative assessments. I suppose I could devise different ways to test whether the outcomes have been met. But I need to be careful. It's important that they learn about the assessment method that they will be tested on and that they develop their skills at using it. I don't want to confuse them by introducing my methods. Could this be an example of 'learning for assessment'?

SPACE FOR YOUR NOTES

Prompts

- List some positive and negative examples of feedback that you have received. What can you learn from your experiences?
- List some of the skills that are important for learners to be successful at summative assessment.

6.13 Record of mentor meeting

Trainee: Alex Croft

Summary of key learning points

- Initial assessment could be defined as the process of collecting qualitative and quantitative data on someone with a view to determining their suitability and support needs for a programme of study.
- Diagnostic assessment tends to happen once the programme has started and it's very much an ongoing process. It would be used at the beginning of a topic to determine the learner's learning needs.
- Assessment is about gathering data to help you to make informed judgements about learners' progress, whilst evaluation is about using those data to make judgements about the extent to which your planned outcomes have been met.
- The purpose of formative assessment is to develop learners' knowledge, skills and understanding.
- Formative assessment is embodied in the concept of assessment for learning. It's a two-way process and it can include peer and self-assessment.
- Questioning is a complex skill. Aspects of Socratic questioning can provide a useful approach. Questioning is an important means of differentiation as questions of varying difficulty can be used and directed specifically at either stronger or weaker learners. Another common questioning approach is IRF: initiate, respond, feedback.
- Feedback may be informal or formal, direct or indirect. It's a two-way process involving the setting of SMART targets. It can be formative or summative. The approach is important, but this should be varied according to the learner's characteristics. Timing and the environment are important.
- Validity (does the assessment test the right outcomes) and reliability (does the assessment produce consistent results across time and groups) are vital aspects of good assessment.
- Summative assessment is about determining the extent to which the learning outcomes have been met. Norm-referencing, criterion-referencing and mastery assessment are approaches used in summative assessment.

Agreed action points

Alex will:

- Identify where to find and how to use data for initial assessments on learners.
- Incorporate planned questioning in the next lesson plan.
- Reflect on how mentors and tutors provide feedback. What did he/she find helpful/unhelpful? What are the implications of this for his/her teaching?

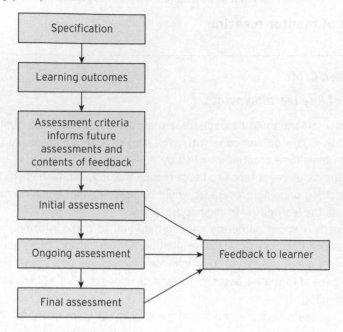

Figure 6.1 Assessment strategy

Optional task

Expand and populate the above boxes (Figure 6.1) with actual data from your institution.

HANDOUT 6.1 Example of Socratic questioning

Q: Why is it important to discuss questioning? *(Initial question)*

A: Because it can be used to enable learners to make links with prior experience.

Q: Give me an example of how links could be made with prior experience. *(Seeking clarification.)*

A: A learner could be asked to describe a previous incident relating to the topic under discussion.

Q: Suggest some assumptions made in your answer. *(Asking what assumptions have been made – assumption probe.)*

A: An assumption could be that the learner has had a relevant experience.

Q: What evidence do you have that questioning is an effective teaching method? *(Seeking evidence – evidence probe.)*

A: I remember that it has helped me to learn in the past.

Q: Can you predict how learners could respond to the use of questioning? *(Implications of the topic under discussion.)*

A: They may find it challenging, or become frustrated, because I don't immediately provide answers.

Further reading

www.routledge.com/cw/mcgrath

Black, P. and Wiliam, D. (2006), *Inside the Black Box, v. 1: Raising Standards Through Classroom Assessment*. Cheltenham: NFER Nelson.

Cohen, L., Manion, L. and Morrison, K. (2010), *A Guide to Teaching Practice* (5th edn). London: Routledge.

Tutorial 7 How to deliver a highly successful lesson

Aim of tutorial: To identify what teachers need to do to transform an adequate/good lesson into a successful or highly successful lesson.

Tutorial overview: Returning to the issues discussed in Tutorial 3, suggestions are made for how a teacher can turn an adequate/good lesson into one that contains the elusive WOW factor. It is suggested that this is best achieved by improving each aspect of the lesson rather than by adding a single new feature or gimmick.

Contents

7.1 Alex's reflection

My meetings with Jane are proving to be much less formal than with Sue. So far we have met in the canteen, the staffroom and the main foyer, as well as in Jane's postage stamp-sized office. Today we're meeting in a classroom between lessons. It just goes to show how busy she is. I'm not even sure that she gets paid much, if anything, for acting as my mentor. Yet she's been great. A real friend and support. I don't know how I would have survived without her.

(continued)

(continued)

Today we're looking at how to deliver a highly successful lesson. It should be interesting. I'd be happy to deliver a satisfactory lesson consistently. From my perspective all the really successful lessons I've ever attended have been delivered by eccentrics – teachers whose larger-than-life personalities and love of teaching and learning seeped into everything they did. Their enthusiasm for their subject just overwhelmed me and dragged me along. I don't have that type of personality, so I'll be interested to see what I can do to improve my performance in the classroom.

7.2 Tacit knowledge and the teacher

Jane was organising her resources for the next lesson when I entered. *'Hi,'* she waved. *'Give me a second and we'll get started. How have you been getting on?'*

'Not bad,' I said. 'I'm still struggling to be consistent. One day my lesson is fine, the next it's verging on poor. I just don't understand how I can be so variable.'

'There is nothing unusual in that. One of the hardest things for new teachers to achieve is consistency. Part of the problem is that their knowledge is new and they have to access it consciously to make use of it. It's not part of their embedded knowledge. Experienced teachers have passed that stage. Much of their knowledge, as I previously said, is tacit and they access it at a subconscious level. Indeed, if you asked them why they did something they would often find it difficult to explain.'

'It must take a long time to achieve that level of expertise.'

'Yes and no. If you constantly use reflection in action and **reflection on action** *to explore your teaching, you will be surprised how quickly you build up an experience bank that you can draw on in moments of need. You need to make deposits into that bank of embedded knowledge constantly. You can then draw on it every time you prepare a lesson plan or hit a problem in the class.'*

'By consciously studying your own experiences?'

'The quickest way to wisdom. I'd suggest that you keep a learning log or reflective journal to record ideas. That will help you consciously examine and commit to memory your insights and inform your future teaching.'

7.3 Starting a highly successful lesson

'Speaking of which, what do you think you need to do to deliver a really great lesson?'

'I imagine you would have to demonstrate that your session had delivered a high level of learning to each member of the class. But that's really tough to achieve.'

'Indeed it is. So let's break it down. Where does a great lesson start?'

'A few weeks ago I would have said that it starts with the lesson plan. But now I realise that I need to know and understand the strengths, weaknesses and needs of my learners before I can draw up an effective lesson plan. So it starts with knowing my learners.'

'And if they are new to you?'

'I can look at their SAT results or other test scores. I can also chat to their previous teacher and review any special needs statements that individuals might have. I can also take account of the learners' preferred learning style as we discussed a couple of weeks ago.' (See Tutorial 4.)

'Good. So you have a clear understanding of your learners; what next?'

'Using the scheme of work, I need to produce a lesson plan that will meet the learning needs of each individual in the class, while at the same time ensuring that I cover any syllabus I'm working to.'

'So you're going to use differentiation to meet individual learning needs?'

'Yes.'

'What else?'

'My resources. They have to support the learning that is taking place, but they also need to add something to the lesson.'

'How do you mean?' Jane asked.

'My PDT told me of a trainee who was teaching health workers about the need to wash their hands properly. Of course, all the learners thought that they knew how to wash their hands. So the trainee brought in a blindfold, some liquid dye and a couple of wash basins. She then blindfolded each learner in turn and asked them to wash their hands thoroughly using the dye. When they took the blindfold off they could see which parts of the hands and wrists they had not washed/covered with dye. From all accounts there were a few embarrassed faces.'

'I bet there were. So the message is, be creative. But in addition to such learning resources, don't forget that the learning area is also a resource. Think about how you can make best use of the space available. Organise the room layout to achieve maximum impact. If students have been sitting in a horseshoe for six weeks, change it and observe the effect it has on them as they walk in the door. Immediately they are engaged, wondering what is going on. "Why has the teacher changed the layout?"'

'OK.'

'So you have prepared well for the lesson. How are you going to kick it off?'

'I need to be enthusiastic and come to the session with high energy levels. But I must also do the mundane things. Like take the register early on and challenge any latecomers appropriately.'

'You've been reading the school policy.'

'Yeah, I find it helps me sleep at night.' Jane smiled and I continued. 'After that I would recap what we covered in earlier sessions.'

'And how would you do that?'

'I'd use a mix of whole group and individually directed questions. That way I could make an assessment of prior learning and identify any areas that I needed to revisit. It would also reinforce the group's previous learning.'

'Why not talk about the aims and objectives of the current session before you get into a recap?'

'Well, personally, I think it's logical to discuss what you have previously done before talking about what you are going to do. In addition, it means I can show how the aims and objectives for the current session build on or link to previous learning.'

'So you wouldn't just read the aims and objectives from a sheet of paper or PowerPoint slide?'

'No, I'd explain what they meant and I'd pin a hard copy of them to the wall so that everyone could see them throughout the session.'

7.4 Alex's reflection

I like the idea of tacit knowledge. Actors, when asked why they did something, often reply that they felt it was the right thing to do at the time. But to reach their decision they probably accessed, sub-consciously, a huge library of memories. I can't amass such memories overnight, but if I reflect on my teaching after each session I will be explicitly 'filing away' memories and ideas for future use.

The rest of what Jane said really boils down to planning carefully with the needs of the learners in mind at all times. I've only been teaching for a few weeks but I can already see how easy it is to view lesson plans and resources as something you have to prepare, as a chore. But in reality they are an essential part of delivering a really effective lesson because they force you to think about what you want to achieve and how you are going to do it. Mind you, it does remind me of a poster I saw in my father's office: 'It's difficult to remember that your job is to drain the swamp when crocodiles are biting your bum'. Teachers have so many demands on their time that it's easy to let lesson planning slide. I need to resist that particular temptation.

SPACE FOR YOUR NOTES

Prompts

- Think of a physical or mental activity that you are really good at, such as football, chess or drawing. When you are immersed in the activity, how many of your decisions are made consciously?
- Identify three weaknesses in your lesson planning and consider how you might eliminate them.

7.5 How to continue a highly successful lesson

'You mentioned being energetic and enthusiastic – what exactly do you mean by that?' Jane asked.

'Well, I think it is really important to show enthusiasm for your subject. After all, if you're not interested, why should the learners be?'

'But if you're like Tigger all the time you'll be worn out by 12.30!'

I suspected that Jane, one of the most enthusiastic teachers I knew, was playing devil's advocate. 'You don't have to bounce around like Tigger to show your commitment. You can demonstrate it by preparing an interesting and lively lesson which actively engages all the learners.'

'And how are you going to do that?' asked Jane.

'You need to grab their interest. So, if I was talking about the Romans I might show them a short clip from *Gladiator* or some copies of actual Roman coins. Then once I have their attention I can build on it.'

'How?'

'By using a range of teaching methods that match the learning styles in the group. They need to be student-centred and enable the learners to become part of the learning process. The three most important things I've learnt on this placement are this. Firstly, always have a good balance between teacher- and learner-centred teaching methods; secondly, good teaching is not something I do to learners, it's something I do in partnership with them; and thirdly, planning for individual needs is really difficult.'

'If you're talking about differentiation, I agree it's difficult. However, there are a range of strategies that you can use. For example, you could differentiate your objectives by using such phrases as "some/most/all learners will be able to . . ." Similarly, you might provide different levels of support for individual learners during the session or pair strong learners with weaker ones. You could also differentiate your resources, providing extension activities that the more able learners can undertake once they have finished the basic task, and use assessment tools that test a wide range of abilities. But perhaps one of the easiest strategies to use is differentiated questioning. You should use both general and directed questions during the session, and the level of difficulty should range from the easy to the very challenging. This will give everyone in the class a chance to answer at least some of the questions.'

'But won't the brighter ones answer all the easier questions before . . .?'

'Not if the easier questions are directed questions. That way you choose who gets first chance to answer them. While we are discussing Q&A, remember that by itself it's not enough. As discussed in our last session (see Tutorial 6) you also need other assessment activities during the lesson to monitor that learning is taking place.'

'You mean like pair or group activities where the learners have to feedback their answers or findings to either me or the class.'

'Yes. But you can also use gapped handouts or tasks, the completion of which you can check as you move around the class. The more assessment you build into your lesson, the more feedback you can provide to learners. It's this reinforcement that cements the learning.'

'I'm getting better at Q&A, but following on from last week, I'm still trying to think more creatively about the types of assessment that I use.'

'While you are at it, think about your communication skills. Do you use the most appropriate language to communicate with the learners? Is what you say clear and simple? Do the learners know what you mean/understand in your instructions? Do you allow the learners an opportunity to seek clarification? I can't stress enough how important it is that all the learners know what is expected of them. If they are unsure, this will be reflected in their performance and their ability to complete your assessment activity.'

'Generally my instructions are clear, but when I differentiate an activity I do sometimes confuse the learners because I have to deliver slightly different instructions to each group,' I said defensively.

'Unless your instructions are clear and unambiguous you will never deliver an outstanding lesson. The best example of giving clear instructions I have ever seen was from a PGCE trainee delivering a session on photography. The class was split into three groups and each group had to move around the room and perform a different task at three separate work stations. She explained the individual tasks to the entire class and told them she would blow a whistle as the signal to move from one work station to the next. So far, so ordinary. But then instead of asking the group a general question such as "Do you all understand?" she asked a series of directed questions to discover if individual learners understood exactly what they had to do at each stage. She must have asked 12 or more questions. It was simply brilliant.'

'That's a very forensic approach,' I said. 'She's probably a *CSI* fan.'

'Possibly, but the important thing is it worked. She also used a variety of resources that engaged the learners' senses.'

'It must be hard finding smelly resources.'

'Don't give up the day job for stand-up just yet,' Jane said witheringly. *'You know perfectly well that I am talking about VAK. Try and develop resources that engage the visual, auditory and kinaesthetic. Too often we rely on the auditory. Yes, we need to speak to our learners and get them to talk to us, but we need to provide the eyes with food and the bodies with movement if we want to give them a holistic learning experience.'*

'You sound passionate about VAK?' I said.

'I am. For years I sat in secondary school and was talked at by a long line of teachers. For example, I remember a lesson on the history of modern art. The teacher spent an age talking about the various movements and how art influenced early twentieth-century design. It was a full 20 minutes before he showed us the first picture.'

'I've noticed the reverse, where some teachers use too many pictures or group activities and not enough verbal instruction. What's going on there?'

'As with my teacher, I'd say they were teaching the session according to their own learning preferences.'

'A case of what is good for them is good for their learners,' I said.

'Exactly. They are happy working within their comfort zone and have forgotten that it's the needs of the learner and not their needs which are paramount.'

'What about using stories to enliven your teaching? Do you think they are a good idea?'

'My MA leadership lecturer uses stories all the time. He previously worked in industry and local government and he constantly uses stories, based on his experiences, to exemplify what he is saying. Occasionally they become a bit self-indulgent, but the odd thing is that I remember the stories and what they represent a whole lot better than many of the theories that we cover, especially the funny ones. So I think it's really valuable to use tales of previous experiences to exemplify points. However, not every teacher is comfortable using personal examples; each of us has to decide how much personal information we are willing to share with our learners. What about you?'

'I like stories but I'm not confident enough to use them at the moment.'

'Don't rush it. Start with a few short anecdotes that exemplify the points you're making. Avoid telling funny stories or jokes, because if they go flat it can be very embarrassing. Gradually over time your confidence will grow and your repertoire will increase.'

7.6 Alex's reflection

I'm glad I'm not the only one who has trouble with differentiation. I need to think more about how I differentiate and what aspects of the lesson I differentiate. I do use a variety of extension activities and my assessment tools are differentiated to some extent, but my resources tend to be undifferentiated.

One thing that really worries me about differentiation is that some learners might find it a turn-off to discover that they are being given easier tasks to complete because I think they are struggling. They could be embarrassed or even annoyed. I know I wouldn't like it. I should raise this with Jane or, better still, I could pose it as a question on the VLE discussion forum. That way I can pick the brains of tutors and other trainees back at the uni and share what I learn with Jane.

What I really need to improve is my use of directed questions to discover if learners have under-stood my instructions. Usually I get by with a peremptory 'Do you understand?' or 'Is that OK?' I'm definitely going to try task-specific directed questions during my next session.

Jane's comment about VAK has also pricked my conscience. I know that I am only too happy to be lectured by someone who knows what they are talking about. I learn through the spoken and writ-ten word. But not everyone is like me. I need to use more images in my teaching and get people doing things rather than just talk about them. Maybe I could talk to some of the other students on the course and see how they use images in their sessions. Again, I could post a query on the VLE and see what replies I get. After all, a good teacher pinches ideas from wherever they can find them, including pages left on the photocopier as I have already noticed!

Until last week's session (see Tutorial 6), assessment was not an area I had worried too much about. Well, that's changing. But I now realise that not only do I need to be assessing the students' learning throughout the session, the approaches I use have to fit seamlessly into my lesson strategy. They can't just be last-minute add-ons which I dream up after I've written the lesson. They must be an integral part of the session.

This lesson planning malarkey is not as easy as it seems! How am I going to make the whole process appear seamless and still feed in a couple of stories to exemplify what I'm saying? This is a three fig roll problem! Time for tea and biscuits.

SPACE FOR YOUR NOTES

Prompts

- What strategies do you use for differentiation? How could they be improved?
- Are you guilty of teaching the way you like to be taught?
- Are your lessons a series of disjointed activities or a unified whole?

7.7 How to end a highly successful lesson

'OK, let's look at ending a lesson. How do you wind up a session?'

'I tend to use Q&A. If I ask the right questions I'm able to check out what has been learnt while at the same time recapping what we've covered. Sometimes I'll vary this by giving them a pop/pub quiz or a mini-written test.'

'And what if you find that their understanding of an issue is vague or non-existent?'

'If I can't clarify the matter there and then, I make a note of it and include it in my next lesson. But I never try to cram an issue in. If it needs further consideration I carry it over.'

'Good.'

'I wind up by referring back to the aims and objectives of the session and explaining how we met them and set any homework that is required.'

'Do you give written guidance on the homework?'

'When it's complicated I do.'

'Well, think about always providing written guidance. It will help anyone who was absent from your session and reduce the number of learners claiming that they didn't understand what was required. I'd also end with a very brief indication of what the next lesson will be about. That way the stronger learners can forge ahead. OK, I think we can end it there. Any questions?'

7.8 Adding the WOW factor to your lessons

'Well, what we've done is examine closely the elements of a lesson. But I've been reading about the need to make your session sparkle if you want to achieve a grade 1. How do you ensure that your lesson has this sparkle or the wow factor?'

'Good question, and I wish I could give you a simple clear answer. It's a bit like beauty and justice, easy to recognise when you see it but horrendously difficult to define. In this country when we are dissatisfied with a system we identify the worst performing aspect of the process and try and improve it by 10 per cent to 20 per cent. The Japanese look at the whole process and try and improve each part of it by 1 per cent. In this way the entire system can be improved. That's what we've been doing in this session. Examining each aspect of a lesson and trying to improve it slightly.'

'And if each aspect is improved slightly, the overall learning experience is improved considerably,' I said.

'Exactly. But in addition you need to bring to the lesson a feeling of excitement and fun. Learning can be hard work at times and learners need to realise that there is a time and place for some fun. If you are upbeat and encouraging, the learners will pick up on this and it will be reflected in how they interact with you and in their work. You also need ways to excite them. How you do this depends on you, the subject you teach and the learners you have in front of you. What will work for one group won't work with another. You have to find the key. That's what makes teaching a profession. You have to exercise your professional judgement as to what is the best way to reach your students. Some of the best films about teaching and teachers have had as their central story line the teachers struggling to reach the learners and turn them on to education.'

'Such as?' I asked.

'To Sir with Love, Freedom Writers, Stand and Deliver, Knights of the South Bronx, even Prez in the fourth season of The Wire. The teachers in each of these dramas are trying to find the way to make learning relevant and interesting to their students.'

'And of course they all succeed?'

'If they didn't, there wouldn't be a film.'

7.9 Alex's reflection

OK, I definitely need to increase my use of assessment during sessions. I'll also try to do everything just 1 per cent better. So I'll take a little more care in how I draft my lesson plan, design my teaching strategy and resources and use differentiation. But I have to find my own way to inject some piz- zazz into the proceedings. Again, I could post a message on the VLE and see what ideas the other trainees/lecturers use. Between us we must be able to come up with a few fresh ideas. Then I'll need to test them out, preferably in a safe environment where failure won't be too embarrassing.

Maybe story-telling is the answer. Trouble is I don't have a stock of stories that I can use. Hang on, who says they have to be my stories. Maybe I can use the stories told to me by other teachers and lecturers. They'll probably need amending a bit to bring them up to date but that could be a way of making them my own. Or better, I could use incidents I saw during my schooldays but tell them from the teacher's perspective. That way they would be more real to me and therefore my learners.

One area we didn't cover in the session was inclusivity. I was reading about it today. Leave that out of a lesson and it's unlikely to be outstanding. I need to check that my use of language, teach- ing and learning approaches and resources promote a learning atmosphere that respects and promotes diversity in terms of gender, ethnicity, religious belief and sexuality. I could ask Jane to look out for this specifically in my next observation. I also need to monitor and pick up on any inappropriate or stereotypical views expressed by learners verbally or in writing. Mind you, I've already noticed that the learners police themselves in terms of racial or gender bias. Occasionally an inappropriate comment is made but very often the learners deal with the issue themselves.

I've earned a cup of tea. I'll have a think about stories I could use and jot a few ideas down.

SPACE FOR YOUR NOTES

Prompts

- Which strategy do you think will improve your teaching the most? Change one or two things substantially or improve several things very slightly or a mixture of both? (**Note:** there is no right or wrong answer to this question. It is all about what suits your personality and style of teaching.)
- What aspect of your teaching are you most concerned with? Why? Who could you discuss this with?

7.10 Record of mentor meeting

Trainee: Alex Croft

Summary of key learning points

- Inexperienced teachers find it difficult to maintain consistency in the quality of their teaching from session to session.
- One reason for this inconsistency is that they have very little tacit knowledge to call upon. The most effective way to increase your level of tacit knowledge is to use reflection in action and reflection on action during and after each session. After every session, always consider what went well, what went badly and, most importantly, ask yourself why it went well or badly.
- The analysis of critical incidents is an invaluable way of increasing both your conscious and tacit knowledge. Record key ideas and events in your learning log or reflective journal.
- As far as possible try to know and understand the strengths, weaknesses and needs of your learners. What makes them tick? What demotivates them? What is their preferred way to learn?
- Ensure that at a minimum you differentiate your lessons to take into account the needs of strong, average and weak learners in your class.
- Differentiation can be applied to the resources you use, the tasks you set and the assessment strategy you design.
- Demonstrate enthusiasm, energy and creativity in your teaching. Spring surprises on your students! Don't fall into a rut.
- Always recap prior learning before starting the current session. Use individually directed and whole group questions.
- State your objectives for the lesson clearly and refer back to them as you achieve each one. Don't treat them as something you have to do but as an aid to monitoring what learning has taken place.
- Use a range of teaching methods to complement the range of learning styles that your learners have.
- Consider what role VAK should have in your lessons.
- Don't use teaching methods just because you find them easy or because they reflect your own learning style preferences.
- Always programme a range of activities for your learners to undertake in each session, e.g. pair or group working, completion of gapped handouts, searching the Internet, discussion, presentations, etc.
- Ask your mentor or a critical friend to assess how well you communicate verbally and in writing with your learners. How easy is it for your learners to understand what you are saying and follow your instructions?
- Always provide a short written brief for any homework that you want your learners to complete.

(continued)

(continued)

- Consider using stories and anecdotes to enliven your teaching. Don't tell jokes!
- Good teachers constantly assess the level of learning that is taking place in their lesson. They identify problems as they arise and resolve them in real time. In addition to Q&A, always include a range of assessment techniques in your lesson plan.
- Constantly refer back to the objectives for the session and confirm that either they have been achieved or that they are being addressed and will be achieved.
- When ending the session, recap/summarise what has been covered in the session.
- Make a note of anything that the learners have found difficult and return to it in the next session.
- Try to improve every aspect of your teaching by just 1 per cent or 2 per cent rather than seek a 20 per cent improvement in just one area.
- Learning is, at times, hard, but you should try and instil some excitement and fun into every session.

Agreed action points

Alex will:

- Review two old lesson plans, the resources used and the written reflections made immediately after the session and identify how the lessons could be materially improved.
- Draw up a checklist of the issues that need to be considered when writing any future lesson plans.
- Consider what strategies could be used to engage and enthuse the group.

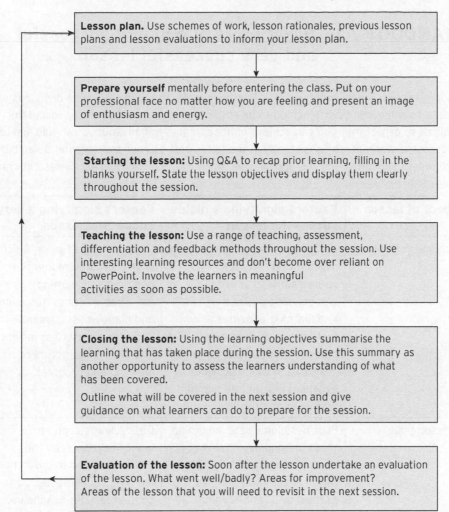

Lesson plan. Use schemes of work, lesson rationales, previous lesson plans and lesson evaluations to inform your lesson plan.

Prepare yourself mentally before entering the class. Put on your professional face no matter how you are feeling and present an image of enthusiasm and energy.

Starting the lesson: Using Q&A to recap prior learning, filling in the blanks yourself. State the lesson objectives and display them clearly throughout the session.

Teaching the lesson: Use a range of teaching, assessment, differentiation and feedback methods throughout the session. Use interesting learning resources and don't become over reliant on PowerPoint. Involve the learners in meaningful activities as soon as possible.

Closing the lesson: Using the learning objectives summarise the learning that has taken place during the session. Use this summary as another opportunity to assess the learners understanding of what has been covered.

Outline what will be covered in the next session and give guidance on what learners can do to prepare for the session.

Evaluation of the lesson: Soon after the lesson undertake an evaluation of the lesson. What went well/badly? Areas for improvement? Areas of the lesson that you will need to revisit in the next session.

Figure 7.1 Stages in a highly successful lesson

Descriptors of a highly successful and very successful lesson

Breaking the average lesson down into 18 components, the following table describes what you have to achieve in your teaching to be either highly successful or very successful. It is unrealistic to expect that you can achieve either category initially, but you should aim to hit the successful descriptors consistently in the latter part of your training and be ambitious and confident enough to aim for, and achieve, some of the highly successful descriptors.

Aspect of lesson	Factors signifying a highly successful lesson	Factors signifying a very successful lesson
1. Schemes of work	Comprehensive scheme of work that includes course aims/objectives and sequenced teaching and learning activities, methods, resources and planned assessment. Detailed information which provides excellent insight into planned learning and progress.	Good scheme of work, which clearly records sequenced teaching and learning activities, methods, resources and planned assessment. Provides a very clear insight into planned structure of learning and progress.
2. Lesson plan	Provides highly detailed timing, structure and description of methods to be used. Excellent range of activities planned to meet different learning styles/needs. Excellent links to scheme of work. Detailed and informative rationale.	Good, clear structure – identifies resources and activities linked to different learning styles/needs. Clear contextual links to scheme. Strong rationale.
3. Learning environment	Learning environment is fully exploited to enhance learning.	Learning environment exploited to some extent to enhance learning.
4. Introduction, aims and objectives	Comprehensive introduction – aims and objectives explained, shared and displayed. Learners demonstrate very clear understanding of the purpose of the session.	Clear aims and objectives shared with learners at beginning of the session. Learners clear about learning purpose.

5. Pace and structure of the lesson	Pace clearly matches subject and learner level. Activities very well structured and timed to maintain interest and stimulate learning for all learners. Learning buzz evident in session.	Pace matches subject and most learners' needs and level. Most activities well timed and structured.
6. Identification and support of individual learning needs	Highly effective identification of individual learning needs through use of learning style analysis/ILP or other means/initial and diagnostic assessment techniques. Excellent support provided through differentiated resources and activities – extension work, structured group/individual work and in-class customised support (as appropriate).	Good identification of individual learning needs through learning style analysis/ILP or other means/initial and diagnostic assessment techniques. Good individual support evident through development and use of resources, activities and support in lesson (where appropriate).
7. Skills for life – key/basic skills – identified and cross-referenced	Highly effective embedding of skills for life in planning, delivery and resources.	Effective embedding of skills for life in planning, delivery and resources.
8. Learning methods	Excellent range/creative approaches used to maximise learning and involve learners; highly appropriate for subject.	Good range of learning methods used to engage learners and promote learning.
9. Checks on learning/questioning skills	Highly effective, clearly focused questioning skills used to check all learners' knowledge/progress throughout the lesson.	Good questioning used to enhance and check learning throughout the lesson.
10. Links in the learning	Previous knowledge and experience referred to throughout. Very clear links drawn out to reinforce/promote learning, especially in relation to linking theory and practice in vocational areas.	Previous experience/knowledge referred to and used to introduce new material in the lesson. Links between theory and practice stressed throughout and some examples elicited.

(continued)

(continued)

11. Learning materials/resources	Excellent range of high-quality (creative) materials clearly presented and well-used to promote learning. Very effective (extensive) use of learning technologies.	Good range of materials and resources effectively used to support session content and promote learning. Effective use of learning technologies.
12. Inclusive learning strategies	All teaching and reference materials promote inclusion through highly effective use of diverse examples. Teacher models best practice through use of inclusive language, attitudes and terminology.	All teaching and reference materials support inclusion through effective use of diverse examples. Teacher models good practice through use of inclusive language, attitudes and terminology.
13. Teacher style and communication skills	Passionate about subject. Outstanding oral presentation skills that engage learners and promote sustained motivation and concentration. Positive verbal/non-verbal communication – strong voice, fluent speech patterns, clear eye contact, enthusiastic manner and open body language and expression.	Animated delivery shows a good level of interest in subject and holds learners' interest. Good presentation skills that promote innovation and concentration. Teacher demonstrates effective verbal/ non-verbal communication skills.
14. Teacher knowledge	Very knowledgeable and up to date in subject area. Very effective reference to appropriate examples which interest learners and extend their awareness.	Clearly knowledgeable in subject area and uses relevant examples to good effect in the classroom.
15. Management of learning	Highly effective group/ individual management. Clear directions and health and safety stressed throughout. Behaviour and standards of a very high order, demonstrating a high mutual teacher/learner value/respect. Highly effective ground rules established and referred to as appropriate.	Good management of group activities. Clear instructions and good emphasis on health and safety. Appropriate standards of behaviour, demonstrating that teacher and learners clearly value and respect each other. Effective ground rules established.

16. Review/recap/ summary of learning	Highly effective review of learning at intervals throughout the lesson. Very clear (and creative) summary linked to learning aims/ objectives and to next lesson.	Good review/recap at points in the lesson plus clear summary of learning progress at end of lesson with reference to next lesson.
17. Learner involvement and response	Learners actively involved and engaged. Highly motivated/ interested. Asks and answers questions well. High levels of cooperation and interaction, plus learners use/take initiative in learning and take responsibility where appropriate.	Good involvement and engagement of learners. Good level of interest and concentration. Some examples of effective cooperation, interaction and initiative.
18. Attendance and punctuality	Highly effective response to issues of attendance and/or punctuality with consistent use of a range of strategies to reinforce good practice among the learners.	Good response to issues of lateness and/or absenteeism. With some strategies in place to support improvement.

Adapted from Birmingham City University Lesson Observation Grid.

Further reading

www.routledge.com/cw/mcgrath

Cohen, L., Manion, L. and Morrison, K. (2010), *A Guide to Teaching Practice* (5th edn). London: Routledge.

Haigh, A. (2008), *The Art of Teaching: Big Ideas, Simple Rules*. Harlow: Pearson Longman.

Part II
Managing your studies

In Part I we looked at how various education ideas and theories can be applied in schools and how you can manage your placement. This part looks at how you can successfully navigate your way thought the academic side of your course. Most, but not all, pathways into teaching require you to undergo training in the theory of education at a recognised partner organisation. Often this is a university.

Some people, including politicians, think that such training is unnecessary. They see teaching as a craft and believe that the best way to learn it is to do it. I have some sympathy with this view. Teaching can't be learnt from a book. You have to practise teaching in order to become expert at it. However, if all your learning takes place at a specific school or college, how do you know that what you have learnt is any good? You've nothing to compare it with. You're like the carpenter who only has a hammer in their tool kit and therefore every problem they see is treated as a nail.

Those organisations that are involved in the academic training of teachers are staffed by ex-teachers. They have a wealth of experience to draw upon and share with trainee teachers. They have also studied education as an academic discipline and can introduce you to the latest thinking in education and learning by explaining both old and new education ideas and theories.

Armed with this knowledge you have choices about how to deal with problems that you encounter, rather than just relying on what has been done in a single setting since Queen Victoria suggested that she was not amused. Effectively, academic knowledge provides you with a range of options you can choose from. That's the value of studying education theory. Of course, you will have to amend many of the ideas you learn to fit the unique requirements of your setting, but that is what all professionals have to do. They find a way to apply best practice in their work.

To ensure that you have understood these ideas and theories you will be required to complete a number of assignments. This section provides the essential advice and guidance you need to successfully complete any academic assignments that are required by your course.

Finally, always remember: Teaching is like riding a bicycle. If you have the training but no theory to back it up or theory with no experience to support it, you'll find yourself riding a unicycle. It can be done but it's a lot harder than riding a bike.

Tutorial 8   How to make time and space for your studies

Aim of tutorial: To help you identify the time and space you require to successfully complete your studies and to suggest that a daily timetable is not the most effective way to manage your workload.

Tutorial overview: This tutorial looks at time management and identifies what you require in terms of accommodation to study effectively. It also makes suggestions for how you might organise the time you spend studying in order to maximise learning.

Contents

8.1 Alex's reflection

What's with these education lecturers? I've only been here a week and already I feel as if I'm back in school. First I'm told that I have to see my PDT, Dr Susan Storm, once a week up to Christmas. Then they tell us that these meetings and any future meetings we might have with our mentor on placement have to form the basis of a reflective diary which we use for our final teaching portfolio. Oh, for the days when I just turned up to lessons, did my assignments and sat the year-end exams.

And if all this extra work wasn't bad enough, I now have lecturers correcting my spelling, grammar and use of syntax. The last time anyone did that I was studying for my GCSEs. Of course, Dr Storm tells me that these corrections are made because as teachers we have to model good practice for our learners at all times and that this includes dress, behaviour, and written and spoken English. Personally, I think it's because most of the lecturers here are ex-teachers and can't break the habits of a lifetime.

Ah, what's the point of getting irritated? I want to be a teacher. I want to pass the course. Besides, Dr Storm seemed friendly enough when I saw her on Monday for our first PDT meeting, even if she did criticise me for making a couple of silly mistakes on my pre-entry task and not taking any notes during the tutorial. Well, I'll blow her away today. Not only am I going to take notes during today's tutorial – I'm going to record it. Then I can replay it at my leisure and pull out the important learning points.

People have told me that any teacher training course is tough. I've just started but already I can see that it's not going to be easy to balance uni with working at my placement, completing my assignments and preparing lessons. The thing is, I can't fail. This course is costing me a small fortune in fees, living costs and lost income. I have to come out of it with a qualification and a job and not just increased debt.

8.2 Are you on the right course?

I'd hardly sat down before Sue asked me, *'How's the course going?'*

'Fine. I'm only in uni three days a week at the moment and my placement doesn't start for a while so things are quiet,' I said, turning on my digital recorder.

'I see you came prepared this time,' Sue said approvingly before continuing. *'At the moment you're in the lull before the storm. Most trainees find the course very demanding once it gets under way. Possibly for the first time in your life you'll have to balance the competing demands of a university course, a placement, preparing lessons, completing assignments and trying to maintain some kind of social life. It can get tough if you're not organised. Where are you living? Are you in halls of residence?'*

'No, I'm sharing a flat with my partner.'

'Is your flat local?'

'It's ten minutes on the bus.'

'Good. The last thing that you want to do is use up time in unnecessary travel. Time is valuable – that's why I like to discuss it with all my PDTs at the start of the course. When considering time management, what is the first thing that you need to confirm?'

'Your timetable,' I suggested tentatively.

'That's a fair answer. But I suggest that the first thing you need to do is confirm in your own mind that you are on the right course. Time management is about remaining motivated enough to stick to a timetable. If you hate the course you're on or believe that it's not for you there's no chance that you will stick to the timetable. But you need to give both yourself and the course a couple of weeks before you decide. If you have doubts, speak to me or the course director before you make a final decision. If there is a specific problem or problems that are making you unhappy, we can often help. And if we can't, we can usually redirect you to someone who can. You are not alone on this course. But we can't do anything to help unless you tell us there is a problem. OK?'

'I'm fine. I'm enjoying the course so far.'

8.3 Introduction to time management

'Well, if you are enjoying your course and want to finish it, never tell me that you don't have enough time to do the work. As Seneca said 2,000 years ago: "Life is long enough, and a sufficiently generous amount has been given to us for the highest achievements if it were well invested. But when it is wasted in heedless luxury and spent on no good activity, we are forced at last by death's final constraint to realise that it has passed away before we knew it was passing" ' (Seneca 2005: 1).

'I take it he would not have approved of computer games,' I said.

'Not much. What he was saying was that we need to prioritise our activities and guard our time. We don't let other people steal our money or property. Yet we are happy for people to steal our time, involving us in activities that might be important to them but are of no value to us. And, unlike property or money, you can never recover time. Therefore guard your time. It's the most precious commodity you have.'

'So I need to be assertive. To say no to people when they want me to spend time on activities which are of little value to me.'

'Correct. But there will be times when your studies should rightly take second place to other important activities.'

'You mean like maintaining good relationships with family and close friends?'

'Yes. Studying for a teaching qualification is a time-consuming activity. Students can become very stressed and find that they're spending all their waking hours studying, teaching, preparing to teach or talking about teaching. It's very easy for them to forget that their family, partners and friends are not as excited as they are about what is happening at school or university. Indeed, friends and family can quickly feel excluded from your new life. This can place a strain on the best of relationships. Don't let this happen to you. So build in some time every day for the people who are important to you. Years ago I had a student who broke up with his fiancée. Both of them were in a terrible state and she went home to her parents in

York. He wanted to go after her but was worried that if he did he would miss an assignment deadline. I told him to forget the deadline. There is always another deadline.'

'What happened?'

'*He went. They made up and I get a Christmas card from them and their two children every year. She is also one of the most successful head teachers in the Midlands.'*

'We're back to Seneca, aren't we?' I said. 'We need to spend the limited time we have on what is most important to us.'

'*Precisely. Always remember that no one ever lay on their death bed and wished they had spent more time in the office.'*

8.4 Planning your timetable: the calendar and the clock

'*OK, with that understood you can start to plan your timetable. Too many people draw up a really detailed weekly timetable and then feel like a failure when they fail to stick to it. I suggest that you use both the calendar and the clock as ways of keeping on track. But always remember that the calendar is more important than the clock.'*

I must have looked blank, because, without waiting for me to respond, Dr Storm continued.

'*The calendar tracks your long-term aims while the clock keeps tabs on daily tasks that you have to complete. I suggest that at the start of a course you jot down your long-term aims. What are yours?'*

'To pass the course and get a job,' I stammered, surprised at the question.

'*That's fine. What are your aims for this term?'*

I had to think about that before replying, 'Complete, submit and pass all my assignments on time and establish myself on placement.'

'*Again, they are a good set of aims because they feed nicely into your overall aim for the course. Now what I would suggest is that every Sunday you sit down and work out what you need to do in the week ahead to help you achieve your "calendar of general aims". So that might be to attend the sessions at uni, start your second assignment, and plan and deliver two lessons on placement. The important thing to remember is that your aim is to complete the tasks and not spend a specified number of hours doing the task.'*

'That doesn't sound like good time management,' I said, doubtfully.

'*It's not time management. It's aims and objective management. Stay with me and you'll see what I mean. What you also need to do on the Sunday is prepare a timetable for the week ahead. I suggest that you have a seven-day planner with each day divided into hours. This handout shows you what I mean. (See Handout 8.1.) Start by selecting one day on which you will do no work. This is important as you need a day a week to do the things that you want to do. To sleep, watch a film, or spend quality time with your partner, family or friends. On all* the other days fill in the hours that are occupied by sleeping, eating, attending university and working at your placement. What is left is the time available for starting that assignment, preparing your lessons and socialising.'

'I think I see where you are going. I can now identify the time slots that I have available to work on my aims and objectives for that week. I don't have to use up all the time available on my studies or study for a specified period each week. I just need to complete the tasks that I have set for myself. If I complete the tasks ahead of schedule, I can have an extra night out, but if I need to sacrifice a night out I have to do it.'

'You've got it. You need to exercise a sort of tight/loose control over your activities. You need some structure but you also have to allow for some flexibility. Provided you're constantly moving towards your objectives, it doesn't matter greatly if you are blown off track for a day or two, provided you recover your bearings and press on. The problem with just relying on a weekly timetable is that it can become a strait-jacket, where putting the hours in becomes more important than achieving your aims and objectives. Now, many of your learners will be unfamiliar with time management, and if they have a timetable it will only be concerned with the clock. Tell them about the calendar and the value of keeping their aims and objectives in mind at all times. It will help them to get organised, complete their work and maintain motivation.'

8.5 Alex's reflection

Well, who would have thought it, a tutor who is a closet romantic, and willing to put relationships ahead of assignments! There can't be many of them around. But Sue is right – work is only part of what makes life worth living. It's important that I don't let it overshadow everything else. I know that I'm competitive and I want to do well, but I shouldn't let that damage other aspects of my life.

I've always associated time management with the use of a daily timetable. But Dr Storm is right. It's vital to use the calendar approach to plot my medium- and long-term objectives. Otherwise I could end up filling every hour of the day with tasks that don't help me achieve my objectives. I need to monitor my progress in terms of jobs done and not just hours spent studying. But I still need to blank out specific periods in the week which I can devote to the completion of these tasks.

I also like the idea of setting aside a day a week for rest and recuperation. I used to do that when I was studying for my GCSEs. It's good to give the mind a rest and it's something to look forward to when I'm stuck in the middle of writing an essay. It's a way of rewarding myself for hard work.

I will do as Sue suggested and tell my learners about time management. I can remember when I started my GCSEs – a lot of my friends found it really difficult to get organised. Fortunately my Dad helped me to plan a timetable. But he didn't include the idea of long-term objectives. If I handle it right, the kids can use their timetables as a sort of record of achievement, ticking off tasks as they're completed.

SPACE FOR YOUR NOTES

Prompts

- Am I on the right course?
- What are my aims for the year, term, month and week?
- What day will I keep free of study?

8.6 When, where and for how long you should study

'Another thing that you and your learners need to consider is when and where to study.'

'You mean, are they a lark or an owl?'

'That's part of it. Which are you?'

'I'm an owl. I hate having to study in the morning or exercising. My body and mind just don't want to know. My best time is from about 2 p.m. until 10 p.m. I'm definitely not a lark.'

'That's valuable information to know about yourself, because it can help you plan the most effective times for your study. You can do the boring bits that have to be done early in the day, administration, photocopying and arranging meetings, and save the creative parts until later, when your mind is ready to do good-quality work.'

'Sounds reasonable,' I said.

'However, that is not an excuse to stay in bed. I always recommend that students should look on their time at uni as if it was a normal working day. Regardless of how many hours of lectures you have, try to arrive at 9 a.m., and if there is no lecture, go and work in the library. If your lectures finish early, go to the library and study until 5 p.m.'

'You want me to keep office hours?'

'*Exactly. We are creatures of habit. So make study a habit. You will be amazed at how much you can get done if you employ this approach – and the beauty of it is that you then have far less work to do at home.*'

But there are so many temptations at uni,' I said. 'I'm like Oscar Wilde – I can resist anything but temptation.'

Sue laughed and shook her head. '*It might be hard at first but it will get easier. A bit of self-discipline is essential to the establishment of good study habits. And the temptations will still be waiting for you when you have finished. Besides, this working day approach might be something you could discuss with your own learners.*'

'I've never been very keen on working in libraries. For one thing they can be quite noisy and you get people walking past your desk every few minutes.'

'*OK, if that is a problem you need to consider where you will do your studying. What sort of things do you need to consider?*'

'I would want a room with a table and comfortable chair, which is quiet, has good lighting and ventilation, warm but not too warm, and is not too far from a kettle and a toilet.'

'*Why a kettle?*'

'I'm incapable of studying for longer than an hour at a time. After that I have to get up and stretch my legs. I've found that if I make a cup of tea it stops me from turning on the TV or radio and getting interested in whatever is on.'

'*I see. I'm interested in what you say about the length of your study periods. It ties in with what most research in this area says, which is that our span of attention is about 45 minutes to an hour maximum. After that, people need a couple of minutes' break. In fact, our concentration can be plotted on a skewed bell diagram. (See Figure 8.1.) We start off with relatively poor levels of concentration; this gradually improves until after about 10 to 15 minutes we reach our peak and then it slowly declines again.*'

'So it goes through peaks and troughs?'

'*Exactly. Having a little break helps you to reset your concentration. But you need to make sure that the break is not too long, otherwise you can become distracted. Also, if possible, change what you're studying or doing every hour or so. For example, if you need to write an essay and plan a lesson, you might do some reading for your essay for an hour, spend the next hour writing part of your assignment and end by doing an hour on lesson preparation. If you spent three hours writing, you'd probably become bored and disinterested. Which reminds me, after three hours of study, you need to take a longer break – maybe as much as 50 minutes.*' (See Figure 8.2.)

'That would be a good point to make to my learners. They need to mix up their homework. Instead of spending an hour and a half on maths, they could do 45 minutes on maths followed by 45 minutes on, say, history, and end with a another 45 minutes on maths,' I said.

'Absolutely, it works on the same basis as a change is as good as a rest.'

8.7 Monitoring your progress

'Now, there are just a couple more things we need to look at before we finish. Not only do you need a timetable, you also need to monitor your progress and take corrective action if required. I suggest you do this every Sunday when you're planning your timetable for the week ahead. That way you can check that you have achieved all your objectives for the previous week and compensate for any shortfalls by increasing your workload the following week.'

'What happens if I achieved more than I'd planned in the previous week?'

'If that happens you should give yourself a pat on the back and decide whether you want to reduce your workload for the following week or if you want to work as normal and stay ahead of your objectives.'

'Staying ahead of the game might be a good idea as I'm bound to have some weeks when I don't complete all my work.'

'Very true. Of course if you find that week after week you are falling further behind in your work you need to talk to someone. I'm your PDT so normally I would be your first port of call, but if you prefer you can speak to the module tutor, your PM or someone from Student Support. Whom you speak to will depend on the nature of the problem. All I would say is that you must never be afraid to ask for help or advice. There will always be someone who can help you.'

8.8 Alex's reflection

I've always known that I'm an owl and that I study best when I have a short break every hour or so. But no one ever told me about this at school. Maybe I went to the wrong school. Nor did anyone ever tell me to change what I'm studying every hour and to have an hour off after 3 hours. This is information that I will definitely pass on to the learners. I don't just want them to work harder; I want them to work smarter. But will they be interested in developing their strategies for learning? I don't know. Some of them will and as for the rest I can only try my best to get them to engage with learning.

Fortunately I can use the bedroom as a study - it's warm and bright and the neighbours aren't too noisy. But I will try to get at least some of my work done at uni. The library has quiet areas and small study rooms that can be booked in advance. If I could do most of my coursework there and most of my lesson preparation at school, I could minimise the amount of stuff I have to do at home. I'd also be working 'office hours' as Sue calls it.

Anyway, that's the end of the tape. Time for a cup of tea. I wonder if there are any fig rolls left?

SPACE FOR YOUR NOTES

Prompts

- Am I a lark or an owl?
- Where am I going to study?
- What excuses do I use to delay starting work?

8.9 Record of PDT meeting

Trainee: Alex Croft

Summary of key learning points

- Make sure you are on the right course. If you are unhappy with your course it is very hard to keep to a study plan. If in doubt, talk to a member of the course team or student services.
- Perceived lack of time is no excuse for failing to complete your course.
- Good time management requires the identification and timetabling of short-, medium- and long-term objectives as well as daily tasks.
- Always timetable one free day a week for rest and relaxation. We work to live not live to work. Get the balance right.
- The sooner you establish a routine the better. Good study is dependent upon good study habits.

(continued)

(continued)

- View your day as you would a nine-to-five job. Use any spare time you have during the day to study, complete assignments or prepare lessons and teaching resources. This will minimise the amount of time you have to spend working in the evenings and at weekends.
- Find a place that you can use for your studies.
- At a minimum, you need a space with a table, a comfortable chair and computer access which is quiet, well lit and warm.
- Divide your studies into 45-minute sessions. Try whenever possible to change the type of work you are engaged in after every session. Never work longer than three hours without a 50-minute break.
- Monitor your progress weekly. You can do this when you prepare your weekly timetable.
- Ask for assistance if you start to fall behind or encounter any personal, academic or professional problems that impact on your work.

Agreed action points

Alex will:

- Establish a study space at home.
- Complete the draft timetable below for the week, term and year ahead.

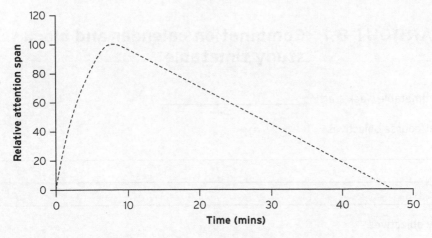

Figure 8.1 Indicative skewed bell diagram showing decline in attention span

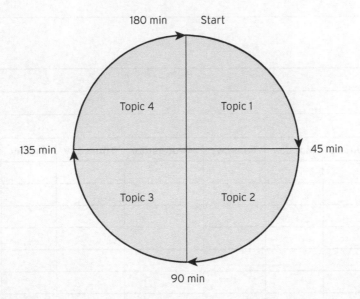

Figure 8.2 Study cycle

Note: Three-hour study cycle showing breaks after each 45-minute period and a change of study topic. Remember, within each period your concentration levels will vary, as shown in the skewed bell diagram.

HANDOUT 8.1 Combination calendar and clock study timetable

Study timetable week starting _____

Annual/course objectives

1 _____

2 _____

3 _____

Termly objectives

1 _____

2 _____

3 _____

Weekly tasks

1 _____

2 _____

3 _____

Time	Sunday	Monday	Tuesday	Wednesday	Thursday	Friday	Saturday
09:00							
10:00							
11:00							
12:00							
13:00							
14:00							
15:00							
16:00							
17:00							
18:00							
19:00							
20:00							
21:00							
22:00							
Notes							

Note: This timetable could be kept manually in Excel or Outlook. Amend/extend as required.

Further reading

www.routledge.com/cw/mcgrath

McMillan, K. and Weyers, J. (2012), *The Study Skills Book (Smarter Study Skills)* (3rd edn). Harlow: Pearson/Prentice Hall.

Seneca, L.A. (2005), *On the Shortness of Life*, trans. C.D.N. Costa. Harlow: Penguin Books.

Tutorial 9   How to find and read the literature you need

Aim of tutorial: To enable you to find and evaluate the literature you need to complete a successful assignment.

Tutorial overview: This tutorial suggests a number of ways that you can find the literature you require for your assignments, including reading lists, search engines and wandering around the library with purpose. It then goes on to explain how to read, critically evaluate and record the all-important literature you need for your studies. It ends by suggesting a few simple strategies that you can use to improve your reading speed by up to 100 per cent without compromising your level of comprehension.

Contents

9.1 Alex's reflection

I'm not sure how useful today's session is going to be. I've never had much difficulty in finding enough literature to fill an essay. In the past my lecturers have normally provided guidance on what to include, which in the main could be found in the standard texts. Still, it might be useful in terms of finding materials that I can use in my lessons. Mind you, I was surprised by how much I got out of last week's tutorial on time management, so maybe I'll find the same today.

9.2 Reading lists

Sue was busy marking some assignments when I entered. She waved me into a chair and with a flourish appended a big tick to the bottom of the page she was reading. Turning the script over, so that I couldn't see it, she smiled and said, *'How have you been? Have you set up your timetable yet?'*

'I'm good, thanks. I loaded your timetable template onto my laptop and I've filled in the data for this week and next. So far it's going OK.'

'That's good. Remember, speak to me if you run into any problems. Today we're going to look at how to find and use literature. Have you ever had a session on finding and using literature before?'

'No. I've never really needed one. I was always given guidance on what to read and I just used the recommended books and articles,' I said.

'In that case, what we cover today will be really valuable, because an ability to find the literature you want and critically evaluate it is an essential component for both your teaching and completion of your assignments.'

'OK, but you have to admit it's not exactly the most exciting subject.'

'I disagree. It's only when you review the literature that you start to uncover the different perspectives on a topic. It's then that you discover that there are numerous sides to every argument and that what you thought was the position is not believed by everyone. So let's start with course reading lists. How useful are they?'

'I would have thought that they were very useful. After all, the lecturer has chosen them based on experience and what is required for the course.'

'Do you ever wonder how many of the books on the list the lecturer has read?'

'I can't say I have.'

'Well, the answer will vary. Sometimes a lecturer will inherit a course and the reading list is not theirs. At other times the list was drawn up when the course was approved and is out of date. To overcome this problem, lecturers often provide students with a list of recommended

texts at the start of the year. I'd use these as your basic texts. They are likely to be highly relevant and fairly up to date.'

9.3 Using search engines

'As well as reading lists how else might you search for literature?'

'I could Google a few keywords and identify some more sources?'

*'That's not a bad idea. However, I suggest that you use Google Scholar because it focuses on academic and **peer-reviewed** sources and includes abstracts. The great thing is that the articles are ranked by the number of **citations** each has attracted, so you tend to get the most popular ones first. You can even click on "Cited by" and see a list of all the documents that have cited the source you are on. However, there is a limited number of full text articles on the site.'*

'That's useful. It must mean that anyone who has cited the entry is writing in a similar area and their work will be more up to date.'

*'Exactly. It's also worth mentioning the **British Education Index (BEI)**. As a teacher you should be familiar with the Index. All you have to do is find the electronic resources button on the library page and look for BEI and you will get a search page up. Enter your keywords on the search page and press find and you'll get back a list of publications. Some returns will only display the abstract for the publication, but many will contain a full text version of the publication. There are other indexes you could search, but I'd concentrate on the BEI and its American cousin **ERIC (Education Resources Information Center)**.'*

9.4 Wandering around the library – with purpose

'So that's why I need my **Athens password**! What about just going to the library and physically looking at the education journals?'

'Actually, that isn't a bad idea. Once you know the subject area that you are interested in it only takes a couple of hours to look at the current copy of the education-based journals in the library and identify which ones cover your specific interests. You can do this by simply checking out the contents page. If you are still in doubt read a few abstracts to get an idea of the type of articles the journal publishes. Once you have identified which journals are useful you can go through the contents page of each edition and identify any articles of interest and follow these up by reading the abstract to confirm that it is relevant.'

'How far back should I go?'

*'If you go back five years you will very quickly identify any **seminal** books or journal articles that were published earlier because they will be referenced in the journal articles. Then, if need be, you can consult them.'*

'The number of citations given to a book or article on Google Scholar would also help me to identify seminal works.' I suggested, diffidently.

'Absolutely.'

Feeling more confident I said, 'A friend of mine says that she finds one really good up-to-date article and then uses the list of references to trace other relevant books and articles. She then repeats the process with the new articles she finds.' *(See Handout 9.1)*

'You can do that, but writers very often reference other writers who agree with their views and arguments. This can result in biased articles which skew the arguments in a particular direction. So don't rely on one major source.'

'Wouldn't this bias be picked up before publication?'

'You would think so. But just as different newspapers support a particular political party or policy, journals can have allegiances to particular academic tribes or ideologies. But don't worry too much about this. Markers are usually delighted to find that a student has accessed any journal articles. Most rely on textbooks.'

'So there are some easy Brownie points to pick up?'

'Indeed. Never miss an opportunity to curry favour with your marker. It's also worth remembering that there is no perfect way to do a literature search. Most students use a mixture of wandering around the library with purpose and using the various electronic search engines that are available. What's important is searching with a purpose in mind. The problem with relying on keywords alone is that sometimes you don't know what the keywords are until you have read up on the topic, hence the value of browsing the shelves.'

'What if I miss a vital article?'

'That's unlikely. If you read four or five relevant articles that are up to date, they will contain 80 or more references between them. Any seminal work in your area is very likely to be in that extended list and you will quickly identify who the key writers are because their names will also crop up more than once in your list.'

9.5 Alex's reflection

If I'm not careful I could be drowning in literature. There's an awful lot of stuff out there. I can't read it all. I have to be selective. With so much to plough through I can see why it's important to be very clear about the key terms that I want to explore. Knowing the correct keywords and combination of words will limit the amount of material that I have to look at. I could find out what the keywords are by looking at the journals in the library. Or maybe I could just ask the other trainees by posting a question on the uni's VLE.

SPACE FOR YOUR NOTES

Prompts

- Do I need any training in how to search for literature electronically?
- Do I know where to find the educational journals in the library?
- Do I know which journals are likely to be useful?

9.6 How many references do I need and how do I keep track of them?

'So how many books or articles do I need for an assignment?'

'That's impossible to say, but I would think that anywhere between 6 and 12 references should be enough for most assignments, more for a dissertation or project. But to get those 6 or 12 references you might need to review 20 articles or books so you'll need some sort of filing system to keep track of everything you've read.'

'Everything?' I said, despairingly.

'Yes, everything. Don't look so worried. What you need to do is record the full reference of the article or book, a brief summary of its contents and jot down its keywords. You should aim to get all the information on one side of a 6 x 4 index card or a half-page record in Word. Remember, you don't need to summarise the whole article or book. You just need to summarise what is relevant to your studies.'

'But how do I know what's relevant?' I asked.

'You must keep referring back to the focus of your assignment. It helps to break down your question into its component parts. Often the question will have two parts to it or refer to two or more issues. For example, "How can the use of learning styles theory help improve children's behaviour in the classroom?" Can you see that before you can answer that question *you need to discuss what is meant by learning styles and a range of theories about the causes of poor behaviour in the classroom. So underline these key terms.'*

9.7 The academic standing/provenance of literature

'There's lots of good stuff on both behaviour management and learning styles on the Web and in government reports. Can I use them as literature?'

'Of course you can. Too often students limit the literature they use to a few books and articles. Here's a list of sources from which you can select literature.' (See Handout 9.1.)

I looked at the list for some time before noticing the heading. 'Oh, I see,' I said. 'The list is in order of academic respectability, with the good stuff, like journals and books, near the top and the less respectable stuff at the bottom – like TV, radio and the Internet.'

*'Correct. Each source has been listed according to its **provenance**.'*

'Provenance?'

'Yes, where it came from and who has approved it. So the literatures with the best provenance are articles that have been published in academic journals of international renown, followed by journals with a national reputation. Books appear below these because they have not been peer-reviewed, although some chapters may have been reviewed by the publisher's advisors prior to publication.'

'Do I have to use at least one paper from each of these sources?'

'Absolutely not. What you need is a good selection of articles, books, reports and reputable websites. Increasingly, examiners expect to see a couple of Web addresses amongst the list of references. That's what we call using diverse sources and it's something that markers will look for.'

'You mentioned peer review, is that where other academics read and approve the article prior to publication?'

'Indeed it is. But even with peer-reviewed journals you need to be careful. As we said, some academics are only published in certain journals because they belong to a specific academic tribe and their views are not shared by others outside that tribe.'

9.8 How to critically evaluate literature used

'So how do I know which articles and books to trust?'

'You shouldn't trust anything you read. Instead, you should try to critically evaluate it. Never expect any book or article to contain the unvarnished truth. You can reasonably expect every journal in the university library to be academically respectable, because someone will have made a case for buying it. But that is not the same as saying it is unbiased and contains universal truths. It will contain weaknesses.'

'But how can I critique any piece of work when the writer will always know far more about the subject than I do?'

'What you can do is find another writer in the same field who holds a different viewpoint. For example, if you're writing about learning styles I would expect you to look at the Coffield Report (2004), because Coffield calls into question the validity of many, if not most, learning style theories.'

'What if I can't find any dissenting views?'

'Then you have probably not looked hard enough. You may still pass but with a low mark. Quoting and summarising the writings of others is not a high-level academic activity, and even at undergraduate level will not attract high marks. What is required is an element of critical evaluation. Without that you will only score in the 40s or low 50s.'

'Other than using different writers, how else can I critique a writer's views?'

'You can examine the provenance of the work. Has it been peer-reviewed? Very often education theories are put forward on the basis of personal experience and insight. This doesn't mean that they are rubbish, but it does mean that they are the unproven opinion of someone. So they are worth challenging. And even where some **empirical research** *has been carried out you might find that the approach was inappropriate, weak or on too small a scale to produce reliable evidence. For example, instead of speaking to the learners, the researcher may have spoken only to teachers about the teaching methods that students liked best . . .'*

'And in doing so they are only discovering what methods the teacher thinks the students like,' I said.

'Exactly.'

'What else can I do to give my work a critical edge?'

'Here, use this,' said Sue, handing me a diagram headed *Evaluation of literature.'* (See Figure 9.1.)

'Do I have to evaluate every article or book using each of these approaches?'

'Of course not. You could use one approach with one piece of literature and a different one with the next. All I'm giving you is a range of approaches to choose from.'

'And if I can't identify the most suitable approach?' Sue looked at me with something approaching exasperation.

'Look at how reasonable and logical the writer's arguments are, especially with regard to the interpretation of any data collected. It's very easy for a researcher to interpret the data in such a way as to support their own pet theory. Often this is done quite innocently, but such bias needs to be exposed. Finally, look at the literature the writer has cited to support their arguments. Are these authors well known and respected? Do they all share a similar education philosophy or ideology?'

'We're back to academic tribes . . . ?'

'In truth we can never get away from them. One last thought before we finish. You can use phrases such as: "X agrees with Y on this issue because . . ." or "in contrast, Z took a different view, namely . . ." or "X argues against this, suggesting that . . ." or "this view is contested by Z" while "in contrast with . . ." or "moreover, . . . ". Can you see what I'm doing?'

I had to think carefully about how to phrase my reply. Finally, I said, 'You're littering your discussion on the literature review with doubts and objections and by doing that you are advertising your critical credentials to the marker. Now you're being Machiavellian. I like it.'

9.9 Alex's reflection

I reckon that I learnt a lot in this part of the tutorial. When I write my assignment on learning styles it's not enough to outline the various theories that writers have developed and how I'll use them in the class. I have to identify the strengths and weaknesses of each theory and compare competing theories. Hang on, I've just had a thought. If I want to be really clever I could look at the whole concept of learning theories. Everyone says how useful they are, but is it a case of the 'Emperor's New Clothes'? Sue mentioned something about the Coffield Report on learning styles. I'll track it down and have a read.

As for how many references I need, that's difficult to estimate. I suppose it's however many I need to answer the question. But they have to be right on the button. So I need to analyse the question that has been set, make sure I know exactly what is required and then find the literature that addresses those precise points. I'm back to looking for keywords and terms.

*From what Sue says I'll need to access literature from a range of sources, including peer-reviewed articles, respectable websites, government reports, reports from **quangos**, such as Ofsted, and a few good textbooks. That should give me a nice range of references and viewpoints for most assignments. Variety - the spice that makes a good assignment. Did I really write that? Time I had a cuppa.*

SPACE FOR YOUR NOTES

Prompts

- Do I rely too much on one source of literature for assignments?
- Do I just report what writers say or do I challenge it?
- What can I do to improve the level of critical evaluation in my assignments?

9.10 Improving your reading skills/speed

'With all these sources to consider I'm going to have too much to read and record in the time I have available,' I said.

'Not so,' said Sue, smiling. *'I've always thought it strange that once we have taught a child to read we never go back and tell them how they can improve their reading speed and comprehension. Yet today teachers and other professionals are deluged with stuff they have to read. Probably the easiest way for any professional to save time is to improve their reading speed.'*

'A few of my friends have gone on speed-reading courses. They were very disappointed with the results. They thought it was money for old rope.'

'So, you're not a fan. Never mind, I won't put you through a full course. I'll just give you some ideas that you can try out between now and Christmas. Firstly, you need to develop a range of time-saving **reading strategies***. The first is* **discrimination***. Instead of reading every document that crosses your path, think, "Do I need to read this document or do I just need to know that it exists and file it where I can find it?" Asking this simple question can save you hours reading stuff that you are unlikely to ever use.'*

'I can't see how that helps me, particularly with my work at uni?'

'Perhaps not. But at work you are going to be inundated with reports and documents from the government, local authority, the Teaching Agency and Ofsted. Not to mention the meaningless emails sent out globally by people too stressed or lazy to address it properly.'

'It sounds like you suffer from global-email syndrome.'

'Doesn't everyone?'

'So effectively we're back to Seneca and not letting people steal our limited time. But why the filing system?'

'We all make mistakes, and when we do we need to be able to find the document in question and read it.'

'Got it. But what of the stuff that I do need to read?'

'Firstly, decide what you want to get out of a source before you read it. List these points. You will find that similar points relate to several sources, so you won't need to do this for every document. Then **selectively read** *the parts of the document that are relevant to your needs. What parts do you normally find in a journal article or report that could help you find these sections?'*

'Well, the abstract summarises the whole article so I could read that to see if it was relevant; maybe the introduction would do that too. Or I could just read the conclusions and skip the rest!'

'Good, or you could use the subheadings and skip those that seem irrelevant. The problem is that you can't always be sure what is irrelevant, so try skim reading some sections and reading others more carefully. For example, read the first and last sentence of each paragraph. The first sentence will tell you what the paragraph is about and the last will often sum up the writer's conclusions on that issue. If it's a report, check to see if it has an executive summary; if so, read that first.'

'Effectively what I need to do is read with a specific purpose in mind and look out for key-words and phrases that tell me if the book or article is relevant to me. If it is, I can then read the entire document more carefully.'

'*Correct. But with books, don't forget the index. Indexes can take you straight to the key issues you are interested in. Once you have identified the important information, remember to highlight it. You can do this with a highlighter pen on hard copies but you can also do it electronically. But use different colours – that way you can colour-code different themes.*'

'I hadn't thought of that,' I said.

'*You can even copy selected quotes directly into a literature file, but be very careful and use a different font or colour so that you don't include someone else's work as your own because you don't want to be accused of* **plagiarism**.'

'Why is there such an emphasis on plagiarism all of a sudden?'

'*It's about academic integrity and it has come to the fore recently because of the Internet. It has never been easier to find an article or essay on the Net and pass it off as your own work. Plagiarism is the greatest academic crime and the way to avoid it is to be scrupulous in your referencing. We'll talk further about referencing when we look at writing for different audiences.*'

'So how do I increase my basic reading speed?'

'*In addition to skimming you need to change the way you read words.*'

'Surely there is only one way to read a word?'

'*Now there we have the problem in a nutshell. You said "read a word". You have to get away from reading single words and learn to read three or four words simultaneously.*'

'That can't be that easy,' I said, defensively.

'*You'd be surprised just how easy it is. There are a couple of simple things you can do which can double your reading speed without decreasing your level of comprehension. They are easy to learn but you have to practise them daily to change your lifelong reading habits.*'

'OK, what are they?' I asked.

'*First, find a passage in a book and see how many words you can read in a minute while still understanding what the passage says. Get someone to time you for exactly a minute and count how many words you have read in that time. This is your baseline reading speed. The average person reads about 200 to 250 words per minute. Once you have this baseline, try to get rid of* **sub-vocalisation**.'

'Sub-vocalisation?'

'*Yes. When you learnt to read you read aloud. When you progressed to silent reading, you continued to hear the sound of the word in your mind. This listening for the sound of the word is sub-vocalisation and it slows you down almost as much as if you had read the word aloud. Yet there is no need for it because your mind registered what the word meant long before you heard the sound.*'

'So why do we still do it?'

'Habit – and like most habits it is very difficult to break. What you need to do is force yourself to read so quickly that you don't have time to hear the word. At first it will feel unnatural but if you stick at it for six weeks you will have replaced an old habit with a new one and it will feel entirely natural.'

'Do I read everything like that?'

'Start off slow. Try "soundless" reading for half an hour a day for the first week, then slowly introduce it into your ordinary reading. At the same time try to read two or more words simultaneously. Again, because we learnt to read by pointing at single words, we tend to continue reading one word at a time. This slows us down further because we move our head or eye to focus on each word. It is this mechanical movement of the head and the eyes that wastes time. We are perfectly capable of seeing and comprehending four or five words simultaneously, but we persist in reading each word because we think we have to. If you don't believe me, consider how quickly you read instructions flashed up on computer games.'

'So how do I practise reading groups of words?'

'Easy. Get a newspaper and, using a ruler, run the rule down a column while keeping your head still and your eyes focused on the centre of the column. You will be amazed at how much information your peripheral vision picks up when you try this, and because you are reading more than one word at a time it will assist you in getting rid of sub-vocalisation.'

9.11 Alex's reflection

Perhaps because my friends have had such poor experiences of speed-reading courses, I've not given much thought to how I could increase my own reading speed. I suppose I had assumed that it was something I couldn't change. Daft really, because you can train yourself to become better at most things. All you need is practise, but that requires patience and persistence. Persistence I have but patience, well that's another story.

I like the idea of having a range of reading strategies, especially discrimination. I need to be more discriminating and not feel guilty when I don't read everything. But the sad fact is that I am one of those people who feel they must read every line of a book. In fact, I often go back and read the same sentence twice, not because I didn't understand it, but because I don't think I've read it properly. How crazy is that? I've got to break that habit.

As for skimming, I probably already do a bit of that. But I need to be more consistent in how I apply it. At the moment I probably only skim when I'm in a rush or under pressure. But if I used it consistently, I would save way more time.

I'm definitely going to try and improve my reading speed. Sue said I needed to practise for about a month and that then my new approach would become ingrained. An idea! I'll record a short comment in my reflective journal every day, saying how my speed reading is progressing. That way I can track my progress. And if I fall back into bad habits I can remind myself that every day is a new start. Help, I sound like one of those American self-help gurus.

I'll certainly share some of this information with my learners. It could be really useful to them. Anyway, enough work for today. I've earned a reward. A cup of tea and maybe one or two episodes of 'The Wire'.

SPACE FOR YOUR NOTES

Prompts

- Do you know how fast you read?
- Do you have any bad reading habits that you need to address?
- How would increasing your reading speed help you?

9.12 Record of PDT meeting

Trainee: Alex Croft

Summary of key learning points

- Course reading lists may be out of date but they can still be useful.
- Use the list of recommended texts given to you at the start of the course or module as the starting point for your literature search.
- Visit the library and spend some time just reviewing what journals and books are available in your area of interest. Explore what electronic resources and searches are available to you and remember to 'act with purpose'.
- Identify keywords and phrases that you can use in your searches.
- Undertake a series of electronic searches using the keywords that you have identified. Searching is an art, so play around with different combinations of words.
- Initially, restrict your search to material that is less than five years old. You can also use seminal material which is older than this.

(continued)

(continued)

- Remember that many academic writers have a particular education philosophy or ideology that they seek to promote in their writing. Don't become tied to the views of one academic tribe until you have surveyed all the competing arguments.
- There are numerous sources of literature that you can use. See the handout which accompanies this tutorial for a full list. Try to use literature from a variety of sources.
- Be critical:

    1   Don't accept on face value what any writer says. Ask yourself why s/he has said it. Is it based on evidence or is it their bias, ideology or pet theory talking?
    2   Consider to what extent the work is based on empirical research or on the writer's own experiences.
    3   Decide to what extent the interpretations placed on the data are logical and reasonable. Could the data have been interpreted differently?
    4   Are the arguments made and conclusions drawn from the data or theories discussed reasonable and logical?
    5   Were appropriate **research tools** selected to collect any empirical data used?

- Identify the key themes in your work and organise a filing system for recording relevant material. As an aid to identification, use colour coding.
- Follow referencing conventions. Obtain a copy of the university's referencing guide from the library, and study and apply its contents.
- Avoid plagiarism at all costs.
- You should use speed-reading strategies such as discrimination, selective reading or skimming to decide if a document needs to be read in its entirety.
- When reading, avoid sub-vocalisation. Read blocks of words (three to five) simultaneously and minimise head and eye movement, which is associated with reading one word at a time.

Agreed action points

Alex will:
- Manually review the education journals held by the library and identify those that are relevant to the course.
- Undertake a range of electronic searches using the BEI and Google Scholar, and refine the searches using a variety of keywords.
- Start to apply the reading strategies discussed.
- Practise reading quickly for half an hour a day, steadily increasing the use of these approaches until sub-vocalisation and head/eye movement have been reduced/eliminated.

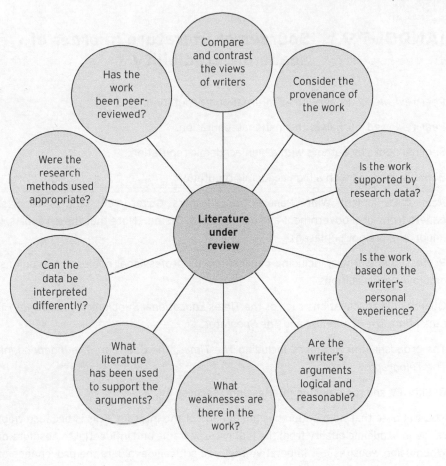

Figure 9.1 Evaluation of literature

Note: Use one or more of the following strategies to critique any piece of literature.

HANDOUT 9.1 Sources of literature in order of academic credibility

- Peer-reviewed journals with an international reputation.

- Peer-reviewed journals with a national reputation.

- Seminal books by authors with a high academic reputation.

- Books by authors with a high academic reputation.

- Acts of Parliament, White Papers, Green Papers, Government reports, reports and papers from local government and quangos, e.g. Ofsted. (Note that these reports, while important, are not unbiased).

- Professional journals, including publications by professional bodies, trade unions and employer organisations.

- Quality press publications such as the *Times Educational Supplement*, the *Times Higher Education*, *The Economist* and *The Spectator*.

- The broadsheet newspapers, including *The Times*, *The Guardian*, *The Independent* and *The Telegraph*.

- Quality TV and radio documentaries and Teachers TV.

- You will note that no mention has been made of the Internet. This is because websites range in academic quality from the highly respectable and influential to absolute dross. When using websites it is imperative that you critically evaluate the provenance of the site. For example, who funds and runs the site, what is its editorial policy and how often is the material on it updated.

Further reading

www.routledge.com/cw/mcgrath

McGrath, J. and Coles, A. (2013), *Your Education Research Project Companion* (2nd edn). Oxford: Routledge.

McGrath, J. and Coles, A. (2015), *Your Education Masters Companion*. Oxford: Routledge.

McMillan, K. and Weyers, J. (2012), *The Study Skills Book (Smarter Study Skills)* (3rd edn). Harlow: Pearson/Prentice Hall.

Tutorial 10   How to improve your writing skills

Aim of tutorial: To improve your academic writing skills in preparation for the assignments that you will be required to submit.

Tutorial overview: This tutorial explores what constitutes good academic writing. It argues that accuracy, brevity and clarity are more important than the use of big words or jargon. The need to reference material correctly is emphasised if charges of plagiarism are to be avoided. It also suggests that you should always ask a critical friend to read your completed assignment before submission. The tutorial ends with a short discussion about the difference between working at **Level 6** (undergraduate level) and **Level 7** (postgraduate level) in your studies.

Contents

10.1 Alex's reflection

Following last week's tutorial on literature searching and reading, today it's writing. It's like being back in junior school – 'and today Miss McCreech will be looking at . . .' That said, I have been surprised at how many of the people on the course are concerned about writing. And some of those most worried are the brightest. For example, one guy, who is a wiz at maths, is terrified of writing essays. It's all about comfort zones, I suppose.

10.2 Writing in the first or third person

Sue was on the phone talking about the new Ed.D. that the university was starting. When she saw me she hung up and said, '*I hope you have been practising your speed reading.*'

'I have, actually. Every day I try to read a couple of pages of the newspaper using the approach you suggested. I'm just starting to feel comfortable reading three or four words simultaneously.'

'*Very good. Keep at it and it will become second nature. Today it's writing. We've previously discussed your pre-entry task, so some of what I'm about to say you already know. But on the basis that there is always room for improvement and that you can pass on some of what I am going to say to your own learners, let's make a start. OK?*'

'Fine.'

'*Right. We're not going to discuss how to write an assignment today. We'll cover that next week when we take another look at your pre-entry task. Instead, we'll take a step back and look at some of the mechanics of writing well.*'

'I hope that doesn't mean that we're going to discuss grammar.'

'*Have no fear. I'm not a grammarian. Indeed, several of my colleagues regularly pick me up on my misuse of apostrophes.*'

'Sounds like a hanging offence,' I said.

'*It is to them. No, what I'm interested in is communicating clearly, and to do that you need some basic grammar and a few guidelines.*'

'What's the difference between the rules of grammar and guidelines?'

'*Why not judge for yourself at the end of the tutorial? But before we launch into the guidelines, let's deal with a pet hate of mine – should you write your assignment in the first or third person?*'

I was surprised by the question. 'Well, I've been told that it is more academic to write in the third person, especially when you do research.'

'Oh, I hear that so often. Your assignments are all focused on your professional practice. Therefore, I strongly advise you to use the first person in all you write. It's just plain silly to say something like "The teacher in question used differentiation to meet the needs of learners," when all you need to say is "I used differentiation . . ." Such an artifice hinders communication between writer and reader. I often find that students with a maths, science, psychology or sociology background find this quite hard at first.'

'Why's that?'

'The sciences and some social sciences writers seek to remain detached from the issues that they are discussing, believing that this will make them more objective.'

'But what you are saying is that a teacher can't remain detached from their own professional practice. So why pretend they can?'

'Exactly. Of course, some tutors, and indeed universities, disagree with me. So always check out what your marker wants and give it to them.'

10.3 The ABCs of good writing (accuracy, brevity and clarity)

'With that out of the way, let's consider the ABCs of good writing.'

'ABCs?'

'Accuracy, brevity and clarity. Now, while I recognise that there is some overlap between these terms, what do you think accuracy covers?'

I paused before answering. 'Accuracy implies that what you have said is factually correct and that there are very few spelling or grammatical errors.'

'That's not bad. Certainly you need to get your facts right. But let me extend it a little. Start by asking "What is the purpose of this piece of writing and who am I writing it for?" That will help you decide the level of detail you need to go into and the type of language to use. For example, if you are giving written feedback to a 12-year-old, you will use a different vocabulary than if you are writing a report.'

'OK. But that isn't really about accuracy? It's more about style.'

'Maybe. But accuracy is also about hitting the target. Your target is the reader. For an assignment, you should imagine that you are writing for a reasonably intelligent non-specialist. That will force you to explain any jargon or technical terms that you use.'

'But isn't that insulting the marker's intelligence?'

'No. Even though they know what the jargon means, they want to see that you understand it – and the only way that they can be sure you do is if you explain or define it. But remember, you can also fail to communicate if your work is badly written, or littered with misspellings and grammatical errors. In this case, factual accuracy becomes almost irrelevant because the reader is struggling to make sense of the English and can't understand the points you are making.'

'OK,' I said, still not entirely convinced. 'I can check my spelling by using the spell checker. What about the rest?'

'Don't become over-reliant on the spell checker. The red wavy line will identify words that have been spelt incorrectly, but it will not confirm that it is the right word. For example, quiet and quite, there and their, loose and lose. You have to check for such errors. As for grammatical errors, when word processing look out for any sentences or words underlined with a green wavy line. A green line is an indicator that there is a possible problem. It may be that what you have written is not a complete sentence, that it's written in the **passive voice** *or that it's unclear. Whatever the potential problem is, you should use the warning as an opportunity to consider rewriting the sentence.'*

'What about the length of sentences? I had a teacher who insisted that sentences should be no more than 20 words.'

'Now we are moving into brevity. Many professional writers argue that a sentence should be no longer than 12 words. So I wouldn't disagree with your teacher. Each sentence should make one clear statement. The chances are that any sentence longer than 20 words will contain two or more sentences. My husband says that the longest sentence he ever marked was 168 words. It is very unlikely that a sentence that long could be clear and unambiguous.'

'He counted the number of words?' I asked, in astonishment.

'Yes, he's a bit of a sad soul,' said Sue, smiling. *'Now you mentioned paragraphs. How long should a paragraph be?'*

'Well, as we're talking brevity I'd say less than 100 words.'

'How easily you fell into my trap,' she laughed. *'Paragraphs can be one sentence long or, in rare cases, more than a page. A paragraph deals with one issue. For example if you were talking about formative assessment, you might define the term in one paragraph, before discussing its strengths and weakness in two separate paragraphs. This approach makes it much easier for the reader to follow.'*

'OK. So it's the content, not the number of words or sentences that determines the length of the paragraph?'

'Yes.'

'What else comes under brevity?'

'Never use a long word when a short word will do. Too many students try to impress by using big words, with the result that the clarity of what they are writing suffers. It's a case of small is beautiful. Also, never use a word unless you are certain that you know what it means. I recently had a student who wrote that they would "Maintain the animosity between the research participants". What they meant to say was "maintain anonymity".'

'And I suppose if we are talking about brevity I have to cut out any padding.'

*'Good point. The golden rule is to "Answer the question, the whole question and nothing but the question." Any unnecessary or extraneous material should be cut from the work. But you also have to ensure that what you have written meets the **assessment criteria**. Read your assignment with a copy of the assessment criteria to hand, and cross out or tick off each aspect of the criteria that you have covered as you come upon it in your assignment. When finished, look to see if there are any aspects of the criteria that you have not met and amend your assignment accordingly. Only then should you start to remove any unnecessary material.'*

'I could also highlight those sections of my assignment that link directly to the assessment criteria. Then I could examine the non-highlighted sections and delete any that were unnecessary.'

'You could indeed. The higher up the academic ladder you climb, the more discerning you have to be as regards what to include in the text, attach as an appendix or exclude altogether. These decisions can be the difference between a bare pass and a good pass.'

10.4 When should you become critical of what you've written?

'But I find that if I become critical too soon and edit what I've written, it slows me down and I end up losing confidence in what I'm writing,' I said.

'That's interesting and raises the point of when do you become critical. Every piece of writing, I think, has three stages: the creative, the organisational and the critical. In the creative stage you need to be uncritical and just get all your ideas down onto paper. At this stage, don't worry about the order, the spelling or the grammar. Just get it written. Once the information is on the page, you enter the organisational phase; this is when you rearrange the sections, paragraphs and sentences into the best possible order and fill in the gaps in the development of your argument. Only when you have done this do you enter the critical phase. In this phase you must ask yourself a series of questions, such as: "Is what I have written factually correct? Have I supported any claims I've made with appropriate evidence from literature or data collected? Have I avoided making sweeping statements or generalisations? Have I expressed my ideas clearly? Is the work structured in such a way as to make it easy for the reader to follow my arguments? Are there any words, sentences or paragraphs that I could amend, change or delete that would improve the strength and clarity of my arguments? Is the work logically structured?" Criticality is the enemy of creativity – it can paralyse you with fear. So don't become critical until you have completed the creative stage.'

'It sounds like you are a believer in multiple drafts.'

'It's true. I do think writing a good assignment requires an element of constant refinement. I had a Ph.D. student who likened writing his thesis to producing a sculpture. The first half-dozen drafts produced a vague outline of the figure contained in the marble. The later drafts chipped away at the remaining marble to . . .'

'Reveal *David*!' I suggested.

'Let's not be too ambitious. There is, after all, only one Michelangelo. But you get the idea.'

10.5 Alex's reflection

Ughh! I've got that sinking feeling. Looking at my pre-entry assignment again I can see that I'm guilty of a few of the crimes against writing that Sue was talking about. In particular, I don't think that I actually answered the question set and I seem to meander all over the place in the first page. Next week's tutorial is going to be tough! Anyway, let's stay positive. What did I learn?

Like Sue, I'm no grammarian. I never did understand what a gerund was. Thank goodness I have a good ear for language. It was James Jameson, a real actor manager type of teacher, who told me that I should always read my assignment aloud before I submitted it. He reckoned that in listening to what we had written we would hear our errors. He was right. I am far more likely to hear an error than spot one on the page when I'm reading silently. Perhaps it has something to do with reading more slowly. The fact that I can't explain in grammatical terms what the error is doesn't matter. It's enough for me to know that there is something wrong and that I need to mess about with the sentence or paragraph until it 'sounds right'. And while I may not understand what the green wavy line in Word means, I can usually play around with the sentence until the line disappears.

I've also tried to write the odd short story over the years, but I've always ended up chucking them in the bin because I lose faith in them. So what Sue said about the three phases of writing really interested me. I don't spend enough time in the creative phase. Instead I move to the organisational and critical phases too early and strangle any creativity that may be emerging at birth. I have to find a way to suspend judgement on what I have written until the work or assignment is strong enough to withstand being reorganised and critiqued. This means that on a long piece of work I have to try to stay creative and confident for a significant period of time until I have completed a good draft. Otherwise I'll never write anything longer than a few pages.

SPACE FOR YOUR NOTES

Prompts

- What type of writer are you? Do you produce multiple drafts or avoid writing a single sentence until you are sure its perfect?
- Do you look at the assessment criteria for your assignment before you start to write, during writing, after you have finished or never?

10.6 Clarity in assignments

'Now onto clarity. Some of what we've talked about under accuracy, brevity and criticality does aid clarity, but in addition you should also consider how much the reader needs to know. If you include too much information you can bamboozle them with unnecessary details or, worse, confuse yourself.'

'So know your audience,' I said.

'Exactly, and write for them. As well as expressing yourself in simple, clear terms, think about the tone of your writing. Ask yourself, does it sound arrogant, ineffectual and apologetic, or assertive and confident. You want to write in a confident manner; after all, you are trying to sell your ideas to the reader.'

'How do you write assertively?'

'Express your arguments in a firm, confident style. For example "I found that ..." sounds a lot more confident than "It's possible that my findings indicate that there is a chance that ..." To be able to write assertively you must have faith in what you have written, the facts presented and the interpretations you have placed on the data collected or literature used. Once you have this firm foundation, you can critique your own work from a position of strength and point out ways in which you would improve the study if you were to repeat it.'

'A case of being confident enough to reveal your own weaknesses,' I said.

'Exactly.'

'There was one thing I did want to check with you,' I said. 'I've always used subheadings in my essays but some lecturers don't approve. What do you think?'

'Always give your marker what they want. Personally I think subheadings help both the writer and the reader, so I'm in favour of them. But if your marker doesn't, write your assignment using subheadings, then remove them as part of the final edit. They will have helped you to organise your material in a logical order, and even when they are removed that order will remain.'

'Which helps the reader.'

'Exactly. I'm often surprised at how little attention students give to the organisation of their assignments. Yes, you need to cover all the relevant points, but you also need to present them in the right order.'

'In other words, I need an introduction, a middle and a conclusion.'

'Precisely, and within each of those sections you need to present your material logically. Exactly what that order is will differ depending on the assignment. But it will always have what I call a narrative flow, with one point leading the reader logically onto the next.'

'So, no jumping around. I need to discuss one issue at a time but link them together using phrases such as "above I discussed the strengths of formative assessment but there are also disadvantages. These include ...".'

'*I couldn't have said it better myself. Now, before we finish talking about clarity, remember that you need to define any terms, jargon or theories that you use because....'*

'If I don't, it may confuse the reader, and whoever is marking my assignment has no way of knowing that I understand the terms unless I define or explain them.'

10.7 Using a critical friend and/or student support

'*Now, before we move on to referencing I want to talk about using a critical friend and your final edit and polish. Critical friends can be a great resource if you choose the right one and a right pain if you choose the wrong one.'*

'Any advice on whom I should ask?'

'*Don't ask your partner or best friend. Neither is likely to be as frank or critical as you require. It is also likely that they will have very little understanding of what is required to produce a good assignment. It's also one sure way to end a beautiful relationship. Instead, see if there is someone on the course whom you respect and get on with and negotiate with them a "buddy relationship" where they read your work and you read theirs. As for what your buddy should look out for: firstly, make sure that they have a copy of the assessment criteria. As you know, ours are in the Course Handbook; secondly, identify your weaknesses. If you know that your use of English is problematic, ask your friend to pay particular attention to the clarity of exposition, grammar and syntax. If you tend to be verbose, ask them to highlight any padding, or if you don't trust your powers of analysis, ask them to concentrate on that.'*

'My school used to have a buddy system, but they didn't explain how we should use it. I just got my best friend to read my work.'

'*Good, so it won't be that strange to you. But while we're on this don't forget that you can also enlist the aid of the student support team (SST). We were one of the first universities to have such a team, and now most colleges and universities have one. They will read your report and comment on the structure of your work, how logically organised the material is and your use of English. However, because they are a non-specialist unit they can't comment on the content of your work.'*

'I probably won't use the SST.'

'*That's your decision. But always remember that, whether you use a critical friend or the SST, you are ultimately responsible for what you submit. Therefore, I strongly recommend that when you have completed writing, editing and checking your assignment and have run it past your critical friend, you put it in a drawer for a week and forget all about it. Then take it out for one final edit and polish prior to submission. You'll be amazed at what you find. Along with convoluted and poorly phrased sentences, missing words, underdeveloped ideas and quotes that aren't linked to anything, you will discover some really good writing, clever ideas and good examples of analysis and linking theory to practice which you can expand on further. But you will only spot these if you give yourself time to stand back from the work and review it with fresh eyes. Anyway, enough about the mechanics of writing. Have a look at this handout, which builds on what I have been saying.'* (See Handout 10.1.)

10.8 Alex's reflection

> *I will find a critical friend from the course. Who, I'm not sure yet. Perhaps I could get someone from a different subject area? They might see things from a different angle, which could provide some interesting insights. But if they are going to read and comment on my work prior to submission, I need to build an extra week into my timetable. I can't expect them to drop everything just to read my assignment.*
>
> *I really like the idea of leaving the work in a drawer for a week. That, combined with reading the assignment aloud, could be very effective.*
>
> *I'm still worried about my entry task. Sue's comment about the assessment criteria being in the student handbook reminded me of the need to 'answer the question, the whole question and nothing but the question'. I've never bothered to study the assessment criteria. Daft or what? That's what I'm going to be marked against, so I need to examine it closely and ensure that I address each of the requirements in my assignment. When I've finished I should be able to go through my assignment and tick off each of the criteria as I meet them. I'll even be able to make some sort of guess at how well I've met each one.*

SPACE FOR YOUR NOTES

Prompts

- What areas of my written work are weak?
- What's the best way to tackle my weaknesses?
- Who would make a good critical friend?

10.9 Referencing

'*Let's talk about referencing.*'

'Do we have to?' I asked.

'*I'm afraid so. Why is referencing so important?*' Sue asked.

'Well, firstly, it helps you to avoid charges of plagiarism. Secondly, the reader can follow up any of your references if they're interested or think that you've misrepresented the text. Thirdly, it gives the reader confidence in what you have written, because if your referencing is correct then it is likely that you have also been careful with the rest of your work,' I said, feeling pleased with myself.

'*Excellent. It's also fair to say that with the growth of the Internet, plagiarism has become a hot topic in universities. Growing numbers of students are downloading material and passing it off as their own.*'

'I suppose most universities are using anti-plagiarism software these days.'

'*Most are. But markers are very experienced at recognising a change "of voice" in a piece of work and they will often Google a sentence to see if it has been copied. If their suspicions are confirmed, they may then check your work against anti-plagiarism software such as Turnitin (www.turnitin.com) to scan and report on an entire assignment in a matter of seconds. So guard against innocent plagiarism.*'

'Innocent plagiarism?'

'*Yes, this is the one that catches out most students. There you are reading a book and making notes and you copy a phrase or section. But you don't include a reference. Three weeks later you're writing your assignment and you copy the phrase from your notes, thinking that it is your own. Innocent plagiarism, but still plagiarism. Good, it sounds as if we can leave referencing . . .*'

'Hang on. I have a few questions.' Sue nodded for me to continue. 'I'm not certain how often I need to reference. For example, if I use the same source several times in a paragraph, do I need to reference it every time?'

'*That depends. If it's clear from your writing that you are still discussing a particular source, then you don't need to reference it again. If desperate you can use ibid. - which means "the same place" - this indicates that the points under discussion have been taken from the previously cited source.*'

'Can I cite a writer whose work I have only read about second hand?'

'*It's good practice only to cite sources that you have actually read in the original. When we find students referencing a source that they haven't read in the original, we say that they have cited "indirectly". It's not a great problem if it only happens on the odd occasion. For example, Banner, cited in Benjamin and Grimm (20xx) - the reference relates to Benjamin and Grimm's work but you are acknowledging that it was Banner's idea originally. However, if you do this too often, or rely a lot on the cited author's ideas, it gives the impression that you are lazy and can't be bothered to read the original source.*'

'I accept that referencing is important. But I find it really annoying when tutors make loads of comments about my use of first names and book titles in the text.'

'Following the conventions of referencing is important because people have an expectation that something will be done in a particular way and, if it's not, confusion can result. For example, it can affect the readability of your work if your argument is interrupted by too much detail, like first names or titles of articles. When it comes to the method of referencing, most universities have their own preferred approach and you must stick to it. This university uses the **Harvard referencing system,** *which is author and date in the text and the author's family name and initials, date of publication, title, and details of publishers and place of publication in a list at the end. This list is always in alphabetical order by author's name. If there's more than one publication by an author, then you list their references in chronological order. If there are two or more publications by the same author in the same year then you use 'a', 'b', etc. to differentiate the texts. In the text you can quote up to two authors for a single source, e.g. Banner and Bruce (20xx), but if there are more than two authors, then you name the first one followed by "et al.", which means "and others". Most people aren't too fussy about detail, such as whether you use commas after names or pg or p, but the important thing is to be consistent, especially when it comes to page numbers. Normally in the Harvard system, page numbers are only required for direct quotes. But if you summarise the writer's words and provide a page number you will have to provide a page number for all references.'*

'Because we must be consistent in how we reference material.'

'Exactly. Anyway, all the details are in the library guide to referencing, so get a copy and read it.'

'I've picked up a copy already.'

'Good.'

'But the guide is not entirely clear about when you should indent quotes?'

'Again, convention varies and the rules aren't too strict on this, but short quotes of fewer than 30 words can be included in the text in quotation marks with a citation and page number. Sometimes italics are used to distinguish such quotes from the student's work. But don't use bold to highlight them. Longer quotes are usually given a separate paragraph and are indented.'

'My teacher once told me not to use long quotes. He said that all they proved was that I could copy.'

'I like the sound of your old teacher. Long quotes should be used very sparingly. Sometimes we get work that consists of a string of quotes. You can imagine that this doesn't score too highly. Or quotes suspended between two paragraphs with no indication of which paragraph the quote refers to. A colleague of mine calls these "hanging quotes" and he hates them. OK, we've covered a lot today. Any questions before we end?'

10.10 Working at Masters level

I looked at my notes and tried to think. Finally, I asked, 'I know what the various levels of study are at university, but in terms of writing what's the difference between Level 6 and **M Level**?'

'*Good question. Undergraduate courses start at Level 4 and finish at Level 6 in the third year. All PGCEs used to be at Level 6, but we now have some that are entirely at Masters level, while others have a mixture of Level 6 and 7 modules. We could spend an entire session talking about the difference, but I suggest that you have a look at the level descriptors on the Quality Assurance Agency for Higher Education website (www.qaa.ac.uk). In terms of writing assignments, the differences are to do with the balance between description, analysis and critical evaluation. In any piece of academic work, you have to report the issues under discussion. You then have to analyse and critically evaluate those issues. The higher up the academic ladder you go, the more the balance shifts from reporting to analysis and evaluation. So while the M Level modules on a PGCE often cover the same issues as the Level 6 modules, you would be required to analyse the issues more thoroughly and apply a greater degree of critical evaluation.'*

'I'd assumed that Masters-level work was all research-based?'

'*Not necessarily – you can do a Masters without undertaking any empirical research. Some studies can be theory-based and only involve reviewing the current theories in a particular field.*'

'I bet that you really have to critically evaluate the literature if you opt for a theory-based Masters.'

'*Indeed.*'

10.11 Alex's reflection

Referencing is such a boring topic. But I need to get to grips with it. Once I know how to do it, it will become second nature, so now, at the start of the course, is the time to master it. So I need to read the guide, remember the guide, apply the guide.

Whenever possible, I'm going to summarise the writer's views in my own words. Not only is that better than just copying what they say, it also means that I don't need to record page numbers as part of my reference. That will save some faffing about.

But I need to avoid innocent plagiarism. It's scary that you could be chucked off the course for making an honest mistake. Mind you, if there were just one or two lines plagiarised, I doubt if they would be too bothered. No, the students they want to catch are probably those who plagiarise huge chunks of their assignment. Still, I need to ensure that whenever I take notes or quotes from a text I jot down the reference.

SPACE FOR YOUR NOTES

Prompts

- What do I need to do to improve my referencing?
- Have I ever been guilty of innocent plagiarism? How did it happen?

10.12 Record of PDT meeting

Trainee: Alex Croft

Summary of key learning points

- Remember the ABCs of good writing: accuracy, brevity and clarity.
- If acceptable to your marker, write in the first person.
- Know the audience for whom you are writing. Do not write at such a level that they won't understand what you are saying nor insult their intelligence by writing down to them.
- Ensure that everything you write is factually correct and unambiguous.
- Avoid using unexplained jargon.
- Whenever possible, use a small word rather than a big word.
- If you have any doubts about the meaning of a word, don't use it.
- Never discuss a theory or issue that you don't fully understand.
- Use short sentences - fewer than 20 words.
- One issue equals one paragraph.

- Answer the question, the whole question and nothing but the question. This means that you must read and understand both the question and the assessment criteria. Ask your tutor for clarification if you are uncertain about what is required.
- Writing a good assignment is a three-stage process involving creativity, organisation and criticality. Do not cripple your creativity by starting the critical phase too early.
- Be prepared to write and rewrite your assignment until it is satisfactory. It is unrealistic to expect that your first draft will be good enough to pass without amendment and/or correction.
- Use subheadings to help organise your work. These can be removed prior to submission if necessary.
- Each section of your assignment should be logically structured and lead naturally onto the next.
- The entire document should have a clear narrative thread that leads the reader through each stage of the assignment from introduction to conclusion.
- Do use a critical friend to check your work prior to submission.
- If your use of English is weak, use the student support services offered by the university. That's what they are there for!
- Once the assignment has been reviewed by your critical friend or student support services, file it away for a week. Then take it out and, read it aloud, conduct a final edit and polish. Be ruthless – cut all unnecessary sections, paragraphs and words, even if you struggled to write them!
- Obtain a copy of the university's guide to referencing. Study and apply the contents of the guide consistently.
- Beware of innocent plagiarism.
- All of the above guidelines apply to all levels of work, including M Level. The mark of good M Level work is the expression of complex ideas in simple terms.
- What distinguishes good M Level work from Level 6 is the level of analysis and critical evaluation that the writer has applied.

Agreed action points

Alex will:

- Study the assessment criteria for the first two assignments on the course and raise any queries with either the module tutor or Sue.
- Study the guide to referencing and raise any queries with either the course tutor or Sue.
- If possible, look at an old assignment and critique it using the information contained in this tutorial.

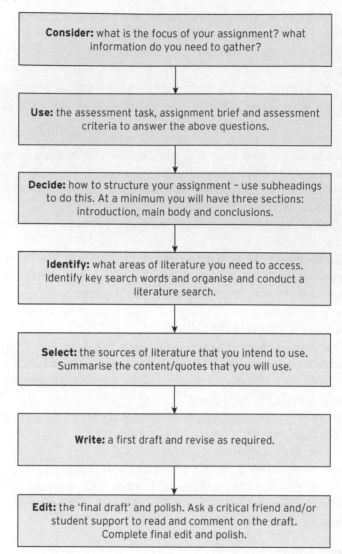

Figure 10.1 Writing your assignment

HANDOUT 10.1　Checklist for final edit of your assignment

By the time you hand in your final assignment you should be confident that you have addressed all of the following questions.

- Is the assignment logically structured? The reader should feel as if they are on a journey of exploration that is clearly signposted and which contains no surprises.

- Did you word-process the assignment yourself? Unless it is absolutely impossible, word-process your own work. The more you engage with your work, the better. As you type you will be thinking about and analysing what you have written. You will also be able to type and retype your work until you are satisfied. If you use a typist, you are unlikely to ask them to carry out multiple retypes.

- Does the assignment contain a balance of description, analysis and critical evaluation, or is it primarily descriptive?

- Is there any irrelevant material in the assignment? If so, remove it.

- Are there any areas of the assignment that are not adequately developed? If they are important, expand on them.

- Have you used any excessively long quotations?

- Have you referenced all materials correctly?

- Have subheadings been used effectively within sections to emphasise important issues and aid the reader's journey through the text?

- Does each paragraph only discuss one issue or idea?

- Are there any incomplete sentences or missing words in the text?

- Does the report contain any sentences that are longer than 20 words? If so, are they clear and unambiguous?

- Have you used any words, phrases or theories in the report that you don't fully understand? If so, double-check that your understanding of them is correct.

- Has each page of the text been numbered?

- Have all tables, figures and appendices been given a number, a title and a legend?

- Has your critical friend read and commented on your final draft?

- Have you carried out a final edit and polish on the assignment, including reading the text aloud?

Further Reading

McGrath, J. and Coles, A. (2013), *Your Education Research Project Companion* (2nd edn). Oxford: Routledge.

McGrath, J. and Coles, A. (2015), *Your Education Masters Companion*. Oxford: Routledge.

McMillan, K. and Weyers, J. (2012), *The Study Skills Book (Smarter Study Skills)* (3rd edn). Harlow: Pearson/Prentice Hall.

Tutorial 11   How to write your assignments

Aim of tutorial: To provide guidance on how to successfully complete four types of assignments that are used widely on teacher training courses, namely, essays, reports, portfolios and presentations.

Tutorial overview: The tutorial starts by identifying why students fail assignments; avoid these errors and you are likely to pass. The need for a critical friend is stressed and advice given on the preparation you need to undertake before you start writing. The actual writing of assignments is then discussed, as are the final checks that you should undertake before submission of your assignment.

Contents

11.1 Alex's reflection

I feel doomed! The more I reflect upon last week's tutorial and look at what I handed in as my pre-entry task, the more I realised how many stupid mistakes I've made. But, I'm here to learn. If I already knew everything I wouldn't need to be on the course. Looking on the bright side, the fact that I can now see where I went wrong has to be a major step forward in my learning and under-standing. Still, it's not going to be a particularly enjoyable 45 minutes with Sue today.

11.2 Why students fail assignments

'Why so glum?' Sue asked.

'After last week's tutorial I looked at my pre-entry task and couldn't believe the number of errors I'd made.'

'It wasn't that bad and, from what you've just said, the exercise has been very useful.'

'How so?'

'It's given both you and me a clear idea of your strengths and weaknesses as regards writing. I'm also delighted that you've spent some time reviewing what you wrote in the light of our last tutorial. That's what I like to see; students actively engaging in their studies and not just passively receiving information.'

'I'm glad someone is happy,' I said, unwilling to reveal how relieved I felt.

'What you have to remember is that people rarely fail assignments, but when they do, there are three main reasons. First, they fail to read the assignment brief and follow the instructions given. You needed to spend more time thinking about what exactly is required. You didn't read the assignment brief that we gave you.'

'But I did,' I said, sounding petulant and defensive.

'The brief we gave you was quite clear about what you had to do and I'm sure you read it, but you didn't read it carefully enough. If you had analysed the task, you would have seen what was required and then when you'd finished you could have made a decent attempt at judging whether you'd met the criteria or not.'

'Are you saying I have to do that with every assignment?'

'Yes, I am. But it's actually easier with the course assignments . . .'

'Because they are marked against a set of criteria which is in the student handbook,' I said, recalling what Sue had said previously.

Sue nodded approvingly. *'The second reason for failure is that students don't follow the guidance given by their tutors; often they rely on asking their peers, so they get really mixed messages about what is required. The result is confusion all round.'*

'So it would be better to ask a tutor or show them a draft of what I've written?'

'That's a reasonable approach, but you should view advice obtained under these circumstances with caution. The first point is that whilst tutors on a programme should have an understanding of all the modules, only the module leader and those personally involved in teaching the module will fully understand all the nuances of the assignment, so ask them. Also, you need to know about the university policy on reading drafts.'

'Policy on reading drafts? Are you serious? I know there's a policy on most things, but reading drafts?'

'It might sound odd, but there is a reason for it. Obviously we want to help you with your work as much as possible, but ultimately it's up to you to act on the advice. We don't pre-mark your work. Our policy is that we read up to 1,000 words and comment on the structure of the assignment. Other universities will have their own policy.'

'So you can't ask the tutor if the assignment will pass or not?'

'It's always tempting to try, but of course the work hasn't been marked, so it's not really a fair question to ask. Now, the third most common reason for failing is that the assignment isn't clear.'

11.3 Study buddy and critical friend

'And that's why getting a critical friend to read your work is so important,' I said. 'Because what makes sense to me when I wrote it may be unclear to my **study buddy** when they read it.'

'Hang on, you have just used the term critical friend and study buddy as if they were interchangeable.'

'Well, they are, aren't they?'

'Not really. A study buddy is someone you work with, discuss issues with and generally share a supportive relationship with. A critical friend is a bit more formal. As we said last week, you are asking them to critique what you have written or done. So the relationship is not so personal. A study buddy is likely to be a friend. A critical friend is more like a trusted peer or professional colleague. And if it doesn't sound too formal, I suggest exchanging a compact with your critical friend at the start of the relationship.'

'Sounds like a contract to me.'

'It is in a way, but of course it's not legally binding. It's just an agreement setting out the ground rules, such as the sorts of things you can both comment on, when and where you'll meet and so on. Many of your assignments will ask for self-evaluation, or evidence of evaluation from others, so the critical friend idea can be very useful. You could even try marking each other's work according to the criteria. You don't have to give a grade, but you could give feedback against each criterion.'

'It sounds scary marking a peer's work, and even scarier having someone else mark mine, but I can see how it would help me to focus on the assessment criteria.' I paused before saying, 'I've just had an idea. I could extend this approach and ask my mentor to comment on the content and clarity of my lesson plans and teaching resources. And when evaluating my lessons I could ask my own learners if they could follow the handouts. Such feedback could be used, along with my assignments, as evidence of my written communication skills against the standards.'

'Good idea.'

11.4 Alex's reflection

After last week's session I tried reading my work aloud and it does work. Mind you, my partner is not too keen on listening to me rattle on. Best to wait until they are out of the flat. It does seem that I haven't been paying enough attention to the criteria, though. I thought that they were just for the tutors. It might even help if I look at these at the beginning of a module and make a note of how they relate to my placement and the taught sessions as they occur. That way I can be sure that I've covered all the relevant points. It's probably best to ask who will be marking my work - that way I can be sure that I ask the right person about the task. If I'm clearer about the criteria, I'll also be in a better position to ask them for some feedback on specific aspects of the assignment.

The problem is that I don't spend enough time reflecting on what I've written. I like to sit down at the end of the module and knock the assignment out in a few days and hand it in. Maybe I under-estimate the task. I'm sure that the key is to plan my time better. I know - I could take a copy of the course timetable and enter my own deadlines on it. In fact, there's one on the VLE, so I could add another column just for me. I'll mention that one to Sue!

I'm still not sure about going to Student Support, but I do need to take more care with my written communications. Teachers have to communicate with learners, colleagues and parents, and it really doesn't put me in a good light if my English is poor or unclear. I suppose that's one of the differences between an 'ordinary' degree and a teaching qualification. I don't just have to persuade my tutors that I have the skills to teach; I also need to show that I have all the other skills required of a teacher, and good written communication is one of those. Maybe I should take this writing lark more seriously.

SPACE FOR YOUR NOTES

Prompts

- Think about an assignment that you either failed or did poorly on in the past. What feedback did you receive - written or verbal?
- How did you use the feedback to improve your next assignment?

11.5 Starting work on your assignment

'It's also important to understand what you've been asked to do before beginning your assignment. You need to identify the keywords. Can you give me an example of some keywords or phrases that might appear in an assignment title/task?'

After a short pause, the best I could come up with was, 'Compare and contrast three theories of learning, illustrating your answer with examples from your practice.'

'OK. So which are the words that tell you what to do?'

'I suppose compare and contrast.'

*'Correct. These are called **process words**. Can you think of similar words that you've come across in the past?'*

'Describe and critique.'

'Good, now let's have a look at this handout. (See Handout 11.1.) It tells you what you're expected to do in relation to those words. For example, take compare and contrast. It's easy to use these words interchangeably, but they do have different meanings. So when comparing ideas, both similarities and differences are discussed, but to contrast ideas means that only the distinctive differences are discussed. You mentioned critique. Can you think how that differs from contrast?'

'They sound similar really, but I suppose that critique might be used when a film critic writes their own opinion about a new film; it's more personal.'

'It is in the sense that it involves a judgement about something based on your understanding of the evidence available. Have a look at the handout for more examples, but the point that I'm making is that you should attach significance to the words used in the question, as they're chosen for a reason, and they will be linked to the assessment criteria. So, if you're asked to critique and you evaluate because you think that they're the same, then you won't be answering the question properly and you will lose marks. Now you've been looking at learning theory. Just in very general terms, how would you go about tackling an assignment on learning theory?'

'I'd find my notes on learning theory and get a couple of books out of the library on the subject. Then I would make some notes on a few relevant theories and write about them. Maybe after writing about each one I'd give some examples from my teaching . . . I can tell by your face that's not right!' I said.

'Well, there isn't really a right way. Writing is a personal thing and different approaches work for different people, but the key thing is to answer the question, and your tactics wouldn't really do that. Can you think why?'

'Because I haven't paid attention to those process words. I suppose that I could highlight the process words in the question. Those would be compare, contrast and illustrate – and what I've just suggested doesn't do any of that, does it?'

'It shows that you've considered the general thrust of the question, but that you haven't really thought too hard about what you've actually been asked to do. The other thing that's missing is a plan, both for the content and the structure. How can you know what sources of information you'll need before you've planned what you want to write? OK, I can see that you look confused,

so let me emphasise the importance of engaging with the task from the start of the module. This analysis of the question doesn't start a few weeks before you have to submit the work, it happens at the beginning of the module. There will be a module launch and the assessment task will be explained. This is the time to consider the different aspects of the assignment and plan your way through it; after all, you don't want to miss important opportunities to gather relevant evidence from your placement. So begin to plan the assignment from the start of the module and be prepared to change the plan as time goes on and new aspects are introduced in the taught session. So, how might you plan your next assignment?' Sue asked.

'I will analyse the assignment title and read the assignment brief. Then draw up a list of topics to be covered and add to this as the module progresses.'

*'Good. That's not a bad approach. But consider using a separate piece of paper for each topic, or better still, a separate Word document. The problem with this approach is that it's not always clear how topics relate to each other and where a new topic goes if you need to introduce one. This is where **mind maps** or **spray diagrams** are useful. Here's an example of one. (See Figure 11.1.) Can you see how it's possible to relate topics to the original idea and each other? I like to do these by hand as it's easy to add things as I get new ideas. A piece of A3 paper works well. You could use text boxes on the computer, though, and there's also software available to create mind maps.'*

'I know that you like colour coding,' I said, 'so I could colour-code different parts of the mind map to show which aspect of the assignment they relate to. I can see from your smile that you like that one!'

'It's certainly a good idea. I'll try using it myself! Another useful exercise is to go back to previous assignments and make a note of the strengths and weaknesses identified by the marker. You could even include these in a separate "bubble" in your spray diagram to remind you that they need to be addressed in your latest assignment.'

'I've never thought of linking feedback from a previous assignment to my next assignment in such a direct way,' I said. 'I'll give it a try.'

'Now we can start to think about your assignment in a little more detail. Let's assume that you have planned the work and have a collection of resources. Have a look at the literature you intend to use and consider whether it's appropriate. It's not just a question of whether it addresses the issues; think about the range of sources that you have covered. You mentioned that you would get some relevant books out of the library, but are books the only source of information? Remember what we discussed in our session on finding and using literature.'

'You said that at this level I should be thinking about a range of sources, such as peer-reviewed journals, government reports, publications from quangos such as the Teaching Agency and Ofsted, and articles from the professional press and specialist publications like the TES, which, by the way, I have now subscribed to at a very favourable student rate.'

'That's a good start. As markers, we want to see that you have gone to the trouble of researching the topic above and beyond the few books and articles on the reading list. It's certainly worth spending some time looking for a journal article, as they often enable you to make a comment on a current issue, or find something relevant to your geographical area. The TES is good too, but also consider publications from interest groups such as unions and subject associations, for example, The Mathematical Association. Or publications from research organisations, such as

the National Foundation for Educational Research – they often provide up-to-date reviews of a topic. Also, as I've previously said, you should work on the assignment as the module unfolds and then pull it all together when the module has ended.

11.6 Alex's reflection

The big message here is that it's never too early to start planning and working on your assignment. If I leave it until the end of the module, I will have forgotten some of the important points from my tutors and lost lots of opportunities to gather relevant evidence from my placement. I'll start the spray diagram for my next assignment now. Hang on, I need some way of relating my planning to the handouts from taught sessions, the information I get from my reading and other relevant documents. I really need a file for each section in the diagram so that I can add the items as they appear. That way I'll have all the resources together in one place ready to write my assignment, rather than having to search through piles of paper in the flat. Friends might actually be able to squeeze in the front door if I do it properly.

As I've noted before, there is a lot to read on this course. No wonder it's difficult at times to see the wood for the trees. I need to apply the advice that Sue gave me about reading at the start of the course. Maybe it's time to revisit that session (see Tutorial 9) and have a look at the transcript and my notes. One thing is for sure – I need to know what the question requires and then read with those requirements clear in my mind. I could even draft out a series of points or issues to look out for as I read. That way I will be actively reading and engaging with the work rather than passively working through a chapter or article simply because I think it might be relevant.

SPACE FOR YOUR NOTES

Prompts

- How do you plan an assignment? Is this the most effective approach? How can it be improved?
- What strategies do you use to ensure that you read actively?

11.7 Writing your assignment

'*So you understand the task, you have the information and you have all the information you need to put it together. Time for another plan, I'm afraid. Go back to the diagram that you've developed during the module, look at any additional guidance that you've been given and plan each section of the assignment. You could begin by writing the headings for the main and subsections. Even if subheadings are discouraged by your tutors, they will help you to organise your writing and you can always delete them later. Don't forget to plan for an intro-duction and conclusion.*'

'I know I need to say what I'm going to say, say it, then say what I've said.'

'*Well, not quite. That implies that you say the same thing three times. Each of these sections has a different function. Let's take the introduction first: the introduction is there to set the scene, so outline the approach that you will take and, because most of your assignments are based on your professional practice, comment on any characteristics of your setting that are relevant. You might also include definitions of any key terms that you intend to use, and give a brief outline of the remainder of the assignment.*'

'So you do tell them what you are going to cover!'

'*OK, yes. The main body of the assignment is where your arguments are developed and you draw on evidence to substantiate them. The conclusion should draw your argu-ments together and summarise the key points. I often use the rule of three here, which is: What were the three most significant learning points or issues that emerged from the assignment? What weaknesses exist in the assignment and how would I address them in future work? What areas would I like to explore further? Then you're ready to start writing.*'

'At last!'

'*That exclamation from the heart implies that you think you've been wasting your time up to this point. You haven't. Think about it: all the groundwork has been done. You have the information you need and the structure of the assignment has evolved and been mulled over for several weeks. All that will make it much easier to write your assignment.*'

'OK I'll believe you,' I said.

'*Oh ye of little faith,*' said Sue. '*When you start to write, it's essential that you have your audience in mind. So for any assignment, who is your audience?*'

'Surely it's the person marking the work. So I won't need to explain every piece of jargon or theory, just the key terms, because, unlike, say, a learner's parent, they will understand the terminology.'

'*Be careful. Remember that you need to demonstrate that you understand certain concepts, and the only way that you can do that is to explain them in your own words. I would suggest* that, unless the term or theory is common knowledge or that it is understandable by the average intelligent lay person, you need to define or explain it.'

'So I'd need to explain common educational terms like "assessment", "behaviourism", "cognitive" and "differentiation"?'

'Yes – and as I've said previously, don't use long words for the sake of it. Good academic communication is about expressing complex ideas simply, not showing that you can use a thesaurus. Also, avoid colloquialisms like "I think that the humanistic school is wicked"; they weaken your argument and we ancient tutors may not even understand them! And, yes, I'm well aware that wicked is so last decade.'

'Got it. But I still can't get over the idea that I can write my assignment in the first person.'

'As we discussed last week, for most institutions it's not a problem. In fact, it improves the clarity of communication as it's much more natural. But not every tutor or university likes assignments to be written in the first person. So check out what's required/ acceptable.'

'OK.'

'Now I must mention the use of quotes again. Can you remember what I said about how they should be used?'

'They should be used when the form of words is important and the message would be weakened by putting it any other way.'

'Correct. As I mentioned, we sometimes get assignments that are little more than a series of linked quotes. The key is to put ideas in your own words when possible and to make sure that you fully reference your sources. We discussed referencing last week. Did you say you got a copy of the library guide?'

'I did, and I have been studying it.'

'Good. As for the style of writing, keep it simple, clear and, above all, try to make the account pleasing to read; after all, your tutor will be marking a lot of the same assignments, and the easier you make it for them the better. Also, remember to use transitions to link sentences, paragraphs and sections.'

'You mean phrases like "in contrast with the above" and "on the other hand"?'

'Certainly, but you can be even more explicit and say "Having discussed X, I will now consider Y." Use the process words from the assignment too; for example, "having discussed the strengths of the cognitive school, I will now consider the weaknesses". Provide a roadmap for the reader. Tell the person marking the work what you have done and will do; convince them that you have answered the question. Make life easy for them.'

11.8 Alex's reflection

Introduction. Main body of assignment. Conclusion. I think that Sue has managed to burn that into my mind. But I do like the rule of three hint for how to structure a conclusion. I've always struggled with conclusions; usually I've just summarised the main points. But the rule of three requires more. You have to decide what the three main points are. That's not always easy but it will force me to distinguish between what is really important and the merely interesting. I'm not sure about exposing the weaknesses in what I've done. But I suppose it shows that I'm capable of critically evaluating my own work. While identifying where I could take the work seems fair enough.

I still find it odd that I have to define all the keywords, theories and jargon. It will take up space, but Sue insists it's essential, so I'll have to apply her ABCs of writing, especially Brevity, if I'm to fit everything in. That means I need to break my habit of using long quotes. I need short quotes that carry a real impact to emphasise important points.

Of course linking paragraphs and issues together will also take up a few words. Quarts and pint bottle spring to mind. I really need to improve my general writing skills in order to answer the question at the right standard and within the word limit.

SPACE FOR YOUR NOTES

Prompts

- List as many useful transition words and phrases as you can. Are there any that you don't fully understand?
- Define each process word or phrase in your own words (after all, you will be using them to set exercises for your learners).

11.9 Final checks prior to submission of assignment

'We're nearly there. You've completed the first draft. Now, as I said in the last tutorial, is the time to make use of your critical friend. Then put the work aside for at least a few days before you start your final edit and polish. So, what are you going to look for when you re-read it?'

'I'll read it again out loud and make any changes that arise and include points made by my critical friend. I'll check for spelling, punctuation and grammar, sentence length and that my paragraphs only discuss one issue or point. Finally, I'll check that my citations in the text agree with those at the end. How's that?'

'Very good. But you've missed two very important things. Check that you have answered the question and that your work meets the assessment criteria. Remember that they're there for you too. It's also worth looking at structure – introduction, main body and conclusion – and the clarity of your layout too. If necessary, have you double-spaced? What about font size? Anything less than 11 point can be tricky for us old-timers to read – 12 point is best. Check whether the work has to be single-sided. Secondly, double-check that you have not exceeded the word count, because usually there is a penalty for going over the limit. We dock 10 per cent but some universities just fail the assignment. So check. It's especially important now, because we ask for a soft copy of students' work and, therefore, it's easy to check an assignment's length.'

'What if I need to reduce the word count?'

'Remember what we said about brevity in the last tutorial. Read the whole account and delete any unnecessary or repetitive words, sentences, phrases or paragraphs, especially if they don't add anything to your argument.'

'But that can be so hard.'

'Maybe, but good writing requires ruthless editing. Also, remember to check your previous assignments for comments to make sure that you're not making the same mistakes again. What about appendices?'

'We were told to keep them to a minimum and be selective about any additional evidence included.'

'Agreed, but do make sure that you actually refer to any appendices in your text and discuss their content. There's no point in including it if you don't use it to support your argument. Check if there are any submission requirements, like spiral binding and the number of copies required. Now you're ready to submit. Don't forget to check the time of the deadline. If you fail to submit before the deadline you may well have marks deducted. So don't miss the bus or train. If you are worried, you can always submit the day before.'

11.10 Alex's reflection

That tutorial was really helpful. I know that a weakness of mine is not looking at my work when I get it back. I usually peek at the mark and, if I've passed, that's enough for me. I need to read the feedback and try and address the weaknesses identified in my next piece of work.

Next time I 'finish' an assignment I'll put it away for a few days and then take it out and do a final edit and check. I'll 'mock mark' it against the assignment criteria and make absolutely certain that I've covered all of them. I may not be able to decide how well I've addressed an issue, but at least I'll know that I have covered all elements of the criteria.

Hang on. What if I did two edits and polishes? The first would concentrate on checking that I've included everything I need to in order to pass. The second would concentrate on the quality of writing. Which means that I'd be checking for accuracy, brevity and clarity. That might work. I'll give it a try.

SPACE FOR YOUR NOTES

Prompts

- Think about how you might make maximum use of the feedback that you receive on your assignments.
- Think about what strategies you can use to ensure that your learners act upon the feedback you give them.

11.11 Record of PDT meeting

Trainee: Alex Croft

Summary of key learning points

- Some of the most common reasons for failing assignments are a lack of attention to the assessment criteria, not following the advice of tutors and poorly written work.

- Prepare a timetable for your work and allow time for your critical friend to review your assignment and for you to put the assignment aside for a week before you take it out, read it aloud and undertake a final edit and polish.
- Use the support services available. Remember that you're taking a professional qualification and that how you speak and write may be copied by your learners.
- Begin working on your assignment at the start of the module. Analyse the question, paying attention to the process words.
- Use a spray diagram or mind map to build your assignment plan.
- Include a range of literature from different sources in your reading and use active reading techniques to gather information.
- Structure your assignment correctly – introduction, main body and conclusion. Use the introduction to set the scene and apply the rule of three when writing the conclusion.
- Write for an intelligent lay person, define or explain all key terms and help the marker to identify points relevant to the assessment criteria.
- Check your work for meaning, correct references and that all relevant points have been covered. Also check layout, presentation and use of transitions.
- Make sure you follow the instructions for assignment submission.
- Review your work when it's returned and make a note of areas for improvement.

Agreed action points

Alex will:

- Find a recent assignment and review the areas for development. Determine how to address the issues identified.
- Look at the assignment brief for the next module and identify the process words.
- Using a sheet of A3 paper, start to draw a spray diagram or mind map of the key areas that need to be covered in the next assignment and identify the relationships between the key factors.

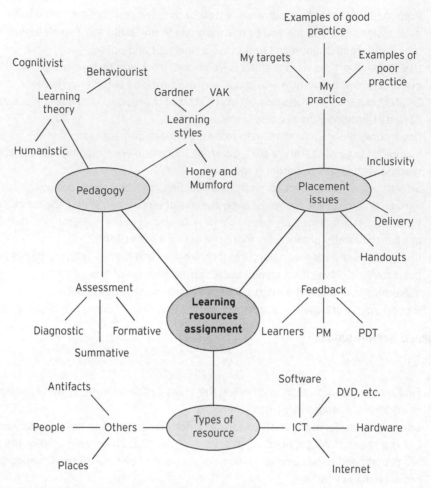

Figure 11.1 Mind map/spray diagram

Note: Mind maps are usually used when outlining your own ideas on a subject; for example, when planning an assignment. Spray diagrams summarise ideas that other people have written or spoken about, but essentially their construction is the same/very similar.

HANDOUT 11.1   What the process words used in assignment questions mean

Analyse	Break the subject down into its different parts – then explain how the parts are connected to each other.
Compare	Summarise both similarities and differences between ideas or concepts.
Contrast	Identify the distinctive features between two or more concepts.
Critique	Make a judgement based on the available evidence.
Define	State the exact meaning of words or phrases.
Describe	Provide an account of a topic based on available facts.
Discuss	Debate the relative merits of an idea or concept by identifying its strengths and weaknesses.
Evaluate	Arrive at a judgement on the value of an idea or concept.
Examine	Describe the material or data in great detail.
Explain	Give a detailed account of the reasons for a particular phenomenon.
Illustrate	Use examples to clarify an idea, often supported by reference to pictures, diagrams or charts.
Interpret	Provide an explanation for something based on available evidence.
Justify	Seek to prove that a claim made by you or another author is reasonable using evidence.
List/enumerate	Provide a series of statements concerning the phenomenon under review.
Relate	Show how the issues under discussion are connected to another set of issues/ideas.
Summarise	Provide a summary of the main points in sequence without going into detail.

Further reading

www.routledge.com/cw/mcgrath

McGrath, J. and Coles, A. (2013), *Your Education Research Companion* (2nd edn). Oxford: Routledge.

McGrath, J. and Coles, A. (2015), *Your Education Masters Companion*. Oxford: Routledge.

McMillan, K. and Weyers, J. (2012), *The Study Skills Book (Smarter Study Skills)* (3rd edn). Harlow: Pearson/Prentice Hall.

Tutorial 12 How to build your teaching portfolio

Aim of tutorial: To provide you with the guidance required to compile a first-class teaching portfolio.

Tutorial overview: This tutorial identifies the sections required in a teaching portfolio, how to organise it and how to demonstrate clearly that you have met all the required standards. The use of *e-portfolios* is also considered.

Contents

Health warning:

Different institutions have different requirements for portfolios. You must ensure that you follow the requirements of your institution.

12.1 Alex's reflection

We're talking about portfolios today. Specifically, my teaching portfolio. I remember doing one years ago for one of my GCSEs, and it was enormous. I collected as much evidence as I could and packed it into a lever arch file. It took me nearly two weeks to complete. I bet they didn't look at most of it. I'm sure they're marked by weight. Still, at least I have the assignment guidelines this time, which gives me a good idea of how to structure it. I'll impress Sue by taking a file to the tutorial with file dividers – one for each section listed in the assignment brief, so that will be:

- Table of contents
- My log of teaching hours
- Paperwork from my PDT and my mentor
- My observed lessons, together with lesson rationales, schemes of work, lesson plans, resources and self-evaluations
- The standards, with items of evidence listed against each one
- Supplementary evidence for the standards
- Critical reflection on my progress

Sue will be impressed!

12.2 Starting to organise your teaching portfolio

Sue was watching Teacher's TV when I entered. Turning, she asked, *'What have you got there?'*

'You're always telling me to read the Course Handbook before coming to see you so that I have an idea of what we're going to talk about. Well, I knew that we were going to talk about portfolios, so here it is! At least it's a start. I'm sure that I'll need another file, though, as I'm likely to have loads of evidence. I'll need a wheelbarrow for it!'

'Hmm, you can put ideas of wheelbarrows out of your mind straight away. Remember I've got to mark a dozen of these and I've already put my neck out practising the tango last weekend. All those sudden jerks. The key to a good portfolio is to be selective. We want to see that you can think about your practice and identify samples of relevant evidence. That is a skill in itself and it's one of the assessment criteria.'

'I thought that you'd be impressed that I've already made a start.'

'I am. It really does help if trainees read the guidelines before the tutorial. Now let's have a look,' she said, flicking through the file. *'This is good. Organising the portfolio like this means that you can put evidence into it as it appears – that way you will hardly notice the time it takes. The worst thing to do is leave it to the last minute. Your mentor and I will want to see regular evidence of your progress, and the paperwork in the portfolio is the best way to demonstrate this. It's not like a traditional written assignment that you can leave until the deadline approaches. It can seem tedious, but little and often is the way to tackle your portfolio.'*

'That's why I've set a weekly target to review my portfolio.'

'That's a good objective. Organising the sections in advance helps you see at a glance where evidence might be lacking, and it will help me when I look at it during our tutorials and also

when I mark it. There's nothing worse than looking at a portfolio and not being able to find the relevant evidence. We have a checklist for each section, so you can imagine how we feel when have to search through plastic wallets for a piece of evidence.'

'It sounds like you're another one of those lecturers who hates plastic wallets.'

'With a passion. It takes forever to mark an assignment where every page is put in a plastic wallet. They really annoy me. One day I swear that I'll put my comments on the plastic wallet with a felt tip pen.'

'If there is one thing I've learnt already, it is to avoid annoying the person who marks my work. I noticed that the checklist you mentioned is in the Handbook. I was thinking I could take a copy and stick it in the file. I can then tick off each item as I put it in,' I said.

'That's a good idea. It also helps to start with a copy of the standards in the file, too, so that you can do the same with them.'

12.3 Alex's reflection

Despite her moan about my wheelbarrow, Sue did seem impressed that I had made an effort to prepare for the tutorial. Reading the guidelines gave me some ideas for questions that I could ask her. Those instructions are always written as if it's obvious what we have to do, when it's not. She liked the idea of the rough checklist too. I'll need to think if there are any other forms I can find that I can copy and put in the file to help me track the evidence as I add it.

SPACE FOR YOUR NOTES

Prompts

- Think about any previous portfolios that you had to compile. How did you go about it? How can you improve on what you did?
- Identify any forms or other documentation that has to be included in your portfolio. Make a checklist of the required documentation.

12.4 The sections required in a teaching portfolio

'Now let's have a look at each of the sections that you need to include in your portfolio and how best to approach them. A detailed table of contents is vital, as it helps the marker to find relevant evidence, so make sure that each section is clearly identified. For example, you could have Section A in your contents for the **log of hours**, Section B for the tutor and mentor paperwork, and so on. Just make sure that you put the section letters on the file divider tabs.'

'So I'd then put the evidence in plastic wallets in each section. Sounds straightforward.'

'Don't mention plastic wallets again. They're the devil's spawn! Use them sparingly, if at all, as we have to take everything out to look at it. If you have to use them, don't put too much in, as it will split. Worst of all, if you overload the file and it bursts, the plastic wallets will slide everywhere.'

'So you really do want me to avoid them whenever possible?'

'Yes.'

'But if I did use some, you would need to know what's in each wallet. I could put that on a label and stick it on the wallet.'

'Good idea. You could even have a list of contents for each section. You could include that immediately after each file/section divider.'

'I could then use the table of contents in each section as a checklist. That would enable me to do all that indexing now and just tick off each item as I put it in the portfolio. That might even convince you that the evidence is there before you look for it.'

'I wouldn't go that far, but your idea would certainly persuade me that you're organised; remember that assessment criterion again – "effective organisation of documentary evidence". But now the log of hours. We need to know that you have completed the requisite number of teaching hours. Most institutions require some record of hours or sessions taught. We have a form for this, so just make sure that you record the hours as you do them and get your mentor to countersign them, and do add them up. The number of times I've had to sit there adding up hours.'

'I suppose the log is a vital part of the paperwork?'

'Absolutely.'

12.5 Evidencing the standards

'So what other paperwork do you have?' Sue asked.

'Well, there are observed sessions, meetings with my mentor and with you.'

'The observed sessions are really important, so give them a separate section in the portfolio and another section for the records of meetings. Most institutions want to see accompanying paperwork, such as rationales, lesson plans and lesson evaluations with the observed sessions. This is because they serve to confirm your competence as a teacher, but also they're one of the few sources of authenticated evidence that you have met the standards. For example, if a standard asks that you have made effective use of ICT in your lessons, how do we know that it was effective just from sources of evidence, such as a lesson plan, or copies of resources?'

'You don't,' I said. 'It needs someone to have been there when the resources were actually used to see that they were effective.'

'So bear this in mind when selecting evidence for particular standards. Some evidence can stand alone, whereas some is stronger when it is the result of an observation.'

'This could apply to other things too, like my use of questions, classroom management and so on,' I said.

'Yes. This is why it's often worth including any resources used in the observed sessions with the observation paperwork. It makes the evidence more authentic.'

'You've started to talk about evidence. I thought that this would be a separate section in the portfolio.'

'Potentially, evidence can be found in any section of the portfolio. But most standards focus on teaching and learning, so a lot of evidence can be found in observed teaching sessions. To maximise the number of standards you address in a teaching session, you have to be familiar with the standards and then logically plan your lesson to cover as many as possible.'

'That sounds very cold-blooded and strategic.'

'Maybe it is. But is it any different than working out what the examiner wants you to write in an exam question and then emphasising these points in your answer?'

'I suppose not. But where else can I meet standards?'

'It's generally the case that your assignments will also provide evidence towards the standards. Some institutions are happy if you simply cite a particular assignment. The assumption is that if you have passed the assignment, then you can claim that you have met the evidence requirements. Most institutions map assignments against the standards, so you just need to follow the map.'

'That sounds straightforward. I may not even have to include the actual evidence. But what about the items that aren't covered in observed sessions and assignments?'

'That's where your supplementary evidence section comes in. If standards haven't been covered by observed sessions or assignments, you need to look for other sources and include these in a supplementary evidence section. Very often these standards can be met if you have engaged fully with your placement.'

'How do you mean?'

'By attending staff meetings, staff development days, exam and assessment meetings, planning meetings, even parents' evening. What you would need to evidence these would be a copy of the minutes from the meeting or a note confirming that you took part, signed by your mentor.'

'I bet it wouldn't harm your chances of a job offer from your placement either!'

'No, it wouldn't. Attending meetings and playing a full part in the life of the school is a great way to get noticed. But coming back to checklists, remember to include a list of the standards cross-referenced to where the marker can find the relevant evidence.'

12.6 Alex's reflection

With Sue's hatred of plastic wallets, I think I'll avoid using them. It's never a good strategy to annoy your marker.

I didn't realise that I could use the whole portfolio as a source of evidence; I thought that I'd have to include every item of evidence in a single section. Some things are still tricky, though: 'communicating and working with others', for example. I suppose emails from people and/or minutes of meetings would be useful evidence. Then there's 'achievement and diversity'. I could use pupils' work to evidence personalisation, but I'd have to make sure that it's anonymous. Perhaps awareness of policy on health and well-being would be difficult. But hang on, there's an assignment on policy, so I could use that. In fact, it must be worth having a good look at the standards now so that I don't miss any opportunities for collecting evidence. I should make that an aim for the next few weeks, 'cos it will certainly help me to achieve my overall objective of passing the course. But whatever I use to claim the evidence, I have to make it easy for the marker to find the evidence, so I need to detail against each standard a clear statement as to where the evidence can be found.

To make sure that I can meet all the standards, what I should do when I get out on placement is to treat it as my job. Then, like any new, enthusiastic teacher I need to volunteer for any jobs, meetings or events that are on offer which will help me meet the standards. If I'm lucky, this will get me noticed and on people's radar for any future full-time vacancies.

SPACE FOR YOUR NOTES

Prompts

- What authentic sources of evidence can you use to claim each standard?
- How are you going to record achievement of standards as you meet them? Would a checklist with space for notes on when and how you met each standard be helpful?

12.7 Critical reflection

'That leaves us with the critical reflection. How will you approach that?'

'We were advised to keep a reflective diary, so that will be a useful source.'

'True, though the word "diary" suggests a description of what has happened. That's fine as a start, but it's really important to consider how experiences have changed your professional practice. I don't just mean practical experiences either. You may read about a particular theory, for example. How has this new knowledge influenced you? This is particularly important if you want to score highly in your assignment. Remember what we said, "description is not enough" – you will be expected to demonstrate that you can critically reflect on the literature and use it to develop your understanding of theoretical principles and illustrate how this has developed you as a teacher.'

'So it's particularly important at Level 6 and Masters level.'

'Yes.'

'Presumably, I could draw on my reflective diary to identify particular experiences. I remember that we had a discussion on critical incidents in class. So I could choose a critical incident or incidents and reflect on how my teaching practice has changed because of my experiences. Also, I could use information from the literature to help with the theory.'

'That's a really good approach. Just remember that critical means that you can critique it. It doesn't have to be critical in the dramatic sense or a world-shattering incident.'

'It could be how one pupil responded to an activity,' I suggested.

'Absolutely, but try to take the discussion further, for example, by asking yourself "what if" the incident had followed a different course. Here's a handout on one approach to analysing critical incidents.' (See Handout 12.1.)

'This session has been really helpful, though it still seems odd that we're asked to collect so much paper.'

12.8 E-portfolios

*'We still use paper-based portfolios, but many institutions are moving towards e-portfolios. In fact we're using one called **Mahara**. This isn't just a repository for files. For example, images, audio and video files, blogs, wikis and **hyperlinks** can be included. In fact, they have been called online personal spaces.'*

'I use one of those already; it's called Facebook!'

'That's actually not a bad analogy. The point about e-portfolios is that they can provide these tools which make them a much more personalised and formative record of progress, which can be shared with peers and tutors as and when appropriate and from wherever you wish.'

'Great. So it would be available in my placement for my mentor to review and at uni for meetings with you without the need for a wheelbarrow. I can see that cross-referencing would be easy too – no more sticky notes.'

'I'm worried about you and your strange obsession with wheelbarrows,' Sue said. *'But there's another advantage, too. I once left my doctoral thesis in a supermarket trolley and only realised on the way home. Luckily, someone had handed it in to Customer Services when I returned. That was before the days of electronic copies. Now, with e-portfolios you could back it up and you needn't fear losing it.'*

I didn't ask how long ago Sue had written her thesis. It sounded as if she had written it on a typewriter. Can you imagine – no cut and paste available! Instead, I said, 'Hmm – I'm not sure about that – I'm always losing USB drives.'

'Me too. So keep it on both your stick and the university system. That way it should be reasonably safe. Before the next session have a look at presentations.'

12.9 Alex's reflection

I've just realised that I could apply the principles of portfolio building to my own teaching file at school. Within the file – paper-based or electronic – I could set up a section or folder for every lesson I teach and significant activity I get involved in. I could then add to the file as I gained more experience/resources. It would be my very own 'portable information bank'.

What Sue said about selectivity is really important. It's already clear that this course is going to produce loads of paper, so I'll need to make decisions about which pieces meet the criteria best. I bet my future learners will also have problems distinguishing between what is essential from what is only interesting. I might be able to pass on what I learn to them.

I never thought that I could get excited about portfolios, but e-portfolios are an interesting idea. I can see that these could be used as a teaching resource, with groups sharing resources and ideas. I suppose one problem of this approach is that a lot of work depends on one piece of software working! Maybe a collection of different tools could be used in the same way.

A blog could be used for reflective diaries. But it could be a problem if students could see each other's contributions. On the other hand this might add an interesting dimension to the diary, and it would be OK if they knew that what they wrote could be seen by others. I could use a wiki to record my evidence for some of the standards as I collect it. I could use it in my teaching to get students to add comments on a particular topic, such as methods of teaching that they liked.

Tutors are already talking about CPD to us. This seems a long way off, but an e-portfolio would be a good way to keep record of my CPD activities, because I could add to it even after I graduate.

SPACE FOR YOUR NOTES

Prompts

- List a couple of incidents that have had an impact on how you teach and which you could critique in your reflective diary.
- List topics that would be suitable for a blog and/or a wiki.

12.10 Record of PDT meeting

Trainee: Alex Croft

Summary of key learning points

- Begin the portfolio as soon as possible.
- Provide a detailed table of contents for the entire portfolio.
- Start to review the standards and identify what evidence you will need to provide as soon as possible. Use this information when designing the layout and content of your portfolio.
- Ensure that all the sections are labelled – use file dividers and checklists.
- Provide a table of contents for each subsection and include a note detailing what standards could be met by evidence filed in the section and where exactly the evidence can be found. Note that there is likely to be an overlap between sections.
- Make sure that teaching hours or sessions are recorded, totalled and counter-signed by your mentor where necessary.

(continued)

(continued)

- Use a separate section for records of your meetings with mentors and your PDT.
- Use a separate section for records of meetings and events attended in the school/college.
- Some institutions allow assignments to be cited as evidence of meeting standards, e.g. for knowledge and understanding.
- E-portfolios can be a creative replacement for paper-based portfolios, and they can incorporate creative tools such as blogs and wikis. The concept can be used to create innovative teaching resources, too.

Agreed action points

Alex will:

- Compile a list of the documentation that is required for the teaching file portfolio and file any material already held.
- Read the standards that must be met and plan ahead for opportunities to gather evidence.
- Ensure that his/her reflections are critical and not just descriptive; using the literature, his/her reflective diary and critical incidents as sources of data.
- Add contents and checklists to the portfolio.

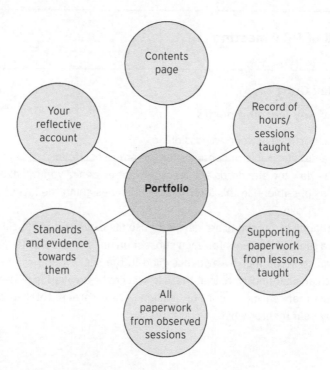

Figure 12.1 Contents of a teaching portfolio

HANDOUT 12.1   Analysis of critical incidents

1. Choose a critical episode: for example, students continually arriving late, students talking during class discussions, behavioural issues or working with other staff.

2. Describe the incident:
    - when and where it happened (time of day, location and social context);
    - what actually happened (who said or did what);
    - what you were thinking and feeling at the time and just after the incident.

3. Interrogate your description:
    - Why did this incident stand out?
    - What was going on?
    - Were there different levels of 'behaviour' or activity?
    - Did I bring personal bias or a particular mindset to the event?
    - Could I have interpreted this event differently from another point of view?
    - What can I learn from this episode?
    - What can I do to progress a resolution of the problems it suggests?

4. Find a friend or colleague to:
    - share your account of the episode;
    - discuss your interpretation;
    - modify your analysis, where necessary, in the light of peer suggestion, advice, perspective.

5. Where appropriate, you may want to compare your analysis with the views of other key people involved in the episode (students or colleagues).

6. Briefly write up your report. Remember that if you name colleagues or students, you need to clarify issues of confidentiality if you wish to make your report public.

Further reading

Tripp, D. (2011), *Critical Incidents in Teaching (Classics Edition): Developing Professional Judgement*. London: Routledge.

Tutorial 13 How to plan and deliver an effective presentation

Aim of tutorial: To enable you to deliver a highly successful presentation and assist your learners to do likewise.

Tutorial overview: This tutorial distinguishes between a lesson and a presentation before discussing the preparation and planning that is required for any presentation. Detailed guidance is given on what to do and avoid during a presentation, and the tutorial ends with suggestions for how you can develop the presentational skills of your learners.

Contents

13.1 Alex's refection

I have to admit I am starting to feel the pressure of the course. It's certainly true what they say - any teacher training course is a full-time occupation. You really can't afford to fall behind, because assignment follows assignment and placements soon take over your life like some

(continued)

(continued)

time-consuming alien monster. I've got to stay the course and to do that I have to stay on top of things. If I fall behind it will be very difficult to catch up.

Well, it's presentations today. I've had a look at the literature on presentations. To be honest I'm not really sure that there is a huge difference between a lesson and a presentation. But Sue will want me to identify the differences that do exist so I'd better review my notes before the tutorial. If only I felt a bit more enthusiastic!

13.2 The differences between a presentation and a lesson

Sue was talking with her partner, Dr Reed, when I entered. They seemed to be talking about the MA Exam Board, which they had just attended. It had gone on for longer than either of them had expected. Seeing me, Dr Reed smiled and left.

'OK, we reviewed portfolios the last time you were here and I asked you to have a look at presentations for this session. So what have you found out?'

I gathered my thoughts for a moment and then replied, 'Well, firstly, they are not the same as a lesson. You are trying to present some information to a group; you are not delivering a lesson. You may want them to remember the presentation, but you don't expect them to learn the content of the presentation. Presentations also tend to be much shorter than lessons,' I said.

'That's pretty good as far as it goes,' said Sue. *'Too often teachers treat presentations as if they were a lesson, often with disastrous results. The aim of a presentation is to provide information. They are **didactic** and very presenter/teacher-centred. The personality and beliefs of the presenter are often the focus of the presentation. This can mean that they lack balance and provide a biased picture of the topic under review. And, unlike a lesson, there is very little attempt to obtain feedback from the audience.'*

'Well, when you put it like that, I can see that my initial response was fairly weak.'

'You did identify that a presentation focuses on the presenter and a lesson focuses on the learners. So don't be too hard on yourself.'

13.3 Preparing a presentation

'Moving on, what is the first thing that you need to think about when giving a presentation?'

'The content. What it is that you want to say,' I said, confidently.

'Most people say that, but I would argue that there are two considerations that come before the content.'

Sue paused, waiting for me to reply. Finally I said, 'The reason for the presentation?' sounding very uncertain.

'*Absolutely. What's the purpose of the presentation? So what might your objectives be?*'

'I might want to sell them something or convince them that an idea I have is worth trying. Maybe I just want to inform them about something, like the dangers of flu. Or I might be trying to sell myself as part of a job interview.'

'*Good. Once you know what you want to get out of the presentation, you can decide how best to go about achieving your objective. The first step in that process is to consider your audience. How well-disposed are they going to be towards you? Are they going to be friendly or hostile? What do they know about the subject? How interested are they likely to be in what you have to say? Why are they there? Have they just eaten lunch and, therefore, will they be ready to fall asleep as soon as you open your mouth? Are they colleagues or strangers? Do they expect a formal presentation or a lively and possibly humorous event? Basically, the more you know about your audience and their expectations the better because . . .*'

'Then you can deliver what they are expecting,' I said.

'*Exactly. The more prior research you can do on the group the better. Once you know your audience, you need to consider how long the presentation will be. Why is that so vital?*'

'I can think of two reasons. Firstly, if it's a short presentation, you won't be able to cover very much ground and, secondly, you will have to simplify what you want to say. Too much depth and you will confuse them. So you probably have to stick to just a few main points. I also read that even in a short presentation it's a good idea to tell the people what you are going to cover, cover it and then end by telling them what you covered.'

'*Ah, we're back to the old teaching adage of "tell 'em what you are going to teach 'em, teach it, tell 'em what you taught 'em". I do think that's a really good way to organise any presentation, because it forces you to structure the presentation into an introduction, the main body of the talk and a conclusion.*'

'Just like any piece of written work,' I said.

'*Yes. But how do you time your presentation?*'

'That's easy. First you develop the slides or materials that you are going to use and then you practise the presentation in front of the mirror and time yourself,' I said. 'You can then add in or take out bits depending on the time it takes to deliver the core presentation.'

'*I like your idea of a core presentation. Whatever happens you are going to deliver that essential message and then, if time permits, you can add in some more stuff that is interesting but not essential. I also think that acting out your presentation in front of the mirror is a wise move, especially if you are nervous. It will give you confidence. However, remember that if you allow questions during your presentation, they can add significantly to the time it takes to complete. Therefore, always ask people to hold their questions until the end. OK, so what types of materials might you use to enliven your presentation?'*

I tried to put my thoughts into some kind of order before I replied, 'Well, depending on the nature of the presentation, you could use PowerPoint, or provide samples, models or pictures of what you are talking about. For example, if the presentation was on a school trip to the First World War battlefields you could show pictures of the children at the main sites that they visited – for example, the Menin Gate.'

'Good, a presentation based on photos would be much more interesting than a series of PowerPoint slides that listed where you went. I've found that people are starting to rebel against PowerPoint. I was at a presentation recently where the presenter said that he had come without any PowerPoint slides and the audience gave him a round of applause.'

'But they are useful sometimes,' I said, defensively remembering how hard I'd worked to master the PowerPoint programme.

'Of course they are. But don't rely solely on them. Try and think, what is the most effective resource that I can use? What resource will capture the audience's attention? One student I had did a presentation on mummification. As well as bringing along copies of the tools that the ancient Egyptians used to extract the heart and brain, she had a large teddy bear which she used to demonstrate how bodies were mummified. To complete the job properly she said that it would take the equivalent of a double sheet for the teddy, while for a person you needed enough linen to cover a football field. Now that presentation took place ten years ago but I still remember it. That's what you call an effective presentation.'

13.4 Alex's reflection

I like Sue's summary of the difference between a presentation and a lesson. The presentation focuses on the presenter and a lesson focuses on the learner. I need to identify my aims for the presentation and then think of the audience, the time available and the key points that I want to deliver in the time available.

But what's more interesting is the idea of using my resources to really engage the audience in the presentation. Yes, I can always use PowerPoint, but before I opt for the default solution I should think how I can add real impact to the presentation. I could use short clips from YouTube, the Internet, TV, even the radio, or present work by students. The list of possibilities is endless. But I must remember that what is most important is the content of the presentation, not the medium used. In fact, if I make the presentation too fancy, I could detract from the message I want to get across.

I think I'll have a look on the Web and review the types of presentations that people upload. Some of the humour sites have great examples of how not to make a presentation, and I could probably learn a thing or three from them. Just as long as I don't end up as a star attraction on one of the 'How not to . . .' sites in the near future.

SPACE FOR YOUR NOTES

Prompts

- Reflect upon your attitude towards presentations. Do you like or dislike them? Do you worry about making a presentation or do you find them easy?
- Consider how your view of presentations might impact on your learners.

13.5 Preparing a presentation continued

'So what else do you need to consider when delivering a presentation?' asked Sue, emphasising the word "delivery".

'If you are going to use any equipment, such as a computer, laptop or whiteboard, you need to check that the facilities are available at the venue . . .'

'And?'

'Get there early to check that they are working,' I said, remembering a **micro-teach** session that had gone badly wrong in the third week because I had arrived to find the projector in the teaching room broken.

'That's right. Always check what equipment is available in advance and, if possible, confirm that it is working. But even then have a fall-back plan. Think about what you will do if you are left with a roomful of people and no mechanical or electrical resources. Again, such planning helps to increase confidence and reduce nerves. What else might you consider?'

'I suppose you need to think about the size of the room, the layout of the furniture and if you will be wearing a microphone, because that will influence how loudly you need to speak.'

'Good point. What else?'

Sue was really grilling me today and I had to think before I replied, 'Consider the type of language I'm going to use. How much does my audience know about the subject I am presenting? Will they understand me if I use technical terms, jargon or big words?'

'That's a very valid point. But never talk down to your audience either. There is the apocryphal story of the research lecturer who told their class "Remember it is no use going to a school during the holidays to collect data, because there will be no one there to answer your questions."'

13.6 Delivering a presentation

'I've noticed that some people just read from a script when making a presentation. That can't be good practice, can it?' I asked.

'Well, I certainly don't think so. But even at international conferences I have seen speakers do that, and I think it looks and sounds awful. Even if the speaker memorises the script and uses no notes, it still comes out sounding like a speech, and a presentation is not a speech. In presentational terms, I think less is more.'

'Sorry, what do you mean?'

'My three preferred approaches to giving a presentation are: in third place, speak from a set of fairly detailed notes, reading directly from them on occasions but also ad-libbing and maintaining eye contact with the group at other times; in second place is using a set of skeleton notes as a guide and structure for your presentation, referring to them as required to keep you on track. In first place, my personal favourite, use the PowerPoint slides, pictures, resources, models or whatever else you have as a series of props on which to hang your presentation. Then talk about and expand on each prop as seems appropriate, depending on the feedback you are getting from your audience and the time available. This last approach really enables you to communicate with the audience and not just speak at them. But it does depend on how experienced you are. If you are new to presenting, it's probably safest to work from fairly detailed notes. As you gain in experience and confidence, reduce the number of notes you use.'

'Hang on, what feedback can I get from the audience? You said that I should ask them to hold off asking questions until the end.'

'That's true, I did. But you should be looking at them throughout the presentation. Try to read their faces and body language. Check if they are restless or engaged – leaning forward listening or slumped down in their chair with eyes closed. If you pick up that they are restless you need to do something to pull them back in. Can you remember what this process is called?'

'Reflection in action,' I said, doubtfully.

'Very good. Reflection in action is all about monitoring what you are doing and the impact your actions are having. This internal monitoring allows you to change your lesson or presentation in real time if things start to go wrong.'

'Unlike reflection on action, which takes place after the event.'

'Correct. At first this can be difficult, but you will be amazed how quickly you adapt to this self-monitoring process.' Sue paused before continuing. *'Now, just like any taught session, you need a structure for your presentation but not a straitjacket. Using a skeleton set of notes or slides to jog your memory enables you to stay on track and cover all you need to while still allowing you to sound natural. So the message is – prepare your presentation meticulously but make the delivery look effortless.'*

'So, not too demanding then,' I said, smiling. 'Any advice on the actual delivery?'

Just the usual stuff that you have covered a hundred times in class. Always aim to make a good first impression. It is still true that people form an opinion of you within the first two minutes of seeing you. So, remembering what Richard Attenborough said, "Good acting is 98 per cent energy and 2 per cent talent", start your presentation with plenty of energy but don't fidget or rock from foot to foot. It will make you look nervous. Plant yourself on the platform and exude confidence even if, no, especially if, you are terrified. Use a friendly, conversational tone, speak clearly and make sure that your voice carries to all corners of the room. Your delivery shouldn't be too fast or too slow, and remember to hesitate after any word or phrase that you wish to emphasise. But whatever you do, do not preach or talk down to your audience.'

'So finishing with a song and a dance is out of the question?' Sue gave me that withering look that mothers reserve for young children who are trying to be clever.

'No,' she sighed. *'Just make sure that you finish on time and with plenty of energy. Personally, I always think it is useful to know what your final sentence is going to be. That way you can end on a powerful note before asking if anyone has any questions.'*

'What about handouts?' I asked. 'Do you think that it is a good idea to provide handouts at the end of the presentation?'

'That depends on the nature of the presentation and the audience you are addressing. If it was a presentation that you did as part of a job interview, then no. But if you were imparting information or trying to promote interest in some issue, then it would be entirely reasonable.'

13.7 Alex's reflection

I may be heading for a fall but I don't think that presentations are all that hard. Like so much in teaching, it is all in the preparation. Get that right and you are almost home and dry. While it's useful to check my timing in front of a mirror, what I really need is some practise with a live audience. I wonder if my **action learning set** *would be interested in doing a series of presentations. We could take turns to either present a subject of our own choice or one suggested by the group. It's worth thinking about, or maybe we can agree to help each other as and when we have to deliver a presentation.*

The other stuff about checking out what equipment is available in the room, confirming that it's working, speaking clearly, appearing confident, even when your legs are shaking, and using language that the group will understand is all standard practice for any teacher. I just need to make sure I do it!

I agree with Sue that the best way to speak to any group or class is to use your resources as prompts for what you want to say rather than read from a script. I read somewhere that 80 per cent of communication is non-verbal, meaning that people not only hear what you say but 'read' both your facial expressions and body language for meaning. And, as any teacher knows, the most powerful way to communicate non-verbally is through the eyes. Therefore, maintaining eye contact with the group is vital, and I can't do that if I have my head buried in a script.

SPACE FOR YOUR NOTES

Prompts

- What was the best presentation you ever saw? Why was it so good?
- What was the worst presentation you ever saw? Why was it so bad?

13.8 Helping learners to deliver a presentation

'You've not mentioned the problem of getting learners to do presentations. From my limited experience, I would say that presentations and role-play are the two most unpopular teaching methods among learners,' I said.

Sue nodded. *'I agree. I think it's because people are terrified of making a fool of themselves. So what do you need to do to encourage them to have a go?'*

It was typical of Sue. She always got me to answer the questions I asked. Maybe I should try the same approach with my learners. 'We're back to confidence. I have to find a way to make them believe that they can deliver a really good presentation.'

'And how would you do that?'

'Well, information is important. So I would share with them all the things you have mentioned, such as knowing your audience, being clear about the purpose of the presentation, how to use PowerPoint and other props effectively, checking out the venue and the equipment in advance if possible, speaking clearly, etc. But, most importantly, I need to get them making presentations.'

'I agree. Here are three things that I would suggest you try. Firstly, let them choose their own topic for the presentation. This probably means that you will get a lot of presentations about hobbies, TV programmes or football teams. But that doesn't matter. At this stage, all you want is to get your learners up and speaking in public. Secondly, the presentations don't

have to be to the whole class. They could be made to small groups of six or seven learners. And thirdly, establish some ground rules in advance so that everyone knows that they need to support the presenter and not make fun of them, even if it goes wrong.'

'Effectively create a safe environment in which the learner can fail but not be destroyed by criticism.'

'*Which is exactly the type of environment you should aim for in your classroom.*' Looking over my head, Sue noticed the wall clock. '*Agghhh,*' she cried, '*I'm late for another appointment. I'll have to shoot off, sorry.*'

13.9 Alex's reflection

I used to worry about doing presentations at school. There was always some idiot, out of sight of the teacher, trying to put me off. Strange thing is, once I'd finished I always felt really good. Maybe I'm a show-off who likes to perform in front of a crowd. Why else would I want to be a teacher? Now, if I felt that way I bet loads of other learners do, too. I just need to give them the opportunity or the excuse to perform.

There used to be a boy in my secondary school that had learning difficulties, but he had one abiding passion - dinosaurs. In his GCSE year he did a presentation on dinosaurs which knocked the socks off every other presentation. It was really fascinating. So I'll use Sue's suggestion and let my learners present on a topic of their own choosing. Knowing my luck, they will all be on soaps or football.

SPACE FOR YOUR NOTES

Prompts

* What ground rules might you agree with the class to help learners feel relaxed and safe when making a presentation?

13.10 Record of PDT meeting

Trainee: Alex Croft

Summary of key learning points

- A presentation is not the same as a lesson.
- The focus of a presentation is usually the presenter and their views, beliefs and opinions. The focus of a lesson should be on the student's learning.
- As a first step, always identify the aim or purpose of the presentation.
- Learn as much as you can about your prospective audience in advance, e.g. their age, reasons for being there, level of knowledge about the topic, etc.
- Use the information obtained above to determine the type of language you will use, e.g. will they understand your use of technical or professional terms?
- Shape the presentation and the material you have to the time available. The shorter the presentation, the less detail you can go into. Do not try and cram a quart into a pint bottle.
- Structure the presentation into three parts: the introduction (tell them what you are going to cover); the main body of the presentation (tell them); the conclusion (tell them what you have told them).
- Leave time for questions at the end.
- Practise your presentation in front of an audience, if possible, and time yourself. If you can't find an audience, practise in front of the mirror.
- Speak in a clear, loud voice with plenty of energy.
- While you can use PowerPoint, consider using more arresting images, e.g. photos, clips from the Internet, examples of work, solid objects or other artefacts.
- Check in advance what equipment is available at the venue and on arrival ensure that it is working. Always have a fall-back position should equipment malfunction.
- Don't speak down to your audience but, likewise, don't baffle them with jargon.
- Don't read from a script. Either use brief notes or, better still, your slides/props as prompts.
- Maintain eye contact with the audience and monitor their body language and facial expressions throughout. Use reflection in action to change tack if you appear to be losing them – just as you do in the classroom.
- Many of your own learners will be concerned about making a presentation. Help them to feel secure by developing a supportive environment in which they can work.
- If they have little or no experience of presentations, let the learner choose the topic for their presentation.
- Establish clear ground rules covering audience feedback and behaviour.
- Allow inexperienced presenters to present to a small group rather than the entire class initially.

Agreed action points

Alex will:

*   Identify one successful and one unsuccessful presentation in which he/she has been involved.
*   Identify the strengths and weaknesses of both and explore how each could have been improved.

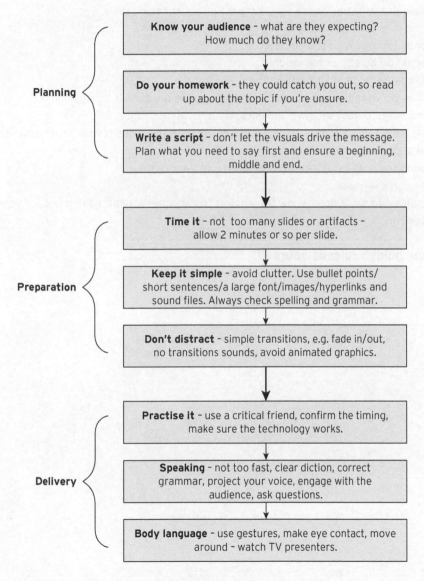

Figure 13.1 Planning, preparing and delivering a presentation

HANDOUT 13.1 Twelve things not to do when making a presentation

If you avoid the most common errors that presenters make, you are well on the way to delivering a good presentation.

Don't:

- Apologise to the audience for your poor public speaking skills.
- Tell a joke to 'break the ice'.
- Speak too slowly or too quickly.
- Speak too quietly or too loudly.
- Mumble or 'er' and 'um' during the presentation.
- Speak down to the audience or use unintelligible phrases or words.
- Avoid eye contact with the audience.
- Hop from foot to foot or pace up and down; both practices reveal your nervousness to the audience.
- Spend the entire presentation reading from your notes.
- Be overly serious.
- Be afraid to say 'I don't know the answer to that question but I'll find out for you'.
- Over-run.

And one golden rule: be yourself.

Further reading

www.routledge.com/cw/mcgrath

McMillan, K. and Weyers, J. (2012), *The Study Skills Book (Smarter Study Skills)* (3rd edn). Harlow: Pearson/Prentice Hall.

Tutorial 14   How to find your first job

Aim of tutorial: To help you get your first full-time teaching job.

Tutorial overview: This tutorial provides insight into the qualities and skills employers are looking for in prospective teachers. It also offers advice and guidance on how to find teaching vacancies, complete job applications and conduct yourself before, during and after the interview.

Contents

14.1 Alex's reflection

It seems ages since I had a tutorial with Sue. But following last week's session on CPD it was suggested that we book in to see our PDT as we need to start thinking about applying for jobs.

I must admit that I have been so busy trying to stay on top of the coursework, lesson planning and delivering sessions that I haven't given it much thought. But it's obvious really, you can't leave looking for a job until you have finished the course. Schools and colleges will be trying to fill their vacancies during the summer term so I need to start thinking about applying in the Easter term.

14.2 Joining a union

Sue was in the middle of sending an email when I entered. Looking up, she smiled and pressed send. '*Done,*' she said.

'Done what?' I asked.

'*Booked my place at the next BERA (British Educational Research Association) conference. Have you ever been?*'

'No,' I said.

'*You should. There is a special students conference held prior to the main event. It's well worth attending. You'll learn a lot about the latest research in education and maybe make a few contacts as well. Anyway, today we need to talk about your future employment. First things first though, have you joined a teaching union?*'

'Not yet, but I'm thinking about it.'

'*Join one this week. You can't afford not to be in a union if you are a teacher. Not only does the union represent you in pay negotiations, they will also represent you in any disputes with your employer. And, even more importantly, if you are accused by any learner or parent of any misdemeanour they will represent you in any disciplinary hearing and pay for legal representation if it goes to tribunal or court.*'

'It sounds like an insurance policy to me. Is there any union you suggest I join?'

'*That's up to you. There's plenty of literature lying around the faculty and on notice boards advertising the various teaching unions. I suggest that you read up on them. Have a look at their websites. See what their aims and objectives are, what political stance they take and then decide which one suits your beliefs and requirements best.*'

'OK. I'll put it on my urgent to-do list.'

14.3 Where to look for jobs

'Good. Right, we're going to talk about jobs. How to apply for them and how to get them. So how do you think teachers get their first job?'

It seemed such an obvious question that I delayed responding. Finally I said, 'By responding to adverts.'

'That's probably true. But you would be surprised how many trainees are invited to apply for jobs by their placement. Why do you think that happens?'

'The placement knows you. It knows what you are capable of.'

'Precisely. Interviews are a notoriously poor way to assess someone's suitability for a job. The skills you require to pass an interview are often very different from those required to do the job. Research shows that the chance of finding the right person for a job, using an interview, is about one in three. These odds are much improved if the managers in the school or college can see you in action over an extended period of time. So, in addition to using your placement as a means of gaining experience, always look on it as an extended interview as well.'

'But not everyone gets a job out of their placement.'

'True, but you need to remember that very often any prospective employer may ask you to provide a reference from your placement, or they might just phone them informally to find out about you.'

'So either way I need to impress on my placement.'

'Yep! But that doesn't mean that you can ignore adverts for teaching posts. The best source for teaching jobs is still probably the TES. It's published weekly and you will find plenty of copies lying around the uni faculty and at school. So get in the habit of reading it. In addition, you should continuously review the local authority's website and local newspapers. Some local authorities have what they call a "pool" which you can register with, and if a job comes up in your area you will be contacted. It will then be up to you to apply directly to the school in question. And, of course, there are numerous privately run teaching agencies that you can register with. Another useful way to keep track of vacancies is to build up your network of contacts. That includes colleagues at your placement and on this course who might hear of an opportunity that they are not interested in but which might suit you. Have you been looking at any adverts recently?'

'Yes.'

14.4 What employers are looking for in a candidate

'So what are the qualities that schools and colleges are looking for in their teachers and lecturers?'

'Well, I have to say that most of the adverts are a bit naff. Lots of them say the same thing, such as, "We are looking for teachers who are adaptable, approachable, enthusiastic, forward-looking and supportive." You know the usual human resources guff.'

'*So young, so cynical,*' Sue sighed. '*But you have missed out change agent.*'

'I would have mentioned it if I knew what it was.'

'*It is someone who is not afraid of change and who can champion change and lead others during a period of change. Which is pretty much all the time in education. What you listed are really the personal characteristics or traits that employers are looking for. On the other hand, the skills that they want prospective employees to demonstrate are the ability to apply good teaching and learning skills; motivate learners; act as part of a team and lead when required; work independently and use their initiative when required; and be creative, analytical, problem-solvers, who can show empathy to staff and learners.*'

'So they don't want all that much for their money then.'

'*That's what they ideally want, but, thankfully for you and every other newly qualified teacher, they usually settle for a little less. But it's essential that you demonstrate these personal qualities and skills in your application form and during the interview day.*'

'And how do I do that?'

'*We'll come on to that in a moment. For the time being, I'm going to get a cup of coffee. Do you want one?*'

14.5 Alex's reflection

I've not given much thought to joining a union, but it's obvious that I need to. I'm not too worried about the pay aspect, but you only have to pick up the paper to read of another teacher in dispute with their school, parents or even police over some alleged incident involving little Johnny. If I'm unlucky enough to get involved in such a dispute I'll need the union's backing.

I didn't tell Sue, but I'm well aware of how important it is to create a good impression at my placement. That's why I've been volunteering to get involved in everything from test marking to the school play and sports day. Every time the head of department turns around I want them to notice me. Then, even if they don't employ me at the end of the year, they will remember me.

As for listing personal attributes and skills in job adverts . . . Hang on, I can feel an idea coming on! I wonder if there is any link between these lists and the standards? I should check that out, see how close the two sets of requirements are and think about how I can demonstrate, in my application, that I have the characteristics and skills required.

SPACE FOR YOUR NOTES

Prompts

- List the sources of job adverts that you regularly review or will review.
- Reflect upon which of the characteristics and skills listed in adverts you have, to a significant extent, some extent, a limited extent.

14.6 Researching prospective employers

Sue blew on her coffee and took a sip before speaking. *'Let's say that you find an advert for a vacancy which appeals to you. What's the first thing you should do?'*

'Send for an application form.'

'Maybe. But I think you could take a step back and do a little research first. Go on the web and find out as much as you can about the school or college. Where is it located? Can you get to it easily by car, bus or train? Would you have to move if they offered you the job? What population does it serve, inner city, suburban or countryside? What is it best known for educationally? What are its future plans? What does the latest Ofsted report say about it? Is there any mention of it in the local press?'

'But couldn't I find that out after I sent off for the application form?'

'Indeed you could. But these things have their own momentum. Once you apply it's very easy to see the process in competitive terms. If this happens you can lose your sense of objectivity. You end up wanting to "win" the job even if it is not the best job for you.'

'So before that happens I need to consider my reasons for wanting to work in that particular school – and they can't just be based on my need to get a job.'

'Precisely.'

14.7 Completing a job application

'*Once you have completed your background research you can apply for the job of your dreams, and the information you have collected will help you to produce a really good application . . .*'

'Because I will be better able to show how my knowledge and skills meet their unique requirements.'

'*Are you related to Machiavelli by any chance?*' asked Sue, laughing. '*Once you receive the application pack you need to read it thoroughly. It will, at a minimum, contain a covering letter telling you what you have to return with your application and details of the deadline for applications. Make sure that you follow the requirements of this letter. If they say you must complete and return the enclosed application form and that no CVs are to be sent, then that is what you must do. You would be amazed at the number of people who send in a CV when they have been explicitly told not to. Such applications go straight in the bin . . .*'

'I can understand that. After all, you have just demonstrated that you can't read simple instructions!'

'*Precisely. In addition to the application form there will be a job description and a person specification. It's essential that you read these documents before you complete the application form.*'

'Why's that so important?'

'*The job description will tell you the duties of the post, and the person spec will list the essential characteristics/skills that each applicant must have and list those skills that are desirable but not essential. Now, this is crucial. All schools and colleges will get numerous applications for each vacancy. But they will probably only interview six or eight people.*'

'Why so few?'

'*Because that is how many people they can interview in a day, and the senior staff won't want to be tied up for longer than that interviewing. To get down to that number and to ensure that they comply with equal opportunities, the school will only interview those people who demonstrate in their application that they have all the essential characteristics/skills. However, it is no use saying "I can engage learners". Instead, you need to demonstrate how you do it. So you might say, "During my placement I engaged my learners by using clips from Apollo 13 to explore the dangers of space travel in a science class." By doing that you are showing that you have the required skills and that you can apply them creatively.*'

'But what if 25 applicants all demonstrate that they have the full range of essential skills?'

'That's where the desirable skills come into play. They can be used to whittle down the number to a more manageable level. So you must never treat the desirable characteristics/skills as unimportant. Treat them seriously and address each one in your application.'

'Sounds like it could be a long application.'

'Maybe. But usually there is a page or so for you to outline your experience, and there is no reason why you can't exceed that using a continuation sheet. But don't write a book. They don't need to know everything about you and your experiences – they just want the relevant stuff. So edit, and edit again.'

'It sounds like I should photocopy the application form and fill the copy in before moving onto the real thing.'

'I'd go even further than that. When you move onto the real thing, complete it in light pencil first. Because even when you copy you can make mistakes. Then when satisfied, go over it in ink, let it dry and rub out the pencil.'

'But what if they ask for a CV, how should I structure that?'

'If they do, then I suggest you follow the guidelines contained in this handout. (See Handout 14.1.) It covers all the essential points. In addition to your application form, what else do you need to include in your response?'

I thought for a moment before replying hesitantly, 'A covering letter and any other documents that they might ask you to enclose.'

'Always include a covering letter. Keep it short. All you need to say is "Please find enclosed my completed application for the post of Supreme Commander of the Universe (or whatever). I look forward to hearing from you in the near future." But it is a business letter, so you need to make sure that it is properly laid out and addressed. If you go to the website www.routledge.com/cw/mcgrath you'll find samples of appropriate letters.'

14.8 Alex's reflection

> The more I think about applying for a job, the more it seems like completing an assignment. The requirements in the job description and person spec are the criteria and the application form is my assignment. Finding out about the organisation is my literature search, and I have to do that before I start writing. Then my task is to ensure that I meet all of the 'criteria' in my response. It also means that I will probably have to complete numerous drafts before I get the application right. When it's complete, I need to go through it one last time and confirm that I have met every one of the requirements. I can do that!

SPACE FOR YOUR NOTES

Prompt

* Think of one successful and one unsuccessful job application that you have made. What were the strengths and weaknesses of each application?

14.9 Preparation for the interview, including presentations and micro-teach sessions

'So you've made your application and waited for a response. Then you get a letter inviting you to attend an interview. What do you do?'

'Start to worry,' I suggested. Sue gave me her best withering stare and waited. Finally I said, 'Confirm that you will attend in writing.' (See www.routledge.com/cw/mcgrath for sample letters.)

'That's better. You want to make a good impression, so write back thanking them for the interview and confirming that you will attend. It is also likely that their letter will contain details of anything that you have to bring to the interview or prepare for the interview.'

'Such as?'

'They might want you to bring your final teaching portfolio, teach a 10-minute session to a group of learners or make a presentation.'

'While being watched by staff.'

'Exactly, so you need to prepare whatever you need well in advance. The better you prepare the more confident you will feel on the day. Do you remember what we covered on presentations?'

'Most of it; I'll review my notes from that session if I have to do a presentation. (See Tutorial 13.) But in all honesty it's not presentations that I find difficult. It's those short micro-teaching sessions that I hate. They are far more difficult to get right than an hour-long session.'

'Most teachers would agree with you. What you have to do is prepare for the session as if it were an assessed task. Do you remember the guidelines you were given for micro-teaching sessions?'

Using my fingers, I ticked off the requirements I could remember: 'Identify clear aims and objectives for the session and share these with the learners. Keep it simple. In a short space of time you can't get involved in detail or complexity. Involve the learners in what you are doing as soon as possible. Allow time for questions and make sure that there is some form of assessment included in the session. Oh! And prepare any resources that you might need for the session in advance.'

'Very good. Also, practise it and ensure that it does not run over.'

14.10 The interview process – remember you are under scrutiny from the time you arrive

'On the day of your interview you will be nervous, so avoid any last-minute panics by arriving in plenty of time. That at least will remove one of your concerns. If you are too early, go for a cup of tea. And remember, you only have one opportunity to make a good impression. So, dress smartly and, if in doubt about what to wear, choose the conservative option.'

'You would think that in today's world we would have got past judging people based on first impressions.'

'Maybe. But there is plenty of evidence that indicates that people make judgements about others within the first two minutes of meeting them. It is then extremely rare for that person to change their minds. When you think about it, in evolutionary terms, our ability to make such quick judgements was a valuable skill when we stumbled upon some stranger in the middle of a prehistoric jungle. In such instances we only had a few seconds to determine if they were a friend or foe. So play the game as it is, not how you would like it to be.'

'So, I'm there. I'm well prepared. I've arrived on time and my mother would be proud of how I look. What then?'

'When you go for a teaching post it isn't unusual for the process to last half a day or longer. Usually all the applicants will be welcomed by the head or deputy and then you will be given a tour of the school or college. It's important to realise that from the moment you enter the building you are being watched and evaluated. The person conducting the tour will almost certainly feedback their views of the candidates to the selection panel. So you need to impress them by asking a few well-chosen questions during the tour.'

'Such as?'

'Here's where your previous research comes in handy. Ask them about the organisation's plans or recent achievements or about the types of learners they have or maybe something about their mission statement. But don't ask questions that are designed to show how clever you are. That will just annoy your guide. Ask questions that you would expect to hear in an intelligent conversation between teachers in any school.'

14.11 More on presentations and micro-teaching

'I suppose after the tour will come the micro-teaching session or presentation?'

'Very likely. You may have to deliver the session to a group of learners or staff. If you have been asked to deliver the session to learners, then you need to concentrate on them and ignore any staff in the room. Treat it, as far as you can, as a lesson and try and relax. The staff may well ask the learners afterwards which applicant they liked best, so try and create a rapport with the learners, but don't risk telling a joke or try to be their buddy. Instead, be approachable, cheerful and encouraging.'

'And if it's a presentation?'

'Do as we discussed in Tutorial 13. Grab their attention and keep it for the duration of the session.'

14.12 The interview

'Then it's the interview?' I said.

'If you are lucky; if you are unlucky you'll have lunch first.'

'Unlucky because they will still be watching me?' I asked.

'Yes. But it is unlikely to be as bad as interviews for the Foreign Office.'

'What?'

'It used to be the case that when candidates were interviewed by the Foreign Office they always had a formal dinner as part of the process at which peas were served. They wanted to see if the applicants could maintain a conversation while faced with the possible embarrassment of chasing peas around their dinner plate. Of course, what they wanted to see was applicants mashing the peas onto the back of their fork with their knife.'

'And in doing so demonstrate that they knew the correct way to eat peas!'

'Don't laugh, on such things was built an empire!' Sue said, smiling.

'I think I'll just avoid the peas!'

'I doubt that there will be any peas in sight. More likely a buffet will be provided at which you will get to meet the other teachers. But they will be looking to see how socially comfortable you are. They will want to judge how easily you will fit into their little world. So don't sit by yourself. Engage in the conversation but don't try to dominate it. And remember, if in doubt, it is better to keep your mouth shut and have people think you are stupid . . .'

'Than open it and confirm their suspicions.'

'*Indeed. Then it's on to the interview proper. Usually there will be a panel of at least three people, and while you are answering the questions of one person the others will be observing you. If they offer to shake your hand when you enter, do so, but don't initiate a round of handshakes yourself. Be confident. Speak clearly and sit upright. Don't fold your arms – it will make you look defensive. Instead, rest your hands in your lap. Remain calm, polite and good-humoured throughout the interview and smile. Always look at the person who is speaking. When asked a question, maintain comfortable eye contact with the questioner, but occasionally catch the eye of other members of the panel as you speak. This will help maintain rapport with all the members of the panel.*'

'So what do I need to do in the interview other than answer the questions?' I asked.

'*Sell yourself! It's not pretty, and many of us find it difficult to do, but basically you have to convince the panel that you are the best person for the job and that they would be daft not to employ you. To do that you need to believe it yourself. So for the week leading up to the interview you need to tell yourself constantly why you are the ideal candidate and that there is no way you are not going to get the job.*'

'Is that what you call positive self-regard?'

'*You could call it that. I think it's about psyching yourself up for the test ahead and visualising your success. As for the questions they ask, answer them in full but be as succinct as possible. To be able to do that, give yourself a couple of seconds to marshal your thoughts before you start to speak. If you didn't hear the question or didn't understand, ask them to repeat it. When you start to speak don't waffle, it will just annoy them. Be positive and assertive when answering, and whenever possible provide practical examples from your own experience.*'

'I'm not sure I understand what you mean.'

'*Let's say they ask you how you would calm an unruly class. You could start by outlining a couple of the techniques that you might use, but it would be a better answer if you described how you had used such techniques to calm an actual incident. That way . . .*'

'I'm saying I have experience in this area and it doesn't faze me. I'm also demonstrating that I have some transferable skills,' I said, pleased with myself.

'*Exactly. Now, never lie in an interview, but a little bit of exaggeration is almost expected. So the minor disturbance that you quelled could be presented as something slightly more substantial in your answer.*'

'But I can't claim that I was involved in a full-scale riot,' I said. Sue nodded, and I continued, 'Sometimes they ask you to describe your worst teaching disaster. How can you put a positive spin on that?'

'*I'd suggest that you say something like "Well, I've never had an absolute disaster, but there was this time when things could have gone wrong and what I did was . . ." and you explain how you avoided the problem.*'

'But what if you did have a disaster?'

'There is nothing in the rules of an interview that says you have to volunteer information that will put you in a bad light. They don't expect you to bare your soul.'

'Anything else?'

'At the end of the interview they are almost certain to ask you if you have any questions. Again, this is where your earlier research can come in handy. Ask one or two thoughtful questions. No more than that. If you have more questions, save them until they make you an offer. Your questions need to demonstrate your knowledge of and interest in the school or college. They should provide evidence of your interest and enthusiasm and, if possible, be forward-looking.'

'Can you give me an example?'

'Let me think. How about "I noticed in your latest Ofsted report that the school has been commended for its teaching strategy. How do you plan to build on that in the next year or two?" '

'Sneaky. You are complimenting them while asking what other improvements they have planned. Then I suppose I just have to wait for a decision.'

14.13 What to do after the interview

'Sometimes they will offer the job to the successful candidate on the day. Other times you'll have to wait for a letter. But however long it takes, use the time to think. Up to the moment you leave the interview you have been working to get the job. Now you need to stop and ask yourself whether you want the job. What were your impressions of the school? Did you like the school and the staff? What were the learners like? Can you get to the school easily in winter and summer? Would you enjoy working there? Interviews are as much about you making a decision as the employers, so don't feel that you have to accept an offer, and never be pressured into giving a quick decision. If they offer you the job on the spot, ask if you can have the evening to think it over and discuss it with your partner.'

'And if I can't make my mind up?'

'That's when you ask those other questions. The ones you didn't ask in the interview. Once they offer you the job, you move from applicant to negotiator.'

'What if they don't offer me the job?'

'Well, you will need a bit of time to lick your wounds. But you should also review the whole process and try to identify what went well and what went badly. Very often schools and colleges offer to give unsuccessful candidates feedback on their performance. You should take up any such offer.'

'You mean, use it as a learning experience?'

'Yes. Especially if you haven't had too many interviews. What they tell you can be very useful. But you will need to decode the language they use. They are unlikely to say that your

presentation was rubbish. Instead, they might say it was "unusual" or "different" or that your answers during the interview were "unexpected".'

'More double-speak,' I said.

'It's just something else you will have to get used to in the world of education. Anyway, that's about it. You need to start looking for suitable jobs and getting your applications off ASAP. So good luck!'

'Thanks,' I said, excited by the thought that my training was drawing to a close and the real thing would start in a few months.

14.14 Alex's reflection

If I follow Sue's advice, I'm likely to be totally paranoid by the time I arrive for my interview. There has to be a happy middle path I can follow. I don't want to be offered a job because people are taken in by some act that I put on. If I have to pretend to be something I'm not to get a job, it's very unlikely that I will enjoy it. No, I have to be true to myself. So what image do I try and project on the big day? Maybe a cup of tea and a fig roll will help me decide.

I'm not sure if it's the tea or the fig roll, but it always works.

The image I need to project is me on a good day! I need to accentuate the positive aspects of my character and minimise the negative. I need to present myself in the best possible light without pretending I'm something I'm not. Then, if they don't like me, any rejection will be for the best, 'cos if they don't like the 'best version' of me they are unlikely to get along with the 'normal version'.

No, I'll be myself and express my own beliefs and values in the most positive way that I can while being respectful of other people's views.

Still, I do need to remember that I will be under scrutiny from the time I arrive to the time I leave. So I need to be alert and on my best behaviour. The world needs more lerts!

I'm not sure how good I am at interviews. I mean, I've applied for a few jobs outside teaching and sometimes I've been successful and sometimes not. I wonder if anyone on the course would be interested in setting up a series of mock interviews where we could interview each other and give and receive feedback. It might be worth posting a message on the VLE message board to see if anyone is interested. A group of about four or five would be best.

The idea of rejecting a job is new to me. I don't think I've ever turned down a job offer. Not that I've had that many. But, thinking about it, there is absolutely no reason why you should accept a job just because it's been offered to you. The application process is a two-way street. The employer wants to see if I am suitable for the job and, while they are making their mind up, I have every right to consider if they are right for me.

I suppose it's OK to make the odd mistake in your choice of jobs, but you can't afford to make too many. Being choosy about which jobs I take will help me build a career rather than just work in a series of jobs.

Anyway, on that profound note I think I'm going to pack it in for the night. Tomorrow I start my job search!

SPACE FOR YOUR NOTES

Prompts

- Reflect on any job interviews that you have had. Which areas of the interviews went well? Which went badly?
- What do you need to do to improve on your performance next time?

14.15 Record of PDT meeting

Trainee: Alex Croft

Summary of key learning points

- For your own protection, join a union.
- Treat your placement as an extended job interview. Many students are invited to apply for posts that become available at their placement. Even if you do not end up working at your placement, remember that it can be a useful source for a reference.
- Review the adverts for teaching posts in the press. What personal traits and skills do advertisers want? Think about how you can demonstrate that you have these traits/skills.
- Before replying to an advert, research the school or college in question and decide if you want to work there. Only if your answer is positive should you apply.
- Read the information pack sent to you carefully, noting the essential and desirable skills/qualities that applicants should have.

(continued)

(continued)

- When completing the application form, ensure that you address all of the essential and desirable qualities required of the candidate. Be explicit – you are trying to showcase your talents, not hide them away.
- If called for an interview, respond quickly and confirm your intention to attend or not. If you are going to attend, start to prepare for the interview, i.e. undertake additional research on the school or college, prepare any presentation, micro-teach or resources that you have been asked to bring, think about the type of questions they may ask you, think of at least two questions you could ask the panel.
- On the day of the interview, make sure that you arrive on time and be aware that you are under constant scrutiny. Therefore, dress smartly and appear confident, cheerful and relaxed at all times – even if you don't feel it!
- In the interview, try to relax, don't fold your arms, engage with whomever asks you a question and, when appropriate, try to contextualise your answer by using examples from your teaching.
- Don't feel under pressure to accept the first job that is offered to you. Accepting the wrong job can seriously damage your career, so give yourself some time to think 'Do I really want to work at that school or college? Why do I want to work at that school or college?'.
- If you are not offered the job, ask for a debrief and use the feedback to improve your performance at the next interview.

Agreed action points

Alex will:

- Start to read the professional press and identify the qualities and skills that schools are looking for in candidates.
- Start to apply for suitable posts no later than 1 February.

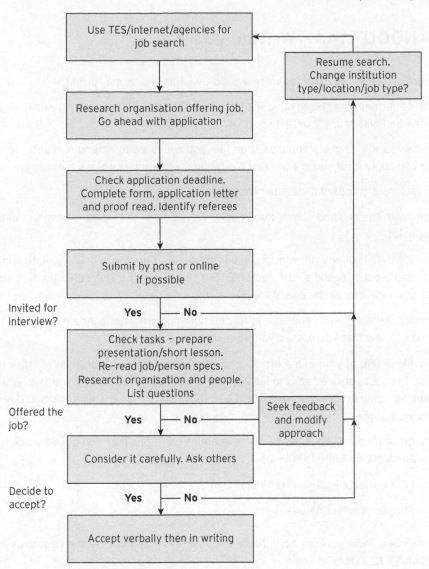

Figure 14.1 Decision tree for job applications

HANDOUT 14.1   Writing your CV

- There are numerous ways to write a good CV – this is just one format.

- If possible, limit the length of your CV to one page. This means that you will have to cut, refine and edit your CV until it sparkles.

- While you will have a standard CV on file, you will need to amend it slightly for every job you apply for if you are to meet the unique requirements of each employer.

- Update your standard CV as life progresses.

- Start with the heading 'Curriculum Vitae of . . .'. Do not provide your contact details at this point.

- Provide details of any relevant previous experience. Employers don't need to know that you had a paper round at the age of 13. But they would be interested if you'd set up a successful IT firm at the age of 14.

- Provide details of your educational/professional qualifications. Again, employers don't need to know that you passed your cycling proficiency test.

- Provide details of your extracurricular interests. Keep this very brief unless they impact upon the post you are applying for, e.g. if applying for the post of PE teacher, you might want to trumpet that you are a Third Dan in karate. Avoid the esoteric and downright strange hobbies.

- A short statement about the personal qualities and skills that you possess which make you an ideal candidate for the job.

- Provide brief details of your referees.

- Provide your contact details.

And remember, while you can accentuate the positives and minimise the negatives in your CV, you MUST NEVER LIE.

Further reading

Job hunting tips: www.prospects.ac.uk
Graduates: www.direct.gov.uk
Careers advice: www.nationalcareersservice.direct.gov.uk
Careers advice: www.targetjobs.co.uk
Your own university's career advice site.

Glossary of terms

Action learning set A collaborative group tasked with solving a series of problems. The set is governed by negotiated ground rules.

Assessment criteria A series of graded statements, linked to the learning outcomes, against which the work of learners is judged.

Assessment for learning Assessments undertaken for the purpose of identifying the learner's current understanding and identifying a strategy for improving their performance using a series of short-term goals.

Athens password A password used by university lecturers to allow students access to electronically held journals.

Behaviourist school The belief that learning proceeds in a step-by-step fashion and that learners are motivated by the receipt of a reward, which should be delivered as soon as possible after the new learning has been demonstrated. Learners remember what they have studied frequently and recently.

Blog An electronic diary updated via a website.

Bloom's three domains There are three domains of learning. The affective is concerned with feelings, values, beliefs, morals and opinions. The cognitive is concerned with intellectual skills and abilities such as analysis, synthesis and evaluation of theoretical constructs and ideas. The psychomotor deals with motor skills, such as those required in sport, craftwork and art. Within each domain there are levels of expertise that describe the stages that a learner goes through, from absolute beginner to expert.

British Education Index (BEI) A specialised search engine usually available at www.leeds.ac.uk/bei/index.html or at most university libraries, designed to search academic works in education.

Citation/cite A reference to an academic source.

Cognitivism Theories of learning that focus on how the brain processes information.

Communities of practice A community can consist of the members of a family, classroom or workplace, the members of which share their knowledge and experience with others in the group and play an active and supportive role in the learning process.

Compact Agreement between two or more people that outlines what each participant can expect from the other in terms of help, support and encouragement.

Conditioned reflex A learned reflex.

Constructivism The belief that true learning involves understanding and that to achieve understanding new learning can only occur if it is built upon the learner's existing knowledge/understanding.

Continuing professional development (CPD) Learning that takes place in a professional context over the period of one's career.

Criterion-referenced assessment Assignment will be marked against a written criteria and all those meeting that criteria will pass.

Critical friend A peer in a similar position to you who provides non-judgemental feedback on academic work or professional practice.

Critical incident An occurrence used for the basis of reflection. 'Critical' is used in the sense of 'to critique' rather than the incident being potentially serious.

Critically evaluate Involves weighing the strengths and weaknesses of an argument using evidence from one's experience, collected data or the writing of others.

Diagnostic assessment Assessment undertaken at the start of a programme of learning to identify what assistance the learner needs to achieve their targets.

Dialectical A series of questions that are used to help the learner access/use their own prior knowledge and learning.

Didactic Teaching in an instructive manner, e.g. lectures and presentations in which learners/audience play a passive role.

Differentiation Differentiation involves the use of different learning strategies, assessment tools and resources to ensure that the differing needs of learners are adequately met.

Discrimination The exercise of choice, based upon professional judgement and knowledge, as to which strategies or documents should be used for a specific purpose.

Education Resources Information Center (ERIC) An American academic search engine for education sources. Available at www.eric.ed.gov or most university libraries.

Empirical research Research involving data physically gathered by a researcher rather than the process of philosophical thought.

Empowered Bestowing on a person some form of autonomy, usually restricted to specific tasks or circumstances.

Entry behaviour The characteristics exhibited by a learner at the start of a learning programme.

E-portfolios An electronic means to collate a range of evidence, such as documents and images, for a portfolio. See *Mahara*.

Evaluation The act of appraising or determining how effective a module, lesson or course of action was in achieving its intended aims and objectives.

Facilitator A person who eliminates/reduces barriers to learning and provides learners with the resources and encouragement required to achieve their learning objectives.

Feedback A written or verbal explanation of how well a learner has achieved against specified criteria and what they need to do to improve future performance.

Formative assessment Assessment used during a programme of study to provide feedback to the learner on their performance to date and to advise on how they can improve.

Formative feedback The advice and guidance given to students during their course and before final assessment with the intention of improving their performance.

Harvard referencing system A system for citation using author's family name and date of publication in the text and an alphabetical list of sources by author's name at the end. **Note:** the system does not allow the use of page notes.

Honey and Mumford learning styles A theory that suggests that there are four broad learning styles, i.e. activist, pragmatist, reflector and theorist, and that each person's unique learning style will be a combination of these descriptors.

Humanistic approach/school The humanistic approach emphasises the need to take account of the learners' feelings and needs and suggests that learning is most effective when undertaken in a non-threatening environment, where learners are self-directed and take responsibility for their own learning and use self-assessment to improve their performance.

Hyperlink An electronic link between documents or files.

Individual learning plan (ILP) A learning plan, with targets, objectives and deadlines, drawn up jointly by the teacher and learner.

Initial assessment Data collected on a learner prior to the start of the course with the intention of determining their suitability for the course and any support needs they may have.

Learner-centred Teaching strategies that focus on what the learners do rather than the teacher's actions and where the learners are actively involved in their own learning rather than passive receivers of information from the teacher.

Lesson evaluations The act of appraising or determining how effective a lesson was in achieving its intended objectives, usually in the form of reflective comments made after a lesson and indicating opportunities for improvement.

Lesson objectives Statements of what learners should know or be able to do by the end of a session.

Lesson plans A detailed plan of what a teacher expects to cover during a teaching session, including information on objectives, lesson content, teaching and learning strategies, activities, assessment and differentiation strategies.

Lesson rationale A description detailing the background to a lesson, the make-up of the learning group, and the teaching, learning and assessment strategies to be used during the session.

Levels 1-6 Descriptors of the stages/levels that learners will pass through during their educational life, e.g. Level 1, foundation; Level 2, GCSE (A–C); Level 3, advanced level; Level 4, undergraduate year 1; Level 5, undergraduate year 2; Level 6, undergraduate year 3.

Level 7 See *M Level*.

Log of hours A record of teaching hours. **Note:** check what is accepted as teaching hours by your university.

Mahara Software designed to enable the compilation of an e-portfolio.

Maslow's hierarchy of needs Maslow's theory suggests that people have five levels of needs (physiological, safety, love and affection, esteem and self-actualisation), and cannot proceed to the next level until the needs of a lower level are fully met. **Note:** Maslow's hierarchy of needs was first published in the 1950s and was based on research conducted with white, middle-class, Protestant, male executives in the United States. While the theory has been widely applied to education, it should be done so with caution, as a whole-life theory of motivation cannot be used to explain the microcosm of the classroom.

Metacognition A high-level mental function which involves the process of planning, assessing and monitoring your own thinking.

Micro-teaching A mini-lesson lasting less than 15 minutes but containing all the parts of a normal lesson.

Mind maps See *spray diagrams*.

M Level Masters level. This is classified as Level 7, one level above final degree year.

Moodle A virtual learning environment used by many schools, colleges and universities.

Negotiated learning Process whereby the teacher and the learner agree on a programme of work that will be completed within a specified period and allows for interim spot checks. See individual learning plan.

Norm-referenced assessment Where the grade awarded for an assignment or exam takes into account the performance of other students sitting the assessment at the same time.

Organisation chart A chart showing the relationships between departments and postholders and their place in the organisational hierarchy.

Pareto Principle The 80–20 rule, e.g., 80 per cent of problems arise from 20 per cent of your learners.

Passive voice A form of grammar in which the process is the focus rather than the people taking part, and the object of the action is the subject of the sentence. For example, 'The interview was conducted in the common room' rather than 'Jane conducted the interview in the common room'.

Peer assessment Process by which a peer of equal standing agrees to evaluate your performance against a previously agreed set of criteria.

Peer review A process by which books and articles are commented upon by respected third parties to confirm their suitability for publication, e.g. sections of this book have been peer-reviewed by other education lecturers to ensure academic quality.

Personalisation A teaching and learning programme designed specifically for the needs of an individual learner.

Plagiarism The act of passing off someone else's work as your own.

Pop/pub quiz Informal formative assessment based on either a short quiz or the popular pub quiz with each round of questions dealing with a different topic. Can be structured as either a team or individual activity.

Portfolio A collection of diverse evidence used to demonstrate the achievement of specified standards. See also *e-portfolios*.

Positive reinforcement Behaviourist strategy used to embed good behaviour/practice by offering praise and reward. See *negative reinforcement*.

Process words Words which tell you what you have to do in order to correctly answer a question.

Provenance The standing of a source. This usually relates to whether an article has been peer-reviewed and the status of the writer and/or publisher.

Quangos Quasi-autonomous non-governmental organisations that enact government policy at arm's length from the respective department, e.g. the Teaching Agency is a quango linked to the Department for Education.

Reading strategies Approaches taken to reading text, such as skim reading, or only reading specific sections of the document, such as the executive summary.

Reflection in action Self-appraisal of your approach to a task whilst the task is being undertaken, e.g. monitoring how effective a teaching method is as you use it.

Reflection on action Self-appraisal of a task following its completion.

Reliable The degree to which the same results would be achieved if the completed assessment task was marked by another person or used with a different group of equally capable learners.

Research tools Sometimes called 'research instruments'. These are the resources used to gather data, such as a questionnaire, interview or observation schedule.

Restorative dialogue The process which follows a strain or breakdown in the relationship between teacher and learner with the intention of re-establishing the previous relationship through dialogue.

Safeguarding Measure put in place to protect children and vulnerable adults.

SATs Tests taken by school children at the ages of 7 and 11.

Scheme of work A summary plan of learning that covers the entire module or course and includes details of the teaching methods, resources and assessment strategies to be used in each session.

Selective reading The practice of reading specific sections of a book or article for the purpose of finding previously identified information. For example, the methodology of an article may be read to determine the approach taken by the researcher.

Self-assessment An assessment approach that allows the learner to mark and assess their own work.

Self-evaluation form (SEF) An evaluation form completed by the organisation and sent to Ofsted prior to the inspection.

Seminal A highly respected source that is relevant to the topic under study. Your work would be incomplete without quoting this source.

Skills audits An exercise to list the skills that a learner has and identify the areas that need to be improve or learnt.

Skim reading A technique of reading in which text is scanned for keywords and phrases.

Socratic questioning A series of questions formulated by an expert that are designed to guide the learner towards understanding by accessing their own prior knowledge and experience.

Special measures A statutory category in which schools are placed when failing to demonstrate that they meet specified standards of learning and leadership.

Spray diagram/mind map Diagram showing the interconnections and relationships between ideas, theories and issues.

Standards Statements related to expected performance criteria – in this case related to teaching and learning.

Statemented A learner who is in receipt of a statement describing their particular learning needs and how these should be addressed.

Study buddy Informal relationship between peers in which each seeks to support and assist the other with their studies in a non-critical way.

Sub-vocalisation 'Hearing' words in the mind when reading without speaking them.

Summative assessment Final assessment undertaken at the end of a module or course.

Summative feedback Feedback given to the learner at the end of the course, usually in the form of a final mark for the course with or without additional written feedback.

Tacit knowledge Knowledge held subconsciously by a person that they would find impossible to express in words but which informs their actions and practice.

Teacher-centred A teaching style that focuses on what the teacher does rather than the actions of the learners.

Unconditioned reflex Unlearned automatic reflex, such as blinking.

VAK A theory of learning that suggests learners prefer to learn in one of three ways: by seeing (visual), by hearing (auditory) or by doing (kinaesthetic).

Valid/validity The extent to which the assessment tool actually measured what it set out to measure.

Wiki A website, the content of which can be edited by any subscribed user.

Zone of proximal development (ZPD) The difference between the child's actual developmental level as determined by their problem solving ability when acting alone and their potential level of development as indicated by their problem-solving ability when working under adult guidance or with capable peers.

Bibliography

Anderson, L.W. and Krathwohl, D.R. (eds) (2013), *A Taxonomy for Learning, Teaching, and Assessing: A Revision of Bloom's Taxonomy of Educational Objectives* (Abridged Edition). Boston: Allyn & Bacon (Pearson Education Group).

Bennett, T. (2008), *Class Act: A TES Essential Guide to Behaviour Management*. London: TES.

Black, P. and Wiliam, D. (2006), *Inside the Black Box, v. 1: Raising Standards Through Classroom Assessment*. Cheltenham: NFER Nelson.

Burley, S. and Pomphrey, C. (2011), *Mentoring and Coaching in Schools: Professional Learning through Collaborative Inquiry*. Oxford: Routledge.

Capel, S., Leask, M. and Turner, T. (2013), *Learning to Teach in the Secondary School* (6th edn). Oxford: Routledge.

Coffield, F., Moseley, D., Hall., E and Ecclestone, K. (2004), *Learning Styles and Pedagogy in Post-16 Learning: A Systematic and Critical Review*. London: Learning and Skills Research Centre.

Cohen, L., Manion, L. and Morrison, K. (2010), *A Guide to Teaching Practice* (5th edn). London: Routledge.

Cremin, T. and Arthur, J. (2014), *Learning to Teach in the Primary School* (3rd edn). Oxford: Routledge.

Fletcher, S. (2000), *Mentoring in Schools: A Handbook of Good Practice*. London: Routledge.

Haigh, A. (2008), *The Art of Teaching: Big Ideas, Simple Rules*. Harlow: Pearson/Longman.

Handy, C. (1993), *Understanding Organisations* (4th edn). London: Penguin.

Martin. K. (1996), 'Critical incidents in teaching and learning', *Issues in Teaching and Learning*, 2(8), University of Western Australia, Centre for Staff Development. Available at www.csd.uwa.edu.au/ newsletter/issue0896/critical.html.

McGrath, J. and Coles, A. (2013), *Your Education Research Project Companion* (2nd edn). Oxford: Routledge.

McGrath, J. and Coles, A. (2015), *Your Education Masters Companion*. Oxford: Routledge.

McMillan, K. and Weyers, J. (2012), *The Study Skills Book (Smarter Study Skills)* (3rd edn). Harlow: Pearson/Prentice Hall.

Petty, G. (2014), *Teaching Today: A Practical Guide* (5th edn). Oxford: Oxford University Press.

Pritchard, A. (2014), *Ways of Learning: Learning Theories and Learning Styles in the Classroom* (3rd edn). Oxford: Routledge.

Rogers, B. (2011), *Classroom Behaviour: A Practical Guide to Effective Teaching, Behaviour Management and Colleague Support* (3rd edn). London: SAGE.

Savage, J. (2015), *Lesson Planning: Key Concepts and Skills for Teachers*. Oxford: Routledge.

Seneca, L.A. (2005), *On the Shortness of Life*, trans. C.D.N. Costa. Harlow: Penguin Books.

Tripp, D. (2011), *Critical Incidents in Teaching (Classics Edition): Developing Professional Judgement*. London: Routledge.

Wallace, S. and Gravells, J. (2007), *Mentoring in the Lifelong Learning Sector* (2nd edn). Learning Matters: Exeter.

Websites

www.businessballs.com: Excellent source of material on personal development and education and training theories.

www.nationalcareersservice.direct.gov.uk: Careers advice.

www.routledge.com/cw/mcgrath: Support site of *Your Teacher Training Companion*.

www.prospects.ac.uk: Advice on searching for graduate jobs and postgraduate courses.

www.targetjobs.co.uk: Careers advice.

www.gov.uk/government/organisations/department-for-education: UK government site for the Department for Education.

Index